THEMATIC GUIDE
TO WORLD
MYTHOLOGY

Lorena Stookey

GREENWOOD PRESS
Westport, Connecticut • London

Library of Congress Cataloging-in-Publication Data

Stookey, Lorena Laura.
    Thematic guide to world mythology / Lorena Stookey.
        p. cm.
    Includes bibliographical references and index.
    ISBN 0–313–31505–1 (alk. paper)
    1. Mythology. I. Title.
  BL312.S76   2004
  201′.3—dc22   2003059528

British Library Cataloguing in Publication Data is available.

Library of Congress Catalog Card Number: 2003059528
ISBN: 0–313–31505–1

First published in 2004

Greenwood Press, 88 Post Road West, Westport, CT 06881
An imprint of Greenwood Publishing Group, Inc.
www.greenwood.com

Printed in the United States of America

The paper used in this book complies with the
Permanent Paper Standard issued by the National
Information Standards Organization (Z39.48–1984).

10   9   8   7   6   5   4   3   2   1

Copyright Acknowledgment

Illustrations by Carol J. Benson

CONTENTS

Contents

PREFACE

The *Thematic Guide to World Mythology* uses a comparative approach to explore patterns that recur within myths gathered from a broad range of cultural traditions. Organized to emphasize the widespread occurrence of repeated elements throughout the myths of different peoples, the guide provides multiple examples of each of the thirty motifs it examines. The motifs, which include instances of the repeated appearances of particular figures, events, or themes found in traditional narratives, are arranged alphabetically by subject for the convenience of the reader. The text includes discussion, for example, of deities, heroes, and tricksters—all significant figures in myths from around the world—and it addresses patterns that emerge in traditional accounts of such mythic events as the creation of the cosmos, the flooding of the world, or the coming of the apocalypse. Because the myth traditions of many different peoples also feature tales of a sacred tree, accounts of a quest, or stories of a journey to the underworld, the guide also includes examples of narratives in which these thematic elements appear.

Designed to provide readers who are interested in myth with an overview of comparative mythology, the *Thematic Guide to World Mythology* is also intended to serve as a reference text for students, teachers, and librarians who are engaged in research. Each entry in the guide offers both explanation and analysis of a motif that appears in multiple myth traditions, and each entry draws from a variety of different cultures to provide illustrative examples of use of the motif. The discussion of the afterlife, for example, outlines patterns that emerge within different peoples' conceptions of an existence beyond death and then examines instances in which the otherworld is represented as a kingdom of the dead, as a place of judgment, or as a site where souls are reincarnated for their return to earthly life. Because descriptions of an afterlife frequently occur in association with certain other myth motifs, readers are referred to additional relevant entries within the guide. For example, myth tradition's references to an afterlife often overlap accounts of an apocalypse or depictions of an underworld, and therefore discussions of these topics are cited at the end of the entry. Similarly, the recurring figure of the trickster can also serve the roles of messenger or culture hero, and thus the entries that examine these related subjects are also cross-referenced.

The *Thematic Guide to World Mythology*'s glossary provides explanation of the specialized terms used both in the text and in other books about myth, and its index is designed to serve readers in several specific ways. As a resource useful to research, for example, the index can be used to find references to particular figures, tales, or themes; to trace different traditions' uses of motifs for purposes of comparison; and to locate myths that belong to a particular culture or that circulate within a geographical region. In addition to the glossary and index, other supplementary materials include the illustrations that can be found throughout the text; examples of mythography, these images depict figures that are emblematic of recurring motifs or portray scenes that embody thematic elements that appear in narratives from numerous cultural traditions. Furthermore, the guide also offers readers a listing of additional resources in the form of a selected bibliography. Chosen in part because they are readily available, the books listed as recommended reading include works currently in print and volumes that can generally be found in collections many libraries possess. Organized to accommodate readers' interests and to facilitate research, the books that appear in the bibliography are arranged in categories that indicate their purposes and their subject matter. Encyclopedias, myth dictionaries, and other general reference texts are all listed together, for example, while books with a more specific focus are also grouped together under headings descriptive of their content.

Several different kinds of resources are available to readers who are interested in mythology. Information about deities, heroes, and other significant figures can readily be found in myth dictionaries, and encyclopedias of myth characteristically provide useful summaries of many cultures' myth traditions. Myth anthologies offer collections of narratives gathered either from multiple cultures or from a particular tradition, and specialized studies of particular myth motifs afford analysis, discussion, and examples of one of myth tradition's recurring elements. For example, books about the trickster figure, studies of creation myths, or explorations of the nature of the underworld all number among focused studies of this kind. The *Thematic Guide to World Mythology* differs from many of these other resources by focusing on multiple patterns that emerge across myth traditions. Like myth encyclopedias or anthologies, the guide draws exemplary tales from many different cultures, but, rather than using such categories as chronology or geography to organize the myths, it arranges them thematically in order to offer its readers an overview of comparative mythology. Indeed, the guide's glossary and index are also designed to serve this purpose.

INTRODUCTION

Myths from around the world address the questions human beings have always posed about their origins, their environments, their ultimate destinies, and the meaning of their lives. Although myth tradition's numerous accounts of the creation of the cosmos, the nature of the afterworld, or the deeds of culture heroes are richly various in their particular details, recurring patterns nonetheless appear in tales that emerge from distinctly different cultures. Many cultural traditions, for example, include an account of a tremendous flood, a deluge that inundates the earth and destroys most forms of life, and stories of a sacred tree, a heroic monster slayer, or a cunning trickster are also widespread throughout myth tradition. The occurrence of repeated themes and motifs within the myths of disparate peoples is a phenomenon that scholars have examined from various perspectives in efforts to identify ways in which experiences that human beings share have been embodied in narratives that circulate within diverse communities.

According to some theorists, for example, myth's recurring patterns reveal features of the human psyche. Thus, from a Freudian perspective, mythic events symbolize the workings of the unconscious mind, and a culture's tradition of myths can be seen as resembling an individual's dreams. The Freudian theory of dream condensation, for instance, might be used to explain the appearance across myth traditions of the figure of the chimera, the fantastic beast that is composed of parts from different kinds of animals. According to Sigmund Freud, condensation takes place when the dreaming mind conjoins disparate elements from the waking world, and indeed this kind of transformation is readily apparent in the characteristics of the mythical creatures that populate tales told by many different peoples. The Jungian theories advanced by Joseph Campbell and other students of myth also afford a psychological understanding of mythic patterns. According to Carl Jung, myth tradition's recurring symbols, figures, or actions are archetypes that arise from the collective unconscious, a repository of timeless images that all humankind possesses. The divine child, one of the archetypes identified by Jung, thus emerges from the collective unconscious to appear in various myths as a symbol of rebirth or the promise of renewal. For Campbell, the hero who undertakes a quest is an archetypal figure whose journey represents the human desire to realize spiritual fulfillment.

Other explanations of myth tradition's recurring patterns focus attention upon human beings' experiences within the natural world. For example, the deification of the earth in many cultural traditions signifies ancient peoples' recognition of its importance as the source of life. The sun, sustainer of all life, is also commonly deified, and in many traditions the earth and the sky are together represented as the primal parents who give birth to the world. Frequent occurrences of stories of the fire bringer—sometimes an animal and often a trickster or a god—underscore the importance of the emergence of fire as a technological development among ancient cultures, and tales of the culture heroes who teach people how to hunt for fish or game or how to plant and harvest crops are also commonplace throughout myth tradition. Ancient human beings' relationship to the animal kingdom is emphasized in the many myths that feature animals as deities, tricksters, helpers, or other significant characters; indeed, in many cultural traditions, a divine animal master oversees the welfare of the earth's wild creatures. The inevitability of death is a common theme within the world's myths, and many cultural traditions include stories of the origin of death that serve to explain why it exists. Most myth traditions also envision an afterlife in the land of the dead, and, according to many different peoples, this place lies beneath the earth, in an underworld.

That an underworld is frequently conceived as the home of the dead is an appropriate expression of ancient peoples' observation that both crops and creatures are absorbed by the earth after death occurs. According to these myths, the dead therefore dwell in a land that lies below the surface of the world, and this conception of the location of the afterworld often plays a role in a society's burial customs. In some cultural traditions, including those of the ancient Egyptians and certain of the indigenous Australians, the sun is described as entering the underworld each day after it completes its journey across the sky. For these peoples and others, the west, the direction of the setting sun, serves as a symbol of the netherworld. The mountain and the tree are among the many other natural features that assume symbolic significance in many myth traditions. Because the mountain and the tree both rise into the sky, the traditional home of the gods, these features of the natural landscape are often represented as sites where the separate worlds of the heaven and the earth are symbolically linked. Thus, accounts of a sacred mountain or tree appear in the myths of a remarkable number of the world's distinct cultural traditions.

Striking similarities among myths' motifs cannot always be attributed to polygenesis, the independent emergence of common themes within diverse traditions. Indeed, scholars have traced many instances wherein stories are apparently carried from one people to another and thus eventually assimilated by other myth traditions. For example, it is believed that the Hebrew account of Noah's flood is a version of a Mesopotamian story that is recounted in *Gilgamesh* (ca. 2000 B.C.E.), an ancient epic, and that a later Greek tale of a great flood is possibly derived from these early sources. Although these particular stories might indeed be related, and would therefore serve as an example of monogenesis, the deluge motif is generally regarded as a universal theme, one that appears in myths from every continent on earth. Many of the tales that describe a devastating flood clearly invite a psychological interpretation, for often the deluge is represented as cleansing the world of imperfections or of evil in preparation for its rebirth. In these myths, the flood's destruction of the world leads to a fresh beginning when the process of creation unfolds anew. In numerous myths, the occurrence of the deluge motif obviously also serves to address one of the great dangers that people must confront in the natural world. It is likely, therefore, that many traditional stories of a flood are mythologized accounts of actual catastrophes.

The *Thematic Guide to World Mythology* introduces thirty common motifs that appear in tales gathered from cultures spanning over four thousand years of myth tradition. While each section offers multiple examples of one of myth's recurring themes, these collections of stories are merely representative of the patterns that emerge from traditions around the world, and readers might therefore readily identify one or more of these motifs in many other myths. Indeed, it is not unusual to find several of myth's recurring themes within a single tale, and therefore some of the stories recounted in the *Thematic Guide* are discussed in various sections of the book. Furthermore, because interrelated or overlapping themes frequently emerge among the categories of myth motifs outlined by the guide, a list of topics provided at the end of each section refers readers to additional relevant discussions within the book. The recurring figure of the trickster, for example, plays many roles in different myth traditions, and some of these roles are elaborated in the guide's discussions of the culture hero and the messenger. Moreover, the trickster is often represented as an animal, and thus references to this figure also appear in the section that considers animals in myth.

Because myths, which generally originate in an oral tradition, commonly undergo changes as they are passed down to succeeding generations, multiple versions of many tales have been recorded. The *Thematic Guide to World Mythology* occasionally refers to two or more versions of a traditional account, and readers might well be familiar with additional examples. Not only do readers of myth encounter variant recordings of tales, they are also inevitably confronted with the range of variations in the spelling of characters' names that is a result of the process of translating phonemes from one language to another. The Greek sky deity Kronos, for example, frequently appears as Cronus, and the Pan Ku of Chinese myth tradition is also called Pan Gu. Yet further confusion arises when a figure from one myth tradition is related to a figure from another who is known by a different name. Thus, in Mesopotamian myth tradition, the Sumerian goddess Inanna is identified as Ishtar by the ancient Babylonians, and, among European cultures, the Greek god Zeus is known as Jupiter in Roman myths. Furthermore, various specialized terms or phrases are commonly employed in the study of myth, and these are not always familiar to all readers. Because the *Thematic Guide* makes use of certain of these terms, a glossary is provided at the end of the text.

The motifs described within the *Thematic Guide to World Mythology* offer an overview of patterns that emerge in myth traditions and trace the repeated occurrence of one of these patterns through several different categories of narratives. Indeed, a remarkable number of myths are concerned with the establishment, the maintenance, or the disruption of order in the world. In tales of the creation or in accounts of the deluge, order arises from a state of chaos, and this recurring theme appears once again in stories of the heroic monster slayer who must confront and overcome the forces of disorder and destruction. Characteristically, the dragon or the serpent serves as the emblem of disorder within these tales, and in several myth traditions, including that of ancient Egypt, the image of a bird carrying a snake in its claws represents the triumph of order over chaos. In tales that depict the separation of the earth and sky, the order of the newly created world is given shape, and in myth tradition's accounts of the afterlife, the idea of order is extended to incorporate the realm of the dead. In many fertility myths, a wasteland is made fecund when order is restored, and in tales that envision the coming of an apocalypse, a new order arises from the chaotic destruction of the world. The world is also reordered in stories of the trickster, the agent of disorder and disruption whose subversive acts are instruments of change. Given the etiological nature of all myths, it is not surprising that an interest in explaining and defining the order of the world lies at the heart of many kinds of narratives.

THE AFTERLIFE

Most of the world's myth traditions include a vision of existence beyond death—existence that continues in an afterlife. While peoples' creation myths explain how earthly life first begins, their stories of an afterlife address enduring questions about what might follow mortal life. Accounts from many cultural traditions depict the land of the dead as a realm that closely resembles the world of the living, but in others it is conceived as a grim, forbidding place where spirits dwell in darkness, often in an underworld. When the land of the dead lies beneath the surface of the earth, the world inhabited by spirits is known as a chthonic realm—a world, in other words, that exists underneath the ground. According to some myth traditions, the netherworld consists of two or more different regions, and the assignment of the dead to one place or another depends upon circumstances that are defined within these cultures. For example, within certain accounts of the afterlife, the destinies of the dead are determined either by their stations in life or by the manner of their deaths. Within other traditions, particularly those that envision a judgment of the dead, a separation of souls also occurs, and, according to the tales that circulate in these cultures, the souls of the wicked are punished in an afterlife of torment, while those of the virtuous are rewarded in paradise or reborn to earthly life. Within the myths of many different cultural traditions, the passage from earthly life to the afterworld is represented as a journey undertaken by souls who must travel to a place of judgment or to their ultimate destination in the land of the dead.

The location of the kingdom of the dead is variously described within myth traditions. Quite frequently the dead are said to reside beneath the earth in an underworld, but some peoples envision the land of the dead as a realm that lies above the earth—a heavenly domain. For those peoples whose conception of the afterlife includes a vision of the judgment of souls, the dead are generally punished for their sins in an underworld and rewarded for their virtues in a celestial paradise. According to a few myth traditions, the world of the dead lies beneath the ocean, and in the tales of many cultures, the realm of the dead is separated from the world of the living by a body of water—a river, lake, or sea. Some myths describe the land of the dead as an island, and, in certain stories from the Irish tradition, the island home of the dead is located in the Otherworld, a magical domain that can be found on the earth. Indeed, according to the accounts of various traditions, the dead inhabit an invisible earthly realm, one that is often represented as lying to the west, the direction of the setting sun. Tales from some cultures describe the dead as spirits that move among the living, sometimes assisting mortals and sometimes preying upon them, and accounts from several traditions represent the journey of the dead as a return to earthly life—a reincarnation of the soul.

THE UNDERWORLD

The earliest writings that make reference to an afterlife come from ancient Mesopotamia and describe the land of the dead as an underworld. Known as the Land of No Return or the Great Below, the chthonic kingdom of the dead, ruled by the goddess Ereshkigal, is depicted as a dark and desolate realm where thirsty shades seek nourishment from the dust or clay. Although a bleak and miserable existence is the lot of the ghostly dead, the Great Below is not a place of judgment and punishment, and all who dwell there, both deities and mortals, share a common fate. (Some descriptions of the Mesopotamian underworld make reference to the seven judges who attend upon Ereshkigal; however, these figures do not serve to judge the dead, but rather to enforce the law of the netherworld that prohibits those who have entered the realm of the dead from ever leaving it again.) To reach their destination in the Great Below, the dead must undertake a journey along the Road of No Return, a path that leads them through seven portals that are all guarded by sentries or demons. As they pass through the gates, the dead are shorn of all vestiges of their earthly lives, for, in accordance with the laws of the underworld, all who arrive there are received as equals in the afterlife.

The Mesopotamian underworld is vividly described in tales that tell of living beings' journeys to the realm of the dead. One myth, for example, relates the story of the goddess Inanna's descent to the Great Below, and another recounts the journey of the god Nergal, who becomes the husband of Ereshkigal when he ventures to the underworld. Like others who take the Road of No Return, Inanna, the sister of Ereshkigal, is stripped of her jewelry and clothing as she passes through the seven gates, and once she enters her sister's dark kingdom, she is subjected to all its miseries. In this tale, Inanna, the fertility goddess and the majestic queen of the heavens, is in fact restored to life and then rescued from the Great Below. Her release, however, comes with a price, for even the great goddess must abide by the laws of the underworld, and therefore Inanna, who is forced to name a substitute to take her place in the land of the dead, decides to choose her lover, the vegetation god Dumuzi.

The ending of the story of Nergal's visit to the underworld is quite different from that reported in the accounts of Inanna's descent. One of the lesser gods, Nergal is summoned to the Great Below after he insults Namtar, Ereshkigal's emissary. Before he sets forth along the Road of No Return, Nergal is warned that he must refuse the food and drink that Ereshkigal will serve him, for those who accept what is offered in the underworld are thereafter subject to its laws. Unlike Inanna, Nergal is allowed to retain his worldly possessions as he passes through the gates, and when he reaches his destination, he is indeed welcomed with both food and drink. Although Nergal does not partake of the repast set before him, he does accept Ereshkigal's offer to become his lover, and, by embracing her, he seals his own fate. Nergal's attempt to escape his lot turns out to be a futile endeavor. He persuades Ereshkigal to allow him to travel to the realm of the gods to announce his betrothal and then fails to keep his promise to return to the netherworld. Ereshkigal, however, sends her emissary to bring him back, and as Nergal makes his final journey through the seven gates, the new husband of the queen of the dead is stripped of all the trappings of his former life.

JOURNEYS TO THE AFTERLIFE

According to the ancient Greek, Norse, and Aztec traditions, the dead are not all subject to the same destiny. Myths from all these cultures describe an afterlife in an underworld, but in both the Greek and Norse accounts, dead warriors or heroes are granted existence in a separate domain. And, in the tradition of the Aztecs, all those who die by violent means are afforded an afterlife in a celestial realm. According to narratives from all three traditions, the spirits of those who die of old age or other natural causes must undertake a journey to the underworld. These journeys are represented as arduous ordeals, and the dead are therefore customarily supplied with the objects they will need to reach their destination. To enter the kingdom of Hades, the Greek underworld, the dead must cross a river barrier by securing passage on the boat that is steered by Charon, the ferryman of the netherworld. In preparation for their trip, the dead are generally given a coin to pay the ferryman and cakes to feed Cerberus, the fierce, three-headed hound of Hades. Likewise, the dead who travel to Hel's kingdom in Niflheim, the Norse underworld, are customarily provided with sturdy shoes. The journey to Mictlan, the Aztec underworld and the kingdom ruled by Mictlantecuhtli, is also fraught with obstacles and dangers, and the dead who travel there are usually supplied with a jade bead that can serve as currency. Like the Greek underworld, those of the Norse and Aztec traditions are bordered by water. According to Norse myths, the dead must cross the river Gjall, whose bridge is guarded by a sentry who must be paid with blood, and, according to the stories of the Aztecs, the dead must seek the help of a yellow dog as they cross the raging waters that surround Mictlantecuhtli's kingdom.

Like the shades that dwell in the Mesopotamian underworld, those that reside in Hades, Hel, or Mictlan lead a dreary existence. With one exception, however, the dead who inhabit these underworlds are not subject to judgment or punishment. The exception appears in the Greek tradition, where Tartarus, the deepest and the darkest region of Hades, serves as the prison where the enemies of the gods endure eternal torture. Three judges preside in the Greek underworld, and their duty is to direct the souls of the dead to their proper destinations: while most shades travel the road that leads to a dismal afterlife in the Fields of Asphodel, the souls of great heroes, leaders, poets, and warriors take the road to Elysium, the realm of the blessed. In Greek tradition, the fate of the dead depends upon their earthly status, and this is also the case in the tradition of the Norse, another ancient warrior society. According to Norse myths, warriors who are slain on the field of battle are led by the Valkyries to Valhalla, the great hall of heroes that lies within Asgard, the heavenly home of the gods.

Whereas the mighty and the valorous gather in Elysium and Valhalla, those who are spared an afterlife in the Aztec underworld include not only warriors, but also many others who suffer violent deaths. According to Aztec tradition, the celestial realm is composed of multiple layers, and suicides, victims of human sacrifice, and women who die in childbirth all ascend to these pleasant, sunny regions. Tlalocan, located on the fourth level of this heavenly world, is under the dominion of the rain god Tlaloc, and all who are killed by his bolts of lightning, drowned in his floods, or stricken with leprosy are granted an afterlife in his paradisiacal domain.

Myths from the Greek, Norse, and Aztec traditions also offer accounts of the "harrowing of hell," the descent of living beings to the underworld. In tales told by the Greeks, for instance, Orpheus ventures to the realm of the dead in search of Eurydice, his beloved wife, and the great hero Herakles travels to Hades to capture Cerberus, the vicious guardian of the underworld. Although the living are usually prohibited from entering the land of the dead, Orpheus is able to charm both Charon and Cerberus with the haunting beauty of his singing, and Herakles succeeds in performing his last labor by using his great strength to overcome the netherworld's ferocious hound in a wrestling match. In a tale from the Norse tradition, the god Hermod undertakes a journey to the underworld after Balder is slain and then sent to Hel's kingdom. Hermod, too, is successful in his endeavor to enter the realm of the dead, for after he explains that he seeks to secure the release of Balder, the most beloved of the gods, the guardian of the bridge allows him to cross the river Gjall without paying with his blood. Quetzalcoatl is the harrower of hell in the Aztec tradition, and he travels to Mictlan to gather bones from which the gods can fashion a new race of human beings. Although Quetzalcoatl encounters no obstacles when he enters the underworld, Mictlantecuhtli is loath to let him leave, and he must therefore outwit the lord of the dead to make good his escape.

DESTINIES OF THE DEAD

Death, according to some cultural traditions, is followed by a reckoning that determines the fate of every soul. Required to account for their earthly lives, the dead are brought to judgment, and the wicked among them are punished for their crimes. In ancient Egyptian tradition, where the land of the dead is conceived as an underworld, there is no afterlife for those who are punished, for, after judgment is passed, the souls of evildoers are consumed by Ammit, the monster whose epithet is "devourer of the dead." The Egyptian underworld is ruled by Osiris, the resurrected god, and the dead must journey by ferryboat to reach the place of judgment at the foot of his throne. There, their hearts are weighed on the Scale of Justice, and those whose hearts are not heavy with their sins travel on to an afterlife in a world that resembles the earthly home of the living. The Egyptian kingdom of the dead shares several features with the underworlds described by other cultures: for example, souls must cross a river on a boat guided by ferrymen, and they must pass through seven guarded gates to reach the house of Osiris. In Greek tradition, the messenger god Hermes serves as the psychopomp, the guide who leads souls to the realm of the dead, and in Egyptian accounts, a similar function is performed by Anubis, the jackal-headed god.

The underworld of ancient Persia's Zoroastrian tradition is also a place of judgment and punishment. Whereas Egypt's tales depict the weighing of hearts, in the

Persian myths the deeds of the dead are entered as credits and debits in a ledger book. The judgment of souls takes place in the underworld, at the Bridge of Chinvat (the "Accountant's Bridge"), and is overseen by three judges, Rashnu, Sraosha, and Mithra. According to the Zoroastrians, three immediate destinies await the souls of the dead. When their good deeds outnumber their wicked acts, souls pass into a heavenly realm that is called the House of Song. When their good and evil deeds are equal in number, souls cross into Hammistagan, a region of the underworld that is a kind of limbo. Finally, when lists of their evil deeds are longer than accounts of their acts of goodness, souls fall from the Bridge of Chinvat into a great abyss, and there they are punished. The punishment of the dead, however, is not a permanent condition, but rather a means of cleansing souls of their wrongdoing in preparation for an afterlife in a perfect world. According to the Zoroastrians, the forces of evil are destined to be defeated in an apocalyptic battle at the end of time, and therefore, on that last Judgment Day, all the dead will be resurrected in an earthly paradise.

PARADISE

Although paradise is frequently conceived as a heavenly domain, according to some of the Arctic region's Inuit peoples, it is located underneath the earth. Paradise, in these accounts of the afterlife, is the destiny of the fortunate, and in an underground world where game and other foods are in plentiful supply, the souls of the dead dwell in comfort and warmth. The souls of others, however, journey to a cold land high up in the frosty sky, and there they are subjected to hardship and starvation. While the traditions of the widespread Inuit peoples characteristically envision a land of the dead, its location varies among the different groups. The Inuits of Greenland, for example, tell stories of the underworld kingdom that is ruled by Sedna, the great spirit of the sea and the queen of the dead. Sedna's domain, at the bottom of the sea, is the destination of many of the dead, but the spirits of those who suffer greatly during their lives on earth enjoy an afterlife in a celestial paradise. Like the underworlds of many other cultural traditions, Sedna's kingdom is separated from the world of the living by a barrier: to enter the realm of the dead, spirits must cross a bridge that is no wider than the edge of a knife. This underworld, too, is guarded by a sentry, a gigantic dog that keeps watch at its entrance.

Hiyoyoa, another underworld that lies beneath the sea, is the land of the dead in the tradition of the Wagawaga people of Papua, New Guinea. A realm of beautiful gardens, Hiyoyoa is ruled by the god Tumudurere, who resides in the underworld with his wife and children. According to the tales told by the Wagawaga, the souls of the dead journey to Hiyoyoa to work in the gardens of the lord of the netherworld. Divers who swim in the depths of the ocean can sometimes catch a glimpse of Tumudurere's exquisite horticulture, and occasionally marvelous plants from the land of the dead are even carried back to the world of the living. Unlike the denizens of Sedna's dark and desolate underwater realm, the dead who dwell in Tumudurere's lush kingdom are surrounded by beauty in the afterlife.

The myths of several cultures describe the land of the dead as an earthly realm, a region that is sometimes conceived as invisible to the living or one that is frequently represented as lying far to the west. In Irish tradition, the home of the dead can be found in the Otherworld, a mysterious kingdom that is also inhabited by various supernatural beings. Although the Otherworld is occasionally depicted as a subterranean realm, one that can be entered through lakes, caves, fairy mounds, or burial sites, it is most commonly portrayed as a collection of magical islands that are located within the western sea. According to some accounts, the dead journey to the Otherworld from the House of Donn, a small island that is the home of the ruler of the dead. Often called the Islands of the Blessed, the land of the dead is generally characterized as a place of plenty, a bountiful world where apple trees are always in fruit and food is supplied by magical cauldrons. In Polynesian tradition, the land of the dead also lies to the west, beyond the edge of the great sea. The legendary ancestral home of the peoples who migrated across the Pacific Ocean, Havaiki is the realm to which their spirits return in the afterlife. Although the dead journey westward in these accounts (as they do in the traditions of several Native American peoples as well), according to the Slavic people, the blissful abode of the dead lies in the east, beyond the rising sun.

EARTHLY AFTERLIFE

According to Africa's Ashanti people, Asamando, the realm of the dead, lies within the world of the living but remains hidden from view. In a tale told by the Ashanti, a grieving husband searches for the wives he has lost to death, and when he arrives in Asamando, he can hear the familiar voices of the wives who nonetheless remain invisible to him. Reassured by them that he will be reunited with his family in the afterlife, he returns to his village and marries once again. Indeed, stories of direct communication between the living and the dead also appear in other myth traditions, and in some of these the spirits of the dead move among the living. In Slavic tradition, for example, souls are not able to journey to the land of the dead if all the rites of burial have not been properly observed. These spirits, and those of suicides, murderers, and sorcerers, belong neither to the world of the living nor to that of the dead—and thus they are regarded as the "undead." According to tradition, undead spirits, or vampires, sustain themselves by preying on the living, drinking their lifeblood or devouring their flesh.

Death, for some cultural traditions, signifies the end of one bodily existence and the beginning of another as souls undergo reincarnation. According to the accounts of the ancient Baltic peoples of Latvia and Lithuania, the spirits of the dead return to the earth in the form of animals or plants. Among the Ma' Betisék people of southern Malaysia, the souls of virtuous people are reborn as human beings while the spirits of others inhabit animals or trees. The dead can be transmigrated into other forms as well, and in the tradition of the Bushmen of Africa's Kalahari Desert, the dead are reembodied as heaven's stars. The souls of the dead can also be reborn to human life, and in other African traditions, people are reincarnated within the clans to which they belong. The concept of the transmigration of souls also appears in the traditions of India and Buddhist China, cultures where the dead are rewarded or punished for their earthly deeds. According to these traditions, souls are judged after death and the forms of life to which they are eventually reborn are determined by this reckoning. Yama, the ruler of the underworld, judges the dead in Indian tradition, and in that of China, the ten Lords of Death decide the fate of every soul.

See also The Apocalypse; Culture Heroes; Descent Motif; The Underworld

ANIMALS IN MYTH

The animals that inhabit the world along with human beings figure prominently in narratives throughout myth tradition. Not only do animals serve as creator gods or other deities, they also frequently play the roles of tricksters or of culture heroes. In many tales animals are the helpers of humankind, and in some stories they are in fact the consorts of people. In large numbers of myths, animals and human beings assume each other's identities through metamorphosis or by the magical powers of shape-shifting, and many Native American myths describe a time when the animal people and human beings are not clearly distinguished from one another. In certain traditions, human beings are spiritually linked to their animal doubles, or they belong to a clan that is said to be descended from an animal or that shares the characteristics and powers of a totemic animal. As in the example of the centaur of Greek tradition, characters in myth can also be therianthropic, or part animal and part human being. Animals in myths commonly serve as messengers, guardians, or protective spirits, and in creation tales from several cultures, it is an animal—characteristically the turtle—that carries the world upon its back.

Human beings' fascination with animal life is clearly expressed throughout myth tradition in the many etiological tales that explain how particular creatures have acquired their behavioral characteristics or their physical attributes. In narratives that describe how the leopard becomes spotted, why the owl hunts at night, or in countless other "just so" tales, the nature of the animal kingdom is addressed and acknowledged through the act of storytelling. Not only do stories about animals express a people's understanding of their fellow creatures by explaining their origins and place within the cosmos, but frequently they also define human beings' relationships to these other forms of life. The importance of respecting animals, for example, is emphasized in the myths of many cultures, particularly those that rely upon hunting for their livelihood. Indeed, tales featuring the figure of the animal master, a protector deity who ensures that the lives of all wild creatures are valued, are fairly common within hunting societies. According to many of these accounts, the animal master punishes those hunters who kill animals wantonly or who fail to show the respect that is due their prey. While these myths and many others express human beings' admiration for the powers and abilities animals possess, in some accounts wild creatures are represented as threatening and fearsome, and thus the animals of myth are sometimes also seen as monsters. Among the most vicious of myth tradition's monstrous creatures are certain instances of the fabulous beasts that are known as chimeras.

MONSTROUS CHIMERAS

Whereas large, predatory animals—often including the lion, the jaguar, or the wolf—are represented as terrifying creatures in some cultural traditions, it is nonetheless telling that myths' imaginary beasts are among the most dreadful of the animals described in peoples' stories. Indeed, accounts of frightening chimeras, fantastic creatures composed of parts from various animals, appear in narratives from around the world. The Chimera, the monster of Greek tales that lends its name to similar hybrid creatures, is but one example of the hideous beasts that threaten human beings. An amalgamation of ferocious lion, lewdly fecund goat, and venomous serpent, the fire-breathing Chimera is, like many other monsters from the Greek tradition, a female creature that embodies the forces of chaos and destruction. Just as such other female hybrids as Medusa the Gorgon and the bloodthirsty Sphinx are challenged and overcome by one of ancient Greece's legendary monster slayers, so too is the deadly Chimera, who is slain by the hero Bellerophon.

While the Chimera represents the threat of disorder, Pazuzu, another hybrid creature, symbolizes the perils of disease and pestilence. According to ancient Babylonian tradition, the dog-headed Pazuzu possesses the talons of an eagle, the claws of a lion, the tail of a scorpion, and four mighty wings. A monster composed of parts from flesh-eating animals, this winged instrument of carnage spreads contagion across the land. Whereas Pazuzu is a flying monster, the Bunyip of Australian tradition lurks in waterholes or swamps. A chimera that possesses the power to threaten human beings with either floods or droughts, the Bunyip is described in several different ways: either feathered or furry, the creature has the flippers of a seal, the hooves and mane of a horse, and, by some accounts, the head of an emu. A flesh-eating beast, it has a large mouth of sharp teeth and two serpent-like fangs. Although the Bunyip eventually devours its victims, it characteristically enslaves them first and uses them as servants. According to most accounts, the Bunyip favors the flesh of women and children, and in this respect the threat it poses resembles that of Um Es Sibyan, a hybrid creature of ancient Arabian lore that seeks out children for its prey. Another monstrous female figure, this winged chimera is a chicken with the torso of a camel and a human face. A composite of seemingly harmless creatures, Um Es Sibyan nevertheless represents human beings' fear of the dangers that threaten their young.

INSECTS, THE SMALLEST OF ANIMALS

The grotesque figures that haunt human beings' imaginations are but one example of the many ways in which animals are represented in storytelling. Indeed, real creatures both great and small appear in peoples' myths, and the many stories that feature insects, the tiniest of animals, number among them. In Navajo tradition, for example, wingless insects are the original inhabitants of the First World, a region deep beneath the surface of the earth, and it is they with whom the people's story of their emergence begins. The insects, after fashioning wings for themselves, first follow Locust in an ascent to the Second World and then travel to the Third World, where human beings are created. When the time comes for all living beings to journey to the Fourth World, and from there to the surface of the earth, Spider creates the ladders used by the people during their ascent. Appropriately, it is Locust, the leader of the insects, who is the first living creature to enter the Fifth World.

According to Navajo tradition, insects play a significant role in the unfolding of creation—as indeed they do as well in several other creation myths. For example, in the earth-diver tale told by the Cherokee, Water Beetle swims to the bottom of the primal sea to find the mud that is needed for the creation of the earth. In some versions of the earth-diver myth, the tiny Water Beetle proves successful in this quest only after larger, stronger animals have failed in their attempts to reach the bottom of the sea. Another insect, Iktomi the spider, is a central figure in the earth-diver story recounted by the Assiniboine people. An animal creator, Iktomi sends several creatures into the primal waters in search of the dirt he needs to make a land where animals can live. The divers are not successful, however, until finally the dead body of Muskrat floats to the ocean's surface. Iktomi removes the mud he finds clutched in Muskrat's claws, and from this material he first shapes the earth, and then he also uses it to create both human beings and the horses they will need. In Egyptian tradition, the scarab (or dung-beetle) known as Khepri personifies the creator Atum-Re in his aspect as god of the morning sun. An emblem of the sun's daily resurrection, Khepri arises each day from the underworld.

OTHER CREATORS AND DIVINITIES

One of the most unusual of myth tradition's animal creators is the praying mantis. In the stories of Africa's Khoisan peoples, the mantis is the first living creature to appear upon the earth and the creator of other living beings, including the people. Cagn, the creator mantis, is also celebrated for inventing words and for providing fire for the people by stealing it from the ostrich. When the mantis creates new animals, he feeds them with various kinds of honey, and therefore each animal acquires its coloring from the red, yellow, or brown honey produced by bees and wasps. The mantis also creates the moon, for when he discovers that hunters have killed one of the animals he has made, he hurls its gall bladder high into the sky, and there it becomes a light to guide those who hunt at night. The praying mantis is not the only insect portrayed as a creator, for peoples from throughout North America's Southwest regard Spider Woman as either the creator of the cosmos or as an animal helper in the process of creation. Birds are also frequently depicted as creator deities: in one of Egypt's several creation myths, the world is called into existence by the cry of the Benu bird (or heron), and in Native American and Inuit traditions, Raven creates the universe. The World Serpent, an emblem of creative energy in the most ancient of myths, is perhaps the animal that most commonly appears as shaper of the cosmos.

Animals in myths from many cultures are deities or semidivine beings as well as creators. Indeed, most of ancient Egypt's gods are personified as animals. Bastet, for example, is the cat goddess (a protective deity), and Heket, a goddess of childbirth, is represented as a frog. The Jaguar, a ferocious deity in myths from Mesoamerica, is the god that rules the underworld. Divine animals in myths often symbolize the power of cosmic forces, and in numerous traditions the figure of the serpent is associated with the underworld or with the earth and its fertility. In Australia and Africa, for instance, the rainbow serpent is an emblem of the fecund earth and of the watery realm of the underworld. In contrast, denizens of the air are usually characterized as sky gods, and therefore mighty birds often rule the heavens. In a recurring motif, the animal deities that represent the upper realm and the underworld battle one another. In myths from North America, the Thunderbird is the powerful sky god whose enemy is the Great Serpent, and in southern Africa it is the Lightning Bird that struggles with the snake. This pattern can be seen in Egypt as well, where each night the snake god Apophis attacks the sun god as he passes through the underworld, and in Norse tradition, where the mighty eagle that nests atop the World Tree exchanges daily insults with Nidhogg, the serpent that dwells at the roots of Yggdrasil.

In some traditions a bull, rather than a bird, is god of the sky, and in these accounts the thunderous roar of the bull echoes through the heavens. In the Mesopotamian epic *Gilgamesh* (ca. 2000 B.C.E.), the hero succeeds in killing the ferocious Bull of Heaven, but pays dearly for his victory over the celestial deity. Other stories of divine creatures can be found in Indian tradition, where the god Vishnu the Preserver often appears on the earth in the form of an animal. As the fish Matsya, for example, Vishnu saves Manu, the first man, from a great deluge, and as Kurma the tortoise he holds the sacred mountain on his back while the gods recover precious treasures from the Ocean of Milk. Vishnu's other avatars include those of Varaha the boar, who uses his tusks to lift the earth from the bottom of the primordial sea, and Narasimha the lion-man, who tricks and kills an evil demon. In a story about Garuda, the divine eagle that serves as Vishnu's steed, the motif of the power struggle between birds and serpents once again appears. In this tale, Garuda's mother, who is the mother of all birds, is captured by his aunt, the mother of all snakes. To free his mother, Vinata, from her sister Kadru, Garuda carries the elixir of the gods to the snakes as ransom. When the snakes lick the elixir from the grass, they slice their tongues on its sharp blades, and this, according to Hindu tradition, is how the snakes all come to have forked tongues.

TRICKSTERS AND CULTURE HEROES

The trickster, a mischief maker or cunning rogue, can also be a culture hero, and animals in myths often serve in one or both of these roles. The animal trickster is commonplace in Native American tradition, where he appears as Coyote, Rabbit, Mink, Beaver, Raven, Blue Jay, Lox the wolverine, or Iktomi the spider. When, more rarely, the trickster figure is not embodied as an animal, he is often associated with one whose shape he assumes, and thus Nanabozho, the Ojibwa trickster, is also known as the Great Hare. As tricksters, animals in Native American myths both boldly test the boundaries of convention and humorously dramatize the follies of immoral behavior. Indeed, the trickster tradition is replete with tales of the wily rascal who outwits himself or whose boundless ambitions and greed lead to his comeuppance. In some accounts of their antics, the tricksters unleash trouble in the world, as indeed Coyote does in a Navajo tale when he steals Water Monster's children and thereby causes the world to flood. In other stories, however, tricksters are the culture heroes who bring fire to the people, who destroy threatening monsters, or who recover the sun when it is stolen from the sky. In a story told by the Crow, Old Man Coyote steals summer and shares it with the people, and in a Kalapuya tale he steals water from the frog people so that everyone can drink and bathe.

Like the animal tricksters of Native American peoples, those from African traditions can be troublemakers or culture heroes, the origins of problems or the sources of great gifts. For example, in a cycle of tales told by West Africa's Ashanti people, although Anansi the spider causes disease to enter the world, he also arranges for the creation of night, an interval when hard-working people can find time to rest. When people then reveal that they fear the dark, he arranges for the moon to shine in the sky at night. In one of the best-known of the trickster tales, Anansi ends up stuck fast to a figure made of sticky gum because he is too greedy. Ture, the trickster of the Zande people, is also a spider, and, like Anansi, he improves people's lives when he uses his cunning to provide them with water. Another animal, Ijapa the tortoise, serves as trickster in a cycle of tales told by the Yoruba, and Yurugu the jackal is the trickster who brings disorder to the world in stories of the Dogon. Hare, the trickster known as Brer Rabbit in North American folklore, is a popular figure throughout Africa. Just as stories of the trickster Hare emerge in the United States in the form of the Brer Rabbit tales, so too do the tales of Anansi, whose name becomes Aunt Nancy. Interestingly, traditional accounts of Anansi and Hare indeed appear to be conflated in the familiar American tale of Brer Rabbit's sticky encounter with the taciturn Tar Baby.

ANIMAL HELPERS

While animals in myths sometimes provide human beings with the gifts of fire, water, or the sun or moon, they also prove to be helpful in many other ways. Among Africa's Bambara people, the divine Antelope is the culture hero who teaches the people how to practice agriculture. In one of the stories of Rome's founding, the infant twins Romulus and Remus are protected and nourished by a mother wolf and a helpful bird. The hero of the *Ramayana* (ca. 300 B.C.E.), the ancient Indian epic, calls upon an army of monkeys led by Hanuman, their chief, to help him find his imprisoned wife and free her from her captors. In Norse tradition, Audhumla the cow plays a part in the unfolding of creation by licking away the ice that covers Buri, grandfather of Odin and the other gods. Animals also lend their assistance in creation stories from North America. In the Iroquois tale of the earth-diver, birds break Sky Woman's fall as she tumbles from the hole in the sky, and Turtle offers his back as a place for her to land. Then, while Sky Woman rests safely atop the waters, Muskrat, Beaver, and Otter dive into the depths of the primal sea in search of the grain of sand that will become the earth. Animals indeed serve as the earth-divers in almost all the Native American myths that feature this motif, and in many of the emergence tales, it is Spider Woman who guides the people during their long journey from the depths of the underworld.

ANIMALS AS KIN

In many myths the creation of human beings follows that of the animals that are therefore regarded as the first inhabitants of the earth. In most Native American accounts, for example, the "animal people" are already present when human beings appear among them. Animals often assist in the process of people's creation or in fact give birth to them. It is not surprising, therefore, that Native American myths emphasize human beings' kinship with the animal kingdom and frequently describe the period just after creation as a time when animals and human beings live together as one people and share a common tongue. Even though the lives of people and animals become differentiated from one another when they can no longer speak the same language, the kinship between them is expressed in Native Americans' practice of treating all animals with respect and in recognizing special relationships with particular animals through membership in clans. In myth, the ancient kinship is reflected in numerous stories wherein people and animals readily assume each other's forms or marry one another.

Although Native Americans are by no means the only peoples who recount stories of marriages between animals and human beings or animals and deities (Zeus, as a swan, is the consort of Leda), almost all of North America's native societies relate versions of this myth. Within these tales people or ancestral spirits marry such animals as the bear, deer, buffalo, whale, dog, raven, eagle, owl, gull, or rattlesnake, and on some occasions new races of beings emerge from these unions. In a tale told by California's Modoc people, all Native Americans are said to be descended from the children born to the youngest daughter of the chief of the Sky Spirits and the grizzly bear she marries. As the story goes, the chief of the Sky Spirits creates all the animals after he and his family move from the heavens to the earth. At this time the bears walk upright and speak the language of the Sky Spirits. When the chief's youngest daughter is lost in a storm, grizzly bears rescue her and raise her as their own. In time the young woman marries one of the bears and gives birth to several children. When, many years later, the chief finds his daughter once again, he is greatly angered to learn of her new life and punishes the grizzly bears by forcing them to walk on all four legs. He also withdraws their ability to speak and drives his grandchildren from their mother. Then, carrying his daughter, he retreats from the earth and is never seen again. The chief's grandchildren, who are soon scattered around the world, are the first people, the ancestors of the Modoc and all the other tribes.

In another tale, a story told by the Brule Sioux, it is a young woman's marriage to an eagle that preserves the human race. In this myth the water monster Unktehi creates a great flood that swells until it threatens to inundate the earth. The people climb higher and higher as the waters rise, but they cannot escape the deluge, and after they are swallowed up, their blood stains the cliffs they climbed and then hardens into the red rock of the Sioux's pipestone quarry. Only one person, a young woman, survives Unktehi's flood, and she is saved when Wanblee Galeshka, the great spotted eagle, swoops down from the sky and carries her away. Wanblee's nest, high atop a pinnacle of stone, remains untouched by the deluge, and it is there that the eagle and his wife make a home with their son and their daughter until the floodwaters recede. When the earth is once again fit for habitation, the children of Wanblee and his wife found the new nation of the Lakota Oyate and thus repopulated the world with the descendents of the eagle. Whereas animals and their spouses do not change their forms in the stories told by the Modoc and Sioux, in a myth of the Pomo people, a young woman is courted by a rattlesnake who takes the shape of a handsome young man when he visits her family to request her hand. On his fifth visit, Rattlesnake appears in his own shape and takes his new wife home with him. After the birth of their four sons, the young mother decides to visit her family one last time to bid her parents farewell, and when she returns to her husband's house, she then becomes a rattlesnake.

SHAPE-SHIFTERS

In some traditions the shape-shifter possesses the sinister power to take the form of a predatory animal. Stories of the werewolf, for example, are commonplace in the folklore of Europe, and in accounts from Mesoamerica and South America the powerful shaman is said to be able to assume the form of the jaguar. The shape-shifter is also a dangerous figure in many myths from Africa and can appear as a lion, leopard, or hyena that preys on human flesh. In a tale told by the Bantu-speaking people, a young woman falls in love with a handsome, well-mannered stranger and agrees to marry him. Her brother, however, is wary of the suitor and insists on accompanying the couple when they set forth into the forest. Although the brother is not altogether certain, he fears that he might have caught a fleeting glimpse of a second mouth—one filled with pointed teeth—under the hair of the stranger's head. When night falls, and the stranger goes off to catch some fish to eat, the brother takes the precaution of gathering spiked thorns to encircle the campfire. Sure enough, the stranger soon returns in the form of a hungry lion with glowing yellow eyes and wickedly sharp teeth. Huddled together inside their ring of thorns, the young woman and her brother must wait until dawn before they can at last make good their escape.

Many of myth's tricksters possess the power to transform themselves, and Zeus and other deities are often shape-shifters as well. Not only does Zeus turn himself into a swan, he also takes the form of an eagle and a bull in myths that afford examples of theriomorphosis, the transmutation of deities or human beings into the forms of animals. While animals like Rattlesnake assume the shape of people, other animals transform themselves into different creatures. Among the Inuit, for example, it is said that Akhlut the killer whale becomes a wolf when he grows hungry, and therefore the sighting of wolf tracks near the sea serves as a warning that Akhlut has come ashore to stalk and kill his prey. Although some characters in myth can change their shapes at will, others are transformed by a power not their own. The maiden Io, for example, undergoes metamorphosis when Zeus makes her a heifer, and in another tale from Greek tradition, Halcyone and Ceyx are changed into birds as punishment for posing as Hera and Zeus. It is indeed not uncommon that metamorphosis serves as a form of punishment, and in the Chinese tale of Chang-e, wife of the heroic archer Yi, it is therefore seen as fitting that the goddess of the moon is turned into a toad after she steals and consumes the elixir of life that was meant for her husband. Similarly, the elder brothers of the Mayan Hero Twins are changed into monkeys as punishment for their greed.

THERIANTHROPIC CREATURES

Myth tradition is also populated by therianthropic beings, figures that are part human being and part animal. In fact, the shape-shifting Zeus transforms himself into one of these creatures when he assumes the form of a satyr, a being that is both man and goat with a horse's tail. The great god Pan is a satyr and a nature deity; with his goat's horns and furry legs, he is appropriately emblematic of the pastoral realm. The god of herds and flocks, Pan sometimes causes frenzy (or "panic") among the animals when he plays upon his pipes. The Greek centaurs, horses with the heads and torsos of men, are, with the exception of the great teacher Chiron, a rowdy and ungovernable race of hybrid creatures. The Minotaur, another legendary figure in Greek tradition, is the bull-man who eats human flesh, and the Harpies, part women and part birds, prey on human souls. In contrast, Ganesha, the Indian god of wisdom and writing, is greatly revered as a symbol of good fortune. Represented as a man with an elephant's head, Ganesha, who has only one tusk, uses his second tusk as the pen with which he writes. In his fourth avatar, the Indian god Vishnu appears as a hybrid creature in the form of Narasimha, the lion-man. In this incarnation he is able to destroy the demon Hiranyakashipu, who is seemingly invulnerable because of Brahma's promise that no god, man, or animal will be able to slay him. However, because Narasimha is neither altogether god, nor man, nor animal, he does save the world from the malicious demon.

AFFINITIES WITH ANIMALS

The bond between ancient peoples and their fellow creatures is expressed in yet another way within myth tradition, for numerous deities are linked to an animal whose attributes they share. In other words, features of the god's identity are symbolically represented through reference to the characteristics of distinctive animals. In some instances a deity is portrayed as having an animal companion, and in others an epithet reveals a special relationship between god and animal. In many traditions, moreover, particular animals are held to be sacred to certain of the gods. Artemis, the Greek goddess of the hunt, is often pictured or described as accompanied by a deer, an animal that is indeed as swift and graceful as the goddess of the woods. The epithet "owl-eyed" links Athena, the Greek goddess of wisdom, with the perspicacity of the sharp-eyed bird that can see in the dark, and "bee," Demeter's epithet, emphasizes that deity's role as the Greeks' goddess of fertility. The cow, an emblem of maternal nurture, is the sacred animal of the Greek goddess Hera, the wife of mighty Zeus, and the horse, a symbol of the power of wind and storm, is sacred to Poseidon, Greek god of the sea.

Tales from myth and folklore preserve a vision of the animal kingdom that appears to be slowing reemerging during recent years. As their narratives indicate, ancient peoples see connections among all the forms of life on earth and regard the presence of animals as inextricably linked to their own existence. Shamans from many ancient cultures call upon animals to mediate between the realms of the material and the spirit worlds, and hunters in traditional societies revere the creatures that they kill through acts of ritual ceremony. Within the traditional societies of Mesoamerica, it is said that each person possesses a *nahual*, an animal double that serves as the protective spirit that lends its special strengths and traits to its human counterpart. Indeed, in the myths of the Aztecs, Tezcatlipoca and the other gods often assume the forms of their animal doubles. Similarly, animals are often associated with the identities of people's clans, either as the ancestors of a lineage or as protective figures. Among the Sioux of North America, the sun god Wi defends and protects the people through his manifestation as the Sacred Buffalo. In India, where the cow and the monkey are sacred animals, customs with legendary roots continue to endure.

EMBLEMATIC ANIMALS

Within the traditions of both myth and folklore, certain kinds of animals are repeatedly associated with particular activities or roles. Myths from Africa, Egypt, India, China, and the Americas, for example, all link the rabbit with the markings on the moon. In Chinese tradition, the goddess Chang-e joins the white rabbit that lives on the moon when she becomes a toad, the figure that appears during the time of an eclipse. In the stories of the Aztecs and Mayans, the moon, once as bright as the sun, loses some of its brilliance when a god hurls a rabbit unto its face. While the rabbit is not always seen as the figure on the moon, the interesting occurrence of this motif within several disparate societies is perhaps explained by that animal's behavior, for the rabbit is a creature known for its nocturnal appearances. Fierce animals, usually predators, appropriately serve as guardians in myth tradition, and birds are often messengers. The turtle (or tortoise), a creature widely regarded as an emblem of stability and longevity, appears in tales from many cultures, and in myths from China, India, North America, and Bali, the turtle is the animal that supports the heavens or the earth. In Chinese tradition, the creator goddess Nu Gua uses the legs of a gigantic tortoise to prop up the sky after Gong Gong destroys the mountain that had supported it, and in the tales told by many Native Americans, the World Turtle carries the earth upon its back. Although the sturdy turtle is often assigned the task of holding up the world, among Japan's Ainu people it is a mighty trout upon whose back the ocean rests, and in Norse tradition the World Serpent supports the weight of Midgard, the land where people dwell.

Many of the animals significant to myth tradition reappear in various genres of the folk narrative and in forms that arise within popular culture. Folk tradition, for example, offers the allegorical tales gathered together in Aesop's collection of animal fables, the bestiaries and the beast epics (such as the tales of Reynard the Fox) popular during the Middle Ages, and numerous Native American accounts of how animals originally acquired their features or their coloring as well as other kinds of narratives. The figure of the animal helper is especially popular in fairytales, including the many variations of the Cinderella story or such tales as *Puss in Boots*. In popular culture, bulls and bears are the talk of the stock market, and doves and hawks debate the policies of governments. Animals of all kinds serve as the mascots for athletic teams or other institutions, and in doing so they continue to share their traits and attributes with human beings. Indeed, the irrepressible animal trickster also appears within popular culture and can be seen there in the form of Bugs Bunny or many other cartoon figures.

See also Earth-Diver Motif; Emergence Motif; Etiological Myths; Guardians; Messengers; Monsters; Tricksters

THE APOCALYPSE

Myths from several different traditions address the subject of eschatology, the study of last things, or ends. Just as creation myths explain how the world came into being, eschatological myths envision the way that it will end. Stories of the apocalypse offer revelations, prophetic visions of the cataclysmic destruction of the cosmos. In many of the narratives, the violent destruction of the universe leads to the birth of a new, and often better, world. In others, the apocalypse either marks the end of all time and a return to chaos, or it heralds the end of all earthly life and the beginning of existence in eternity. In those myths wherein the world is reborn after its destruction, the apocalypse serves a function similar to that of the deluge: like the flood, the catastrophe that destroys the world cleanses and renews it.

Like other apocalyptic literature, the myths that foretell the end of the world frequently make use of suggestive images or symbols. Many of the accounts are particularly interested in interpreting signs that the world's destruction is imminent, and therefore offer vivid descriptions of the events that will inevitably lead to Armageddon. Several recurring themes appear among these visions of the last days of the earth. In many myths, both the disintegration of the world's society and the degradation of the earth's environment signal the approach of the apocalypse. For example, a decline in morality often becomes evident near the end of time. The final age of life on earth is frequently described as a period of confusion, violence, lawlessness, and unremitting warfare. It is also a time of natural disasters: the droughts, storms, volcanic eruptions, and earthquakes that plague the earth during its last days bring with them famine, suffering, and disease. In some accounts, a sign that the end is near appears in the heavens when the sun and moon grow dim and the stars fall to the earth. Sometimes monsters or demons emerge near the end of time, and some myths represent the apocalypse as a great battle between the forces of good and evil. In several myths the end comes when a final reckoning occurs on a Day of Judgment.

RAGNAROK: THE END OF AN AGE

The apocalyptic vision of the Norse tradition that is recorded in Snorri Sturluson's *Prose Edda* (ca. A.D. 1220) provides an extraordinarily detailed account of the end of the world. Because the inevitability of fate is central to the Norse worldview, the particular sequence of events that leads to Ragnarok (the gods' destiny) is represented in their myths as being preordained. As Snorri Sturluson recounts it, long before the actual coming of Ragnarok, the gods are well aware of the natural omens that will signal the beginning of the end, and they also know what must happen when Heimdall's horn summons them to meet the evil monsters and their old enemies, the giants, on the battlefield. Odin and the other Norse gods live with the understanding that their world is doomed, but they are well prepared to meet their destiny with fortitude, for they always know exactly how it will unfold.

Norse myths are interconnected in intricate ways, and it is therefore in the story of Loki and Balder that the stage is first set for the coming of Ragnarok. When Loki, the cunning trickster, causes the death of Balder, the most virtuous and the most beloved of the gods, the world begins to become increasingly wicked. Bloody wars rage among human beings, and the gods must constantly do battle with the giants and the trolls. After three years of violent warfare, a terrible winter called Fimbulvetr marks the next stage of Ragnarok's approach. Fimbulvetr lasts for three long years during which the sun does not shine and no plants can grow upon the earth. After this period, Hati, the wolf that pursues the sun, manages to catch it and swallow it, and a second wolf, Skoll, catches the moon. Surt, the giant who rules the fiery realm of Muspelheim, sends flames into the sky that cause the stars to fall to earth. All of these events signal the coming of the end, and when one morning the golden cock that lives in the home of the gods hears his crowing answered by the black cock that roosts in the underworld called Hel, the last day of the world begins.

On the day of doom, mighty quakes split the earth open and cause mountains to crumble. Loki, securely bound since the death of Balder, breaks free of his fetters, and so too do his son Fenrir, the monstrous wolf with gaping jaws, and Garm, the evil hound of Hel. The World Serpent named Jormungard, another of Loki's sons, rises from his home in the sea, spitting poison into the sky and causing huge waves to wash across the land. The ghostly ship Naglfar, made from nail clippings taken from the dead, rides upon the waves with Loki at its helm. From Muspelheim, Surt and his hordes of fire demons surge across the rainbow bridge called Bifrost, causing it to break. When Heimdall, the god who guards the rainbow bridge, sees all his enemies converging on the battlefield known as Vigrid, he blows upon Gjallarhorn to alert the other gods that Armageddon is nigh.

On the plain of Vigrid, the site of the last battle, the gods and their enemies engage in mortal combat. Odin, the leader of the gods, meets his death when he is swallowed by Fenrir the wolf. The mighty Thor kills the World Serpent, but before he can move nine paces from the corpse, Jormungard's deadly venom causes his death. Freyr, the god of fertility, is killed by the evil giant Surt, and one-handed

Tyr and Garm the hellhound slay one another. Heimdall, the trumpeter, does battle with Loki, and these two age-old enemies also kill each other. Vidar, one of Odin's sons, avenges his father's death when he slays the ferocious wolf by ripping Fenrir's hideous jaws apart and splitting open its head. After the battle is over and corpses litter the plain, the fire giant Surt sets the world aflame.

Although Ragnarok's holocaust brings to its end the world of the gods, in Norse tradition the apocalypse does not mark the end of time. The sun, just before the wolf swallows it, gives birth to a daughter, and after Ragnarok is over, the new sun rises in the sky. A new moon and stars begin to shine as well, and a new rainbow appears in the place of Bifrost. Odin's sons, Vidar and Vali, survive the day of doom, and Balder is freed from his confinement in Hel. Thor's sons, Modi and Magni, also survive, and these two inherit their father's magic hammer, Mjollnir. The last of the gods gather at the place that once was Asgard, the home of the gods, and together remember the times of the past. In addition to the gods, two human beings escape Surt's conflagration. When flames engulf the earth, Lif (life) and Lifthrasir (will for life) seek refuge in the branches of Yggdrasil. There they survive by drinking the life-sustaining dew of the World Tree, and when the new sun rises in the sky, they venture forth to give birth to a new race of human beings.

ETERNAL CYCLES OF DESTRUCTION AND RENEWAL

In Indian tradition, as in that of the Norse, the cosmos is reborn again after its destruction. However, while the Norse apocalypse ends an era that will never be repeated, in the Indian worldview the destruction of the world occurs within an endless cycle of recurring ages. During the Maha Yuga, or the "great age," life on earth becomes increasingly dangerous and difficult throughout the passage of four lesser eras. By the end of Kali Yuga, the last and the shortest of these lesser ages, most of the earth's human population has succumbed to the ravages of warfare, famine, or natural disasters, and many other people drown during the *pralaya*, the period of dissolution that precedes the beginning of another Maha Yuga. At the end of a Kalpa, a cycle of one thousand Maha Yugas, the earth, finally depleted of all its resources, is completely destroyed. The Kalpa is one day in the life of Vishnu, who in the form of Shiva-Rudra takes one night that is as long as the day to destroy the cosmos. In India's vision of the eternal cycle of birth, death, and regeneration, the universe is then re-created at the end of the night, when Vishnu awakens in the form of Brahma.

In Hindu tradition, the apocalypse known as Maya Pralaya, the "great dissolution," begins with one hundred years of drought. Shiva-Rudra, the destroyer of all life on earth, enters the seven rays of the sun and draws up all the water in the world. At the end of this period, called "the sucking of the waters by Rudra," all the moisture in the cosmos is contained within the sky. Shiva-Rudra then causes the rays of sunlight to turn into seven suns, and these suns set the world on fire. After the heavens, earth, and underworld have all been consumed by flames, Rudra, the storm god, exhales gigantic, multicolored clouds that flash with lightning and roar with thunder. Rain from the monstrous clouds quenches the holocaust and then continues to fall for one hundred years, and the heavens, earth, and underworld are all inundated. Vishnu, as Shiva-Rudra, exists alone in the watery void, for all gods and living things perish in the fire and the flood. For one hundred years Vishnu exhales a mighty wind that blows the storm clouds from the sky, and then he sleeps until he awakens as Brahma, the creator of the universe.

Among other stories in which the destruction of the cosmos leads to its rebirth is one from Native American tradition. In a myth of the Cherokee, the world is drowned when the strip of rawhide that holds the earth above the primal waters grows old and finally breaks. Whereas it is a flood that washes the world clean in many other apocalyptic narratives, in this account the earth is cleansed when it is submerged. Like the Norse and the Hindus, the Cherokee people view the destruction of their world as part of the endless cycle of the birth, death, and regeneration of all life, for each time the rawhide breaks, the Great Creator lifts the earth from its watery grave and then refashions the world.

APOCALYPTIC VISIONS OF THE END OF THE WORLD

In other myths of the apocalypse, including examples from Central Asian, Mesoamerican, and Native American traditions, the world is not re-created after its destruction. In these tales, where there is no vision of an afterlife that follows life on earth, the universe ceases to exist when the apocalypse occurs. The world is destroyed, according to ancient Mongolian accounts, when its mountains turn to dust. At that time, Erlik Khan, king of the underworld, at last seeks revenge for an injustice he suffered at the time of creation. Accompanied by nine iron warriors riding iron horses, Erlik Khan emerges from the bottom of the sea on the day of doom. Terrified people seek help from the gods when their slaughter begins, but even the gods cannot stop the bloodshed. When Karan and Kere, Erlik Khan's mightiest warriors, emerge from the underworld to strike down Sagjamuni (the Mongols' name for the Lord Buddha), the earth is utterly destroyed by the flames that erupt from Sagjamuni's blood.

Although the apocalypse envisioned by the Mongols does not come about until all their mountains have eroded eons in their future, the end of all time is nevertheless perceived to be inevitable. In stories told by the Aztecs, Cheyenne, and White River Sioux, the complete destruction of the world is also seen as inevitable, but these myths detail the ways in which the people try to forestall the coming of the day of doom. In the Aztec tradition, the Fifth World is the last one, and after a tremendous quake destroys it, the earth is not re-created. According to the Aztecs, human sacrifice is required to prolong the age of the Fifth World, for the ritual letting of blood keeps the sun in motion—it is when the sun stops that the earth begins to quake and the apocalypse occurs.

In the Cheyenne account, the cosmos is destined to vanish into a bottomless void when the Great White Grandfather Beaver of the North finishes gnawing through the wooden pole that supports the world. Because the Great Beaver gnaws faster when he is angry, the Cheyenne are careful to avoid invoking the wrath of the Beaver: they do not eat the beaver's flesh, and they do not hunt it for its pelt. According to the White River Sioux, the task of prolonging the existence of the world falls to Shunka Sapa, a gigantic black dog. The black dog sits and watches the ancient, wizened woman who has been stitching her porcupine-quill blanket for thousands of years. From time to time the old woman gets up to stir the pot of berry soup that has been simmering on her fire for thousands of years, and each time she does this, Shunka Sapa removes quills from her blanket. As she works on her blanket, the old woman is also stitching the destiny of the world, for as the Sioux tell the story, the day when the old woman completes her design of porcupine quills will be the last day of the earth.

MILLENNIAL APOCALYPSE

In yet another set of stories, the apocalypse that brings about the death of the temporal world also marks the time when eternity begins. Unlike the myths that envision the world's life as cyclical, as existing within the eternal pattern of birth, death, and regeneration, the millennial accounts link the destruction of the world to the end of time itself. In many of these prophetic tales, social order and moral responsibility are described as having given way to confusion and wickedness near the end of time, and the apocalypse, therefore, is frequently regarded as the occasion for a reckoning, a time for final judgments. The reckoning characteristically takes the form of a mighty battle that is followed by the raising of the dead on a Day of Judgment. Virtue triumphs over evil when the old, corrupt world is destroyed and replaced in eternity by a new order of existence.

According to Persia's Zoroastrian tradition, the last days of the world unfold during an epoch called the Age of Iron, a time of ceaseless struggle between the forces of good and evil. On one hand, malicious demons invade Persia, bringing with them earthquakes and drought, starvation and disease, but on the other, three saviors arise to represent the enduring powers of virtue. The sun and moon grow dim during the Age of Iron, a time of darkness in the world, but a shower of sparkling stars signals the birth of Aushedar, the first of the saviors. Like the other holy saviors, Aushedar is born of a young virgin who becomes pregnant while she bathes in a sacred lake that contains the seed of the prophet Zoroaster. A savior is born every one thousand years during the Age of Iron, and each of the holy men advances the cause of virtue throughout his lifetime. During the time of Aushedarmah, the second of the saviors, the hideous dragon Azhi Dahaka is finally defeated and killed. Soshyant is the savior when the world is destroyed, and it is he who presides on the Day of Judgment.

In the Zoroastrian vision of the apocalypse, the old world is destroyed when its mountains are melted and the molten metal from them spreads across the earth. The sheet of molten metal effaces the landscape, smoothing the earth's surface until it assumes the state of perfect flatness it possessed at the beginning of creation. In this fashion the world is cleansed of all evil and its demons are all killed. On the Day of Judgment, Soshyant raises the dead and reunites all people's bodies and their souls. The wicked spend three days and nights suffering in hell to cleanse them of their evil deeds, and then, their virtue restored, they join the righteous in a new paradise on earth. When the hot metal sweeps across the old earth, the people pass through it as though it were water, for in eternity death no longer threatens them. The apocalypse, in the Zoroastrian worldview, expunges evil from the world and thus restores the perfection of the earth's original creation.

Like the Persian account of the apocalypse, millennial narratives from both the Islamic and Christian traditions also envision a great battle between the powers of good and evil, numerous omens signaling the last days of the world, and a final Day of Judgment that marks the end of earthly life. In these apocalyptic tales, however, the wicked are condemned to hell forever as punishment for their evil, and only the righteous spend eternity in paradise. Prophetic writings from both traditions offer warnings about the many dangers of the last days of the earth. Islam's Hadith, for example, predicts the coming of the Antichrist, and Christianity's Gospel of Saint Mark warns of the appearance of numerous false prophets. Monstrous creatures also arise in accounts from both traditions: the Hadith tells of the reemergence of Gog and Magog, monsters once captured and imprisoned by Alexander the Great, and Saint John's book of Revelation describes the emergence from the sea of the blasphemous beast with its seven heads and ten horns. In both the Islamic and Christian visions of the apocalypse, the people of the world's last age are visited by epidemics, plagues, and famines, and catastrophic earthquakes and storms cause them to suffer greatly. In both traditions the righteous are at last rewarded for all that they have suffered when they are granted eternal life in paradise on the Day of Judgment.

Whereas the blessed are immediately separated from those who are damned in the Christian account of the Last Judgment, in Islamic tradition the deeds of all who are judged are weighed on a great scale. When the angel Israfil blows for the third time on his trumpet, the scale of reckoning descends from the heavens. The sins of every person are then balanced on the left side of the scale, and all the good deeds of each person's life are balanced on the right. When one side of the scale outweighs the other, the judgment is apparent, but when the two sides are equally balanced, a penitent soul must cry out for the mercy that is granted whenever the appeal is heartfelt and sincere. The judgment takes one hour, and after the weighing of the souls, all of the judged set out upon the bridge that leads to paradise and crosses over hell. The bridge is sharper than a sword and as narrow as a hair, and while the blessed have no trouble crossing it, those who are damned falter and then drop down into the gaping mouth of hell.

FIRE, FLOOD, AND CHAOS

The earth is destroyed by a variety of means in stories that envision an apocalypse. Accounts of conflagration and deluge are fairly commonplace, and these destructive forces usually serve the purpose of cleansing the earth before it is reborn. This is the case in the Norse tale, where the old world of the gods and giants is immolated before a new sun begins to shine, and in the Cherokee myth, where the world is washed clean when it is submerged in the primal sea. In the Hindu tradition, a new Kalpa begins only when the cosmos has been twice purified, first by a holocaust and then by a cleansing flood. The sheet of molten metal described by the Persians also serves to wash the earth, eradicating its imperfections and purging it of evil.

When the world is not reborn, the means of its destruction bring about the state of chaos that existed before it was created. In the story told by the Cheyenne, the cosmos is enveloped by the fathomless chaos of the void when the Great White Beaver finishes gnawing through the pole, and in the Aztec tale the earth collapses into chaos when a mighty quake shakes it apart. In these myths the apocalypse occurs when the life of the world has run its full course and therefore has come to its inevitable end in the condition of disorder from which it arose. In the myth of the White River Sioux, the world must come to its end when its order is complete, when the last porcupine quill that reveals its design is stitched into place, and in the story told by the Mongols, the history of the world comes full circle when Erlik Khan, who has waited since its creation to destroy it, exacts his revenge.

In the apocalyptic narratives that describe the temporal world's annihilation on the Day of Judgment, the earth and its people are characteristically assaulted by multiple destructive forces during their last days. The wars, earthquakes, famines, plagues, and appearances of monstrous creatures all reinforce the idea that the destruction of the world is a necessary outcome when life on the earth becomes increasingly intolerable. In these visions of the apocalypse, retributive justice restores the order that is lost during the chaos and confusion of the last days of the earth. The wicked, who have fostered the eruption of disorder, are duly punished, and the righteous, who have endured lives of misery, are granted the consolation of eternal bliss in paradise.

See also The Afterlife; Changing Ages; The Underworld

CHANGING AGES

In several cultural traditions, history and myth intersect in tales that express a particular people's conception of time. These accounts characteristically address a culture's perceptions of the changes that occur in the unfolding of time, and, in so doing, offer a worldview that serves to explain the experiences of temporal life. In other words, while creation myths answer the need to understand how life first came into being, myths of the changing ages answer a need to understand the significance of the present era in respect to the past and the future. A desire to define the meaning of human experience within the context of time is not at all unusual and can in fact be seen in the common practice of assigning labels to epochs ("The Dark Ages," for example), to centuries ("The Age of Reason"), or to decades ("The Roaring Twenties"). In similar fashion, the narratives of changing ages name the distinctive periods that comprise a culture's understanding of its own historical identity.

EPOCHS

While accounts of changing ages focus on the temporal experiences of earthly life, they usually reveal a people's conception of the nature of eternity. In Indian tradition, for example, four epochs of human existence are endlessly repeated within the recurring cycle of the birth, death, and regeneration of the cosmos. In the Indian worldview, where time is eternally cyclical, the earth is reborn again each time it is destroyed. In many other traditions, where life on earth is understood to occur in finite time, eternity lies beyond mortal experience, existing both before and after the time of earthly life. Interestingly, both of these worldviews often envision a golden age, a period of existence in paradise or Eden. In Indian tradition, the golden age occurs during the first of the four recurring epochs—and then occurs again each time the cycle begins anew. In many other traditions, the time of creation is also a golden age, but one that is lost when the world falls from grace. The golden age, in these accounts, can only be recovered in the eternal paradise beyond earthy life.

According to Hindu tradition, the four epochs of earthly life occur within a "great age" called the Maha Yuga. The four lesser ages, or *yugas*, are not of equal length; the first age, which comes after a *pralaya* (dissolution) that cleanses the world, is the longest of the *yugas*, and each of those that follow is shorter than the one before it. Through the course of the cycle of the changing ages, the world becomes increasingly corrupt, until, at the close of the fourth epoch, a flood that few survive cleanses the earth. The great Vishnu presides over each of the *yugas*, appearing in the first age as Brahma the Creator and taking the form of Shiva the Destroyer at the end of the cycle. Dharma, the principle of moral order, behavior, and duty, metaphorically stands on all four legs during the first *yuga*, but then loses one leg in each of the succeeding ages. During Kali Yuga, the last period of life on earth, Dharma rests precariously on one remaining foot. After the "great age" ends with the flooding of the world, another Maha Yuga begins with a golden age on earth. At the end of one thousand Maha Yugas, an interval known as a Kalpa, Vishnu, as Shiva-Rudra, destroys the entire cosmos. After the Maha Pralaya, the "great dissolution," Brahma re-creates the universe and another Kalpa begins.

During the Krita Yuga, the first age of life on earth, gift-giving trees provide for all the needs of human beings. No houses are required for shelter, and work is always a pleasurable occupation and never a necessity. There is no hardship or sorrow during the golden age, which is the time of *satva* (goodness), and people live long lives enriched by devotion to Dharma and the virtue of meditation. The first age is a period of brightness, and people accordingly worship a white god. As is characteristic of a golden age, the Krita Yuga is an era of abundance, an age of ethical, social, intellectual, and biological harmony.

The second age, Treta (three) Yuga, is so called because Dharma stands on three rather than four legs. Virtue and devotion still exist during this period, but are diminished by one-quarter. Earthly existence begins to become difficult when the gift-giving trees vanish after greedy people claim them as their own. Great rains produce new trees that replace the trees of plenty, and people turn to them for shelter and for food. People therefore still find their livelihood in the gifts from trees, but their lives are not as long and satisfying as those of the people of the golden age, and they must work hard to answer their needs. Some provide for themselves by stealing from others, and it is not long before greed and thievery inevitably lead to bloodshed. It is therefore during the second age that the Kshatriya, a caste of warriors and kings, is created to protect people from one another. Knowledge is the primary virtue during the Treta Yuga, and it is during this era that people worship a red god.

It is Vishnu the Preserver who presides over both the second and the third ages of the cosmos. During Dvapara Yuga, the third era of earthly life, famine, drought, disease, war, and suffering are all commonplace. People do not live as long as those of the preceding ages, and most endure hardship as they struggle to survive. Because only one-half the virtue present during the golden age still remains in the world, religious texts are produced for the moral instruction of the people. During the Dvapara Yuga, therefore, the great sage Vyasa appears on the earth to write the scriptures known as the Vedas. In the third era the righteous people begin to offer sacrifices to the yellow god they worship, and thus sacrifice becomes the highest virtue of the age.

The fourth age, Kali Yuga, is a time of darkness. Ignorance is widespread, and people's understanding is dulled by a cloud of illusion (*maya*). In this period, people ignore the scriptures written during the Dvapara Yuga. Under tyrannical leaders, nations wage senseless and unending wars against one another, and natural calamities frequently occur. Wicked and dishonest people prey upon others to advance their social standing and then measure their success in terms of their material possessions. Beggars fill the streets of the overcrowded cities where they endure misery and hunger or flee to the countryside where they live as hermits off the land. Life is short for the people of the Kali Yuga, and their god is black. Charity is the one virtue of the age—and is only practiced by the honest poor. According to Indian tradition, Kali Yuga is the current age, a time of darkness in the world.

CYCLES

The recurring pattern of earthly life, the cycle of birth, death, and regeneration, lies at the heart of the Hindu tradition's vision of cyclical time. Indeed, the concept of cyclical time is manifest throughout India, for although Buddhists and Jainists conceive of the changing ages as the eternal turning of the great wheel of time, each revolution of the wheel completes a cycle that will begin again. An account of the changing ages that comes from Mesoamerica's Aztec people offers an interesting variation on the idea of cyclical time. According to the Aztec myth, the world is created and destroyed several times over, but each new world that is born is different from the others. Each world is ruled by a different creator god, and each is governed by its own particular sun. Eventually, each world is destroyed by a means appropriate to its governing sun. Like the Indian accounts, the Aztec narrative of changing ages is informed by the cyclical pattern of birth, death, and regeneration. In Aztec myth, however, there is no conception of a golden age, and the finite history of life on earth does not repeat itself in eternal time. Furthermore, the Aztec history of the ages does not record the pattern of the world's gradual decline into corruption that appears in many other stories of the changing epochs.

In Aztec tradition, the ages of the world are distinguished by the various suns that govern them. Each of the first four suns is associated with one of the four essential elements—earth, air, fire, and water—and for the fifth age, all four elements are combined to create the Sun of Four Movements. The element associated with each of the worlds signifies the mode of its destruction by one of the gods. When a world is destroyed, the people who inhabit it are either killed by the elements of nature, or they are transformed into animals. At the end of each of the first ages, a different member of the Aztec pantheon creates a new sun, and, for the creation of the last world, the gods finally join together and offer themselves in sacrifice. Just as the gods must sacrifice themselves to set the Sun of Four Movements in motion, so too must human beings practice ritual sacrifice to prolong the age of their world. According to Aztec myth, the Fifth World is the present age, and after the destruction of the Sun of Four Movements, the earth will cease to be.

During the first age of the world, known as the Sun of Earth, Black Tezcatlipoca is the presiding god, and the earth is inhabited by giants who live by eating pine nuts. The First World comes to an end when jaguars, creatures associated in Aztec tradition with the earth and its underworld, devour the entire race of giants. Quetzalcoatl reigns over the Second World, which is governed by the Sun of Air. This age ends with the destruction caused by the mighty winds of an immense hurricane. The people of the Second World, who live on mesquite seeds, are transformed into apes by the tremendous winds. Tlaloc, the god of rain, presides over the world governed by the Sun of the Rain of Fire. Many of the people of the third age, who cultivate primitive grains, are consumed by flames when a rain of volcanic ash falls upon the earth, but those who survive become turkeys, butterflies, or dogs. The Sun of Water governs the fourth age, and Chalchiuhtlicue (She of the Jade Skirt) is the presiding god. Chalchiuhtlicue, goddess of streams and ponds, destroys this world by means of a deluge, and the people who subsist on acicintli seeds are then transformed into fish.

To create the fifth and the last of the Aztec suns, the gods gather together in darkness at Teotihuacan, an ancient site northeast of Mexico City. Two gods, the richly adorned Tecuciztecatl and the humble Nanahuatzin, agree to transform themselves into the sun by leaping into a sacrificial pyre prepared by the deities. The noble Tecuciztecatl approaches the flames four times, but then turns away in fear. Finally, after the sickly Nanahuatzin boldly steps into the fire and is instantly consumed, Tecuciztecatl also flings himself upon the pyre. The brave Nanahuatzin rises first in the east and is soon followed by another sun, that of Tecuciztecatl. Fearing that two suns will make the world too bright, the gods hurl a rabbit into the face of the second sun, which then dims and becomes the moon. Further sacrifices are required, however, before the sun and moon will move across the sky, so Quetzalcoatl cuts the hearts from each of the gods in the sacred ritual that the Aztecs, the people who cultivate maize, must themselves repeat during the fifth age. It is said that at the end of this era, when the Sun of Four Movements no longer crosses the sky, the earth will be destroyed by a mighty quake.

GOLDEN AGES OF THE PAST

Greek tradition, too, records a history of changing ages that begins with a people known as the Race of Gold. Older versions of the myth trace a pattern of the world's degradation from an idyllic Golden Age through the lesser ages of silver, bronze, and iron, but Hesiod, writing in the eighth century B.C.E., adds to the four traditional epochs a fifth age, the Age of Heroes, to honor the Greeks made famous by stories of the Trojan War. In placing the Age of Heroes between the Age of Bronze and the Age of Iron, Hesiod interrupts the narrative of social decline recounted in earlier myths, but his version, like the others, concludes with a description of the evil excesses of the current age. In fact, in his *Works and Days* (ca. 725 B.C.E.), Hesiod warns the people living in the Age of Iron of their world's imminent destruction by gods disgusted by the corruption of the earth.

Greece's Age of Gold, dating to the time of Zeus's father, Kronos, resembles the idyllic epochs described by other cultures. During the Golden Age, mortal beings enjoy long, peaceful lives, and the bounty of nature provides for all their daily needs. When the people of this age eventually die, they become guardian spirits who spread their benevolence throughout the world. Zeus creates the people of the Age of Silver—and then later destroys them in anger, for during the second age the people are childish and selfish. When these people die, their spirits enter the underworld. Zeus makes the people of the Age of Bronze from ash trees. The fierce and cruel mortals of the third epoch worship Ares, god of war, and eventually kill one another with their bronze swords. Their spirits, too, go to the underworld. During the Age of Heroes, the era of the Trojan War, the people are nobler and more courageous than those of the Silver Age or the Bronze Age. When the Greek warriors lose their lives on the field of battle, their spirits are transported to the Elysian Fields. In the fifth era, the Age of Iron, the valorous deeds of the heroic period are but a distant memory for those who live in troubled times. Indeed, Hesiod regards his own age as a period of hardship and toil, a time when violent and rapacious people commit crimes more terrible than those of any other age.

History, for the Zoroastrians of Persia, consists of four epochs of equal duration that unfold until the Day of Judgment marks the end of time. In Zoroastrian tradition, the history of the world tells the story of a cosmic conflict between the forces of good and evil, and it is only when that history is over that the battle is won. The Zoroastrians' apocalyptic vision of the end of time is one that is shared by other cultural traditions, and, indeed, scholars see its influence in Judeo-Christian eschatology. The Zoroastrians' understanding of hell, however, is different from that of Christian tradition, where evil people are condemned to eternal punishment. Although the wicked are sent to hell on the Day of Judgment, the three days and nights they spend there purge them of all evil. In eternity, according to the Zoroastrians, all people are made immortal in body and soul, and all dwell together in a paradise on earth.

In the first and second epochs of Zoroastrian history, Ahura Mazda, the great creator god, brings the universe into existence. During the first age, he creates from pure light the *menog*, the spiritual nature of the cosmos, and during the second age he creates the *getig*, the material universe. In the third age of the cosmos, the forces of evil assault Ahura Mazda's creation, and during this period good and evil exist together throughout the world. The fourth era, which begins with the birth of the prophet Zoroaster, is divided into four lesser ages. It is during the first of these, the Age of Gold, when Zoroaster is visited by Ahura Mazda and five of his angels. The Golden Age is the time of revelation, the time when the prophet learns of the good creation and of human beings' role in combating the forces of evil. During the Silver Age, Zoroaster shares his revelations and begins to convert the people, and during the third era, the Age of Steel, Zoroastrianism spreads throughout the entire Persian Empire. The Age of Iron, the last period of historical time, is filled with perils for those who battle evil. Earthquakes and droughts ravage the land and hordes of demons invade Persia. During this age, however, three saviors rise up among the righteous people, and the last of these, Soshyant, finally triumphs over evil on the Day of Judgment.

MYTHICO-HISTORICAL ACCOUNTS OF IRELAND'S AGES

In Ireland, because writing was not widely practiced among the Celtic followers of Druidism, the history of the ages is chronicled by Christian scribes who add a biblical context to myths circulated in an oral tradition. The monks' twelfth-century work, *Leabhar Gabhala* (Book of invasions), describes the six successive periods of Ireland's colonization and details the ways in which each group of invaders contributes to the legacy of Irish culture. Indeed, the *Book of Invasions* tells not only of how the people who settle Ireland civilize the island, but also of how they manage to reconfigure its landscape. To link Ireland's legendary past with the history of Christianity, the monks begin the *Book of Invasions'* narrative during the time of the great flood described in Genesis. According to the account the Christian scribes provide, the leaders of five of the peoples who invade Ireland are descendents of Noah.

The first age in Ireland's history is a short one and abruptly ends when Noah's flood inundates the world. According to the *Book of Invasions*, the first group of people to reach Ireland includes three men and fifty-one women who travel from their homeland in the Near East. Although his name is not mentioned in Genesis, one of the men, Bith, is said to be the son of Noah. Because his father refuses to allow Bith to board the ark, he and Ladhra and Fintan build the boat that carries their families to Irish shores. Shortly after the settlers divide up the land, Ladhra becomes the first human being to die on Irish soil. Bith soon dies as well, and shortly thereafter Ireland's first settlers are drowned in the flood.

Partholon, a descendent of Noah's son Japheth, is the leader of the twenty-four men and twenty-four women who next invade Ireland. When the settlers arrive, they find that the island contains only three lakes, nine rivers, and one treeless, grassless plain, and so they add to their new home seven additional lakes and three new plains to cultivate. They bring cattle to Ireland, introduce agriculture, build the first houses, and brew the first beer. They begin to establish a legal system, and it is during the age of Partholon that the first legal judgment is rendered—ironically, against Partholon himself. It is also during the second era that the inhabitants of Ireland first turn back the assaults of the Fomorians, a race of misshapen monsters descended from Ham, the son Noah cursed. After many battles, Partholon drives the Fomorians to Tory Island off the coast of Donegal. Ireland's second era lasts three hundred years, and during that time its population grows to five thousand. The age of Partholon comes to an end when a deadly plague strikes down all the people.

Ireland's third age begins when Nemed, another descendent of Noah, leads four men and four women to a new home on the island. As the Nemedians grow in number, they add four more lakes to Ireland's landscape and establish twelve new plains to grow their crops. Agriculture flourishes during the third age, and when the Nemedians introduce sheep to the island, their prosperity increases. Like those before them, the Nemedians must stave off the Fomorians, who look with envy at the settlers' agricultural successes. The Nemedians defeat the Fomorians in four initial battles, but when a devastating epidemic kills Nemed and two thousand of his people, the monsters seize their chance to take control of the island. The evil Fomorians demand a tribute from the conquered people: every year on Samhain the Nemedians must relinquish two-thirds of their children as well as two-thirds of their milk and corn. Desperate to throw off the burden of their tribute, the Nemedians attack their enemy's stronghold on Tory Island and succeed in killing the Fomorian's king. However, of the sixteen thousand who go into battle, only thirty Nemedians survive. The third age of Ireland's history therefore ends when the last of the Nemedians flee from their island home.

Ireland's fourth age is the era of the people known as the Fir Bolgs. In the *Book of Invasions*, the Christian monks link the history of these people to the story of Noah's flood by claiming that the Fir Bolgs, or "Bag Men," are the descendents of the Nemedians who travel to Greece when they sail away from Ireland at the end of the third age. Other accounts of their origin suggest that they might have come from Spain or Gaul, or that they might be the indigenous people who inhabited Ireland before the arrival of the Celts. In any case, the Fir Bolgs are the first of the races to survive on Irish soil, for although they are defeated in battle by the invaders of the fifth age, their survivors remain in Ireland, either in Connacht or on the Aran Islands. During the fourth epoch the people maintain the successful agriculture established during earlier periods, and, because the Fir Bolgs are warriors as well as farmers, they introduce to Ireland the heavy spearhead made of iron.

In Ireland's fifth age, the Tuatha De Danann, the people of the goddess Danu, invade the land of the Fir Bolgs. Said to be a race of gods, the Tuatha De Danann bring with them to Ireland the magical powers of their warriors and Druids as well as a legacy of poetry and music. Although several of the leaders of the Tuatha De Danann bear the names of the Celtic gods of Gaul, the Christian monks once again establish a connection between the fifth wave of invaders and the lineage of Noah: as the *Book of Invasions* explains it, the Tuatha De Danann are the descendents of those Nemedians who travel north when they flee from Ireland. Two great battles take place during the fifth age. In the first, the mighty heroes of the Tuatha De Danann defeat the Fir Bolgs, and in the second they finally overwhelm the Fomorians and drive them away from Ireland forever.

The sixth age brings to Ireland the Gaels, the ancestors of the people who currently live there. The Sons of Mil are mortal beings who must defeat the race of gods to make claim to their new homeland. The Milesians invade Ireland with two purposes in mind. On the one hand, they seek vengeance for the death of Mil's grandfather Ith, slain by the Tuatha De Danann, and, on the other, they follow the counsel of their Druids, who believe that Ireland represents the destiny of their people. Their destiny is also recognized by Eriu, a goddess among the Tuatha De Danann, for when the Milesians first come ashore, she foretells their victory and requests that they name their island after her by calling it the land of Eriu, or Ireland. The three kings of the Tuatha De Danann are killed during two great battles with the Milesians, and after their defeat, the survivors of the race of gods move into the fairy mounds of the Otherworld that lies beneath the land seized by the Milesians.

See also The Apocalypse; The Fall

THE COSMIC EGG

The world, in the myths of several cultural traditions, is born of an egg, a natural symbol of the genesis of life. In these creation stories, the image of the egg appropriately suggests a self-explanatory account of the origin of the cosmos—which develops from a primordial seed. Also known as the mundane egg (the world egg), the universal egg, the Orphic egg, or the Golden Germ, the cosmic egg contains the original potentiality of all existence enclosed within its shell. Arising from the precreation void, the egg represents in microcosm all that will come to be when the world assumes its shape. In the process of creation, the oneness of the cosmic egg is broken open to reveal the differentiation that is necessary to order the universe. In the Chinese tradition, for example, the opposing principles of yin and yang come into being when the egg breaks apart. Interestingly, some myth scholars have noted that the Big Bang Theory can be regarded as an analogue of the cosmic egg creation myth. Like the primeval egg, the original fireball described by the theory contains within itself the whole of creation. Just as yin and yang emerge from a broken egg, so too does differentiation occur in the universe when the Big Bang's primeval fireball explodes.

Although the idea of birth is implicit in traditional images of the cosmic egg, some theorists have proposed a more dramatic explanation of the origin of this form of creation myth by suggesting that certain ancient people's conceptions of the birth of the universe might have been inspired by their witnessing a solar eclipse. Indeed, during a total eclipse of the sun, the corona that streams from behind the darkened face of the moon can assume the shape of a mighty bird's wings. Then, as the sun emerges from behind the egg-like moon, its appearance naturally evokes images of birth. The sun, in several cultural traditions, is in fact represented as a bird—the figure suggested by the visual phenomena that often accompanies a solar eclipse. When the great bird that is emblematic of the life-giving sun is born from the cosmic egg, the whole of the cosmos comes into being.

BIRTH OF THE WORLD

In some accounts of the cosmic egg, creation begins when a serpent or a bird lays the fertile egg on the primal waters, while in others an egg simply arises from the empty void. In a few myths, the creator emerges from the cosmic egg or assumes the form of an egg that then gives birth to order as the creation unfolds. Occasionally the human race itself emerges from the cosmic egg. According to the Orphic tradition of ancient Greece, the world born of the oval egg is egg-shaped itself, and, in some of the creation tales, an egg divided in half is used to form the heavens and the earth. The cosmic egg, in certain traditions, is described as being silver or gold, the colors of the moon and sun. Similarities among the accounts of the primal egg found in the Chinese, Mongolian, Japanese, Indian, and Tibetan creation myths suggest the possibility that all originate in a common source. Variations of the cosmic egg motif also occur in the myths of Polynesian and African peoples, and a Finnish account is recorded in the nineteenth-century epic, the *Kalevala* (1849). A cosmic egg is present as well in the creation myth of the Pelasgians, the inhabitants of ancient Greece.

The multiple versions of early Tibetan creation myths represent the regional variations of peoples or clans who were separated from one another by mountain ranges. All of the pre-Buddhist stories, however, describe the original presence of the primal void, and many include accounts of the egg—or eggs—from which the world is born. In one of the most ancient of the myths, five primordial elements (hardness, fluidity, heat, motion, and space) fuse to give form to two great eggs. One egg, named Radiant, is composed of white light, and the other, called Black Misery, is made of darkness. When the god of wisdom strikes Radiant, splinters of light become gods called the *thorsas* (scattered divinities), and Sangpo Bumtri, the shining god with turquoise hair, emerges from the broken shell to make the world and produce its living beings. Another figure, Munpa Zerdan, is hatched from Black Misery, and as the king of nonbeing, he brings ignorance, madness, pestilence, and demons into existence. In a slightly different version, the five elements of earth, air, fire, water, and wood give shape to a single egg that splits into eighteen smaller eggs during the process of differentiation, and in other variations it is a beam of light that originally engenders the cosmic egg.

The Indian tradition, too, offers many distinct accounts of creation, but in one of the best-known among them, Brahma emerges from the Golden Germ to initiate the cycle of creation. In most of the creation myths from India, it is consciousness, or *brahman*, that wills order into being. Through the power of consciousness, the primal waters appear and a seed is made to float upon them. The seed becomes a shining, golden egg that contains Brahma, who remains enclosed within its shell while he meditates for the duration of one year. (It is said that because it requires a year for Brahma to split open the golden egg, it also takes a year for a cow to give birth.) When Brahma emerges from the cosmic egg, he makes the sky and the earth from its two halves, and then, through the powers of meditation, he creates the rest of the world. The process is one that Brahma performs many times over, for in India's vision of cyclical time, the universe is always destroyed before the creator once again splits open the Golden Germ.

ORDER EMERGES FROM CHAOS

Although the earliest of the Chinese creation myths do not mention the cosmic egg, the most familiar account, which dates from the third century A.D., tells of Pan Ku's emergence from a gigantic egg. In the beginning, chaos takes the form of an egg that contains within itself all the elements of the cosmos in the form of the body of Pan Ku. As Pan Ku slumbers inside the egg for eighteen thousand years, he grows to become a giant, and when he breaks forth from the shell, the white of the egg (yin) rises upward to become the sky and the heavier yolk (yang) sinks down to become the earth. To prevent yin and yang from merging into chaos once again, Pan Ku spends another eighteen thousand years pushing them apart. When he at last lies down to rest, and dies in his sleep, the world takes its shape from the parts of his corpse. Because this version of a creation myth includes both the theme of the cosmic egg and that of the body transformed to become the world, scholars speculate that the tale was probably influenced by the Hindu tradition of Central Asia, where these two themes earlier emerge. In its turn, Chinese tradition appears to have influenced the creation myths of Japan, for some of them also feature a primal egg in which the lighter and heavier elements (In and Yo) separate to form the "High Plain of Heaven" and the world beneath it.

In a creation myth that is remarkably similar to the Chinese story of Pan Ku, the people of Tahiti describe the original existence of a cosmic egg within the void known as Havaiki. Tangaroa-tahitumu, or "Tangaroa the origin," resides inside the egg until he grows restless and cracks the shell in half. Finding himself alone, the feathered creator god begins to shape the world from the materials at hand. First he lifts one-half of his shell high above him to create the sky, and then from the other half he creates the earth. He uses his own backbone to form mountain ranges, he makes clouds from his intestines, and from his other organs he creates the creatures in the sea. Tangaroa's feathers become plants, his blood provides the world with color, and his flesh gives form to deities and people. The feathered god indeed uses all of his body except his head to shape the cosmos, and therefore the Tahitians, who worship the head, find their creator and his shells in all that exists. According to the people, the sky is the shell that contains the sun and moon and the earth is the shell of all living things.

Egyptian creation myths are notably complex and various, existing in somewhat different versions at particular times and places. The cosmic egg, however, appears in a version told in Khemenu—or Hermopolis, as it was known to the Greeks. The cult town of the Ogdoad, the eight primeval deities who personify the forces of chaos, Khemenu is said to be the place where the sun first rose in Egypt. In the myth, the cataclysmic coming together of the four male and four female elements of chaos causes a mound of earth to rise up from the primal waters. A cosmic egg of gold rests upon the mound, and Ra, the god of the sun, emerges from it to ascend into the sky in the form of a brilliant sunrise. In a similar account, this time from Heliopolis, a sacred bird called the Benu lays its egg on the primal mound, and when the egg is hatched, the sun god comes forth and rises to the heavens.

BIRDS AND WINGED CREATORS

Another bird, a small duck called the teal, also lays its eggs above the primal waters in a creation myth from Finland. According to the *Kalevala* (1849), the sun, moon, stars, and all the lands appear when the eggs are broken open by a ferocious storm. A bird named Manuk Manuk, the blue chicken that is the consort of the primordial deity, lays the cosmic eggs in a myth from Sumatra. From the cosmic chicken's three eggs emerge the three gods who create the three realms of the universe—heaven, earth, and underworld. And in a myth from Borneo, two creator spirits in the form of birds swoop down to the primal waters and gather up two eggs. One egg is made into the sky, and the other becomes the earth. In a Greek myth told by the Pelasgians, a people who predate the classical Greek tradition, the great goddess Eurynome arises from chaos to dance upon the primal waters. Her dancing stirs up a wind, and from it she shapes a mighty serpent named Ophion. Eurynome assumes the form of a dove and lays a cosmic egg that is fertilized by her serpent consort. When the dove's egg hatches, the heavens and the earth and all the animals and plants come into being.

The cosmic egg is featured in yet another Greek creation myth, that of the Orphic mystery cult of the seventh century B.C.E. In this account, Time (personified as Chronus) creates a silver egg that gives birth to Phanes, the androgynous creator of the universe who possesses two pairs of eyes and magnificent wings of gold. Phanes, in whose dual sexual nature rests the origin of all life, represents the state of oneness that exists before the unfolding of differentiation occurs. The creator's name, which means "shining one" or "the revealer," signifies the appearance of light within the cosmos, and when Phanes then creates his daughter Nyx (Night), the process of differentiation begins. Together, Phanes and Nyx give birth to Gaea and Uranos, the Greek gods of earth and sky, and thus the entire universe is engendered by their union.

Characteristically a symbol of birth, the egg can also signify rebirth, as it does in accounts of the legendary phoenix, the bird that is reborn from its own egg after perishing in flames. Although contemporary scholars offer several different theories to explain the origin of tales about the phoenix, a fabulous creature that bears a Greek name, the classical Greek writers Hesiod (eighth century B.C.E.) and Herodotus (fifth century B.C.E.) both link the phoenix to ancient Egypt's Benu bird. In Egyptian tradition, this sacred bird of Heliopolis—the city of the sun—immolates itself at the end of its long life and then rises again from the ashes of its nest. An enduring symbol of resurrection and immortality, the solar bird of Egypt is first identified as the phoenix in tales told by the Greeks; later on, the image of the phoenix is adopted by the Romans to signify the immortality of their empire, and eventually, the bird that is emblematic of rebirth becomes a Christian symbol. In its service as a Christian emblem, the phoenix shares its symbolic significance with yet another traditional image, that of the Easter egg.

BIRTH OF HUMAN BEINGS

Among the variations within the cosmic egg motif are those accounts in which human beings emerge from the eggs. In a tale from the Admiralty Island, for example, people are born of the eggs laid by the World Turtle, and many similar stories can be found throughout Polynesia. In Tibet, where egg myths abound, some of the narratives recount the origins of different orders of people. One myth, for instance, tells how the water spirits from four original eggs produce the classes of people who make up Tibet's social order. From the water spirit of a golden egg come those who are kings, and those who are servants come from a turquoise egg. An iron egg produces religious leaders or holy men, and social outcasts come from a bronze egg. In similar fashion, another myth relates how Tibet's six traditional clans originate in six yellow eggs that are carefully cracked open by a blacksmith sent by the spirits. According to this tale two great birds lay eighteen primal eggs that are yellow, blue, and white, the colors of the earth, sea, and sky. The clans of people emerge from the six earth-colored eggs after a blacksmith from the gods cracks open six white eggs and a smith from the water spirits opens six blue eggs.

REGIONAL EGG MYTHS

While Tibetan tradition offers accounts of creation from a cosmic egg as well as stories of human beings' emergence from eggs, other egg myths are also commonplace. Indeed, many regional myths describe how eggs give birth to mountains or other features of the landscape. One of these, for example, recounts how cosmic eggs produce the four lakes that lie at the foot of Mount Kailash, one of Tibet's sacred mountains. According to the tale, the four eggs arise from the void and give form to bodies of water with distinctive characteristics. Gungchu Gulmo, born of a silver egg, resembles the moon, and Gurgyal Lhamo, which comes from a white egg, shines like a mirror. The lake of the gods, Gurgyal Lhamo contains the treasures of the water spirits. An island sanctuary lies in the middle of Lake Rakastal, which is born of a golden egg, and people make pilgrimages to the island to seek spiritual enlightenment. Manosawar, the fourth lake, comes from a blue cosmic egg and is known for the medicinal plants that grow near its shores. One of these, a healing flower with eight petals, is the turquoise blue color of the egg and its lake. Because tales of the cosmic egg are widespread throughout the ancient Tibeto-Mongolian culture, it is not surprising that the tradition's greatest hero, the legendary Gesar Khan, is also born of an egg, one that springs from his mother's head.

A particularly interesting account of the cosmic egg comes from the Dogon people of Mali in West Africa. In some versions of their creation myth, the creator god Amma assumes the form himself of a great cosmic egg that contains the potentiality of the entire cosmos. The elements essential for creation—fire, air, earth, and water—all exist within the god, whose name is said to mean "The One Who Holds." Amma is split open by seven tremendous vibrations or explosions, and from him fall the Nummo (water) deities in the form of five sets of male and female twins. The Nummos give shape to the sky and the earth, divide the day from the night, create the changing seasons, and organize the societies of the people they produce. In their representation as twins, these water deities symbolize duality, the differentiation that gives rise to order. Because the Dogon believe that water is the element from which all life arises, the Nummos take the form of that essential element. This myth, with its intriguing description of the explosive shattering of the cosmic egg, is one of those that call the Big Bang Theory to mind. In its emphasis on the importance of water to life, it also resembles scientists' accounts of a primordial soup.

See also Creation Myths; Ymir Motif

CREATION MYTHS

Creation myths, narratives that address the question of how the universe or the earth and its inhabitants first came into existence, can be found in almost all cultural traditions. With relatively few exceptions, peoples from around the world seek to explain their origins and thereby define their cultural identities in their creation myths. In circumstances where a story of creation is not extant, as with the early Celtic settlers of Ireland for example, scholars believe that tales that once existed have in fact been lost. Although Christian scribes of the twelfth century compiled Druidism's legends of Ireland's colonization, the monks did not record any pre-Christian creation myths that might have been part of their ancient culture's oral tradition. Fortunately, stories of creation from Germanic cultures, where a rich oral tradition also flourished before the coming of Christianity, were preserved by Iceland's Snorri Sturluson, who recorded them in his *Prose Edda* (A.D. 1220). In the instance of the Inca, another people whose legends were transmitted by storytelling, the sixteenth-century writer Inca Garcilaso de la Vega chronicled traditional myths in *The Royal Commentaries of the Inca* (1609).

Although the world's creation myths are wonderfully various in their details, myth scholars have identified several recurring patterns among them. Tales of creation, which characteristically depict the emergence of order from a state of chaos, commonly begin with a description of the void; in many if not in most of these narratives, the original chaos is represented as the primal waters that exist before creation begins. In some creation myths, the universe, the earth, the original deities, or the first living beings are born of a cosmic egg. In myths of this kind, an image of the fertile egg serves as a familiar emblem of the source of existence. In other myths, creation arises from a primal mound, a small bit of earth that rests upon the surface of the primordial sea. In creation myths that feature the earth-diver motif, the world grows from a primal mound that is created when a deity, animal, or some other agent swims to the bottom of the primal void to recover and then bring to the water's surface a particle of earth. In this type of myth, creation follows an act of descent, but in another category of tale, the emergence myth, creation is completed only when human beings or animals ascend from the depths of the earth to reach the world that exists on its surface.

The imagery of birth that is expressed in the conception of a cosmic egg is also present in tales of both the earth-diver and the emergence. In myths of the earth-diver, the primal waters give birth to the cosmos, and in stories of the emergence, life comes forth from the womb of the earth. In yet another type of creation myth, primal parents give birth to the world. Primal parents, usually conceived as earth mother and sky father, must be separated before creation can occur, for when they are joined as one they represent the undifferentiated unity of the void. Myths of the primal parents often explain the need for separation by pointing out that when earth and sky are linked together, there is no space for creation to exist or for the parents to give birth. When earth and sky are pulled apart, the order of the world is born out of chaos. Although the earth represents the primal mother in most myths of the world parents, in the creation tale from Egypt, Nut, the goddess of the sky, is separated from Geb, the god of the earth.

ORDER FROM CHAOS

In some creation myths chaos is the state of nothingness that exists before the creator deity brings the world into being. In most creation myths the order of the cosmos is unfolded in a series of stages, and, in tales where the world is shaped from nothing (*ex nihilo*), the creator usually makes the earth, heavens, and living beings by successive acts of thought, word, or deed. In other words, order might arise from creators' thoughts, from words that are spoken or sung, or from an action a creator performs. Sometimes, for example, creators mold human beings from clay, carve them from wood or stone, or fashion them from cornmeal. Sometimes creators make the world from their own secretions, from their sweat, vomit, spit, semen, or breath, and sometimes they perform as *deus* or *dea faber* (deity as maker), the artist who skillfully designs and constructs the world. Sometimes the process of creation requires a sacrifice, usually the offering of a god, and sometimes the cosmos is shaped from the dismembered body of a monster, deity, or primordial being. Named for one of the most familiar instances of this theme, that of the Norse tradition's description of creation from the dismembered corpse of the first Frost Giant, this repeating pattern is known as the Ymir motif.

MULTIPLE MOTIFS

In many myths the recurring patterns of creation from a cosmic egg, from earth-diving, from an emergence, from primal parents, or from nothingness appear in various combinations. For example, in one version of the Hopi people's accounts of their origins, the primal parents separate by dividing themselves into two beings: Spider Woman, the earth mother, becomes both Spider Woman and

Huzruiwuhti, goddess of life's forms, and Tawa, the sky father, makes himself into Tawa and Muiyinwuh, god of life's energy. Tawa and Huzruiwuhti together produce the Sun Twins and the Great Serpent, and then Tawa thinks of the creation of other beings. When Tawa sings of his thoughts, Spider Woman molds his thought into clay and thus brings into existence the birds, animals, and fish. After Tawa and Spider Woman also think the people into being, Spider Woman guides them in the journey that leads to their emergence from their origins in the underworld. In addition to the motif of creation from primal parents, the intricate Hopi tale incorporates the themes of creation by thought, song, and deed, as well as by emergence.

The creation myth recorded in the Babylonian epic, the *Enuma elish* (ca. 1100 B.C.E.), also begins with the motif of the primal parents. Long before the heavens and the earth come into existence, father Apsu, representing fresh water, unites with mother Tiamat, the personification of salt water. From these original parents come the gods who emerge from the primordial waters to produce a pantheon of deities. The gods, however, do not live in harmony with one another, and the next stage of creation occurs when the young gods overthrow the first generation: father Apsu is killed by his descendents, and then Marduk, who aspires to become king of all the cosmos, earns his crown by battling and overcoming mother Tiamat. With Tiamat's defeat a new order is established in the universe, and Marduk creates the heavens and the earth from the two halves of the primordial mother's dismembered corpse. He makes rain clouds from Tiamat's saliva, forms mountains from her skull, and causes the Tigris and Euphrates rivers to flow from her eye sockets. In the Babylonian account, the original void of the primordial waters is represented in the form of the primal parents. The Ymir motif is also present, as is the theme of *deus faber*, or deity as maker, for Marduk, who creates order in the universe when he constructs the heavens, the earth, and the landscape of the world, is indeed the god who configures the cosmos.

CREATION OF THE COSMOS, THE DEITIES, AND HUMAN BEINGS

Cosmogony

While some creation myths describe the birth of the cosmos or explain the origins of the primordial deities who create the world, others emphasize the origins of humankind or account for the history of a particular people. Among myth scholars, a story that recounts the birth of the universe is known as a cosmogony, and one that focuses on the origins of the gods is called a theogony. The tale that traces the origins of human beings (anthropogony) sometimes presumes the existence of the world and its creator deities. The Hebrew creation story recounted in the first chapter of Genesis provides a good example of a cosmogony. In this account, Elohim (or Yahweh) creates the entire cosmos from nothing by speaking it into being. In a series of stages, Elohim makes the heavens and the earth, the light and the dark, the dry land and the sea, the sun and the moon, and all the living creatures. In this account, the first of two versions recorded in Genesis, Elohim completes the process of creation when, on the sixth day, he creates a man and a woman in his own image and grants them dominion over the world.

Theogony

The *Enuma elish*, which describes the Babylonian gods' birth from the primal waters, offers an example of a theogony, an account of creation that focuses upon the emergence of the creator deities themselves. Hesiod, the Greek writer from the eighth century B.C.E., presents another example in his *Theogony* (eighth century B.C.E.). Like the Babylonian myth, the story recounted in the *Theogony* explains how the primordial parents, Gaea the earth mother and Uranos the sky father, arise out of chaos and give birth to the generations of gods that eventually become the Greek pantheon. Just as father Apsu is overthrown by his descendents, so too is Uranos usurped by his son Kronos, and then Kronos is defeated in battle by his son Zeus. Like Marduk, Zeus establishes a new order in the world after he becomes god of the sky and thus ruler of the family of Olympian deities.

Anthropogony

While the cosmogony of Hebrew tradition describes the creation of the universe, and the Babylonian and Greek theogonies explain the origins of the gods, myths from many other cultures emphasize human beings' appearance in the world. The emergence myths of North America's native peoples, for example, recount the journeys of the first people from their origins in the depths of the earth to their ultimate destination, the world they discover when they reach its surface. In these myths the process of creation is completed when the people emerge to inhabit their new homes on the earth. Although Ireland's Christian scribes do not include a cosmogony among their chronicles of early Celtic myths and legends, their account of the settlement of their island, culminating in the arrival of their own ancestors, serves as another example of anthropogony. The monks' *Book of Invasions* (A.D. twelfth century) traces the origins of the Irish people back to the last invasion of the island, the time when the mortal Milesians defeat a race of gods to make claim to their new home. Similarly, *The Royal Commentaries of the Inca* (1609) describes the emergence of the Incan culture as dating to the time when Father Sun sends two of his children to earth to teach the people, who live as wild animals, to grow crops, weave clothing, and build houses, temples, and cities. Under the guidance of their deities, Manco Capac and Mama Ocllo Huaco, the Inca emerge as a people whose destiny it is to create an empire.

MODES OF CREATION

Within creation myths from around the world, the cosmos originally comes into being by a variety of means. In the tale told by the Boshongo people of Central Africa, for example, the creator god Bumba, who at first exists alone in the dark void of the primal waters, vomits up the sun. When the sun begins to dry the land, and rain clouds appear in the sky, Bumba vomits up the moon and stars, nine kinds of animals, and the first human beings. In this myth, Bumba is not the sole creator of the world, for the animals he produces create additional creatures, and then Bumba's three sons complete the process of creation by making ants, the seeds of all plants, and the bird called the kite. The Boshongo tale features the motif of creation by excretion or secretion, and one of the creation myths of the Chukchi people of Siberia offers another version of this theme. The creator, in this Inuit story, is the trickster Raven, who is called upon to make an earth where people can live soon after his wife suddenly gives birth to human beings. As the story goes, Raven does create the world by defecating and urinating as he flies across the sky: the mountains, hills, and valleys are formed from the trickster's excrement, and his urine becomes the rivers, lakes, and seas.

In the myths from many cultures, creator deities think, dream, speak, or sing the cosmos into being. The creator, for example, in the myths of the Laguna people of New Mexico is called both Thinking Woman and Old Spider Woman. As her name indicates, Thinking Woman conceives within her mind the original being of all that exists. Thinking Woman makes the world, including the thoughts and the names of all it contains, and then her twin daughters, Uretsete and Naotsete, contribute to creation by thinking into existence additional names. In the Mayan myth recorded in the *Popol Vuh* (ca. 1558), the creator deities talk and plan together in the darkness of the primal waters. After they have thought about creation, they bring the earth into being by proclaiming their desire. At their word, the world of mountains, valleys, plants, and streams arises from the void. Viracocha, the creator god of South America's ancient Tiahuanaco people, shapes the landscape of the earth by waving his hand as he utters his commands, and Wanadi, the creator in the myths of Venezuela's Yekuhana people, makes the first human beings by thinking, dreaming, and singing as he sits smoking his tobacco and shaking his gourd rattle. When the first people appear, they are exactly as he has dreamed them.

Although Wanadi dreams and sings people into existence, and Raven's wife gives birth to the first human beings, in many other creation myths the first people are shaped from various natural substances. In the Babylonian creation myth, for example, Marduk orders that human beings be made from the blood and bones of Kingu, the defender of mother Tiamat who is slain at the time of her defeat. In Norse tradition, Odin and his brothers create Ask, the first man, and Embla, the first woman, from an ash and an elm tree. According to the Navajo, the first man and the first woman are made from a white and a yellow ear of corn, and, similarly, in the Mayan creation myth the creators shape human beings from a cornmeal dough. In the myth of North America's Chelan people, the creator deity orders the animals to kill the Great Beaver and then make people from portions of its corpse. Eleven different tribes of human beings are created from Beaver's body parts, and a twelfth, the bloodthirsty Blackfoot tribe, is formed from its blood. Viracocha, the creator deity of the Tiahuanaco culture, fashions human beings from stone and then paints features on all of the figures before commanding his divine helpers to bring them to life.

RE-CREATION

Creator deities are not always satisfied with the beings they first make, and some myths describe their efforts to refashion their creations. Viracocha, for example, creates a race of giant human beings when he first shapes the heavens and the earth, but because he is displeased by the behavior of the giants, he turns them into stone and then floods the world to cleanse it of his mistake. The Mayan creators are also disappointed with the beings they originally make, first modeled out of clay and then carved out of wood, and they too create a flood to rid the world of these imperfect creations. Indeed, the deluge motif is often associated with creation myths and frequently plays a role in emergence tales. In those traditions where a flood occurs long after the creation, as in the Hebrew story of Noah and his ark, the world must be created anew when the waters recede. According to Greek myth, Zeus destroys the original creation when he floods the world to punish wicked human beings. Deucalion and Pyrrha, two mortal beings who survive the deluge, follow the advice of the gods and create a new race of people from the stones of the earth.

Other myths, acknowledging the imperfections of creation or the differences that exist among human beings, describe mistakes that occur during the process of creation. In a tale told by Africa's Yoruba people, the creator deity Obatala begins to carefully fashion human beings out of clay. When he eventually grows tired and thirsty, he refreshes himself with wine before completing his task. Unfortunately, the figures that Obatala models after consuming the wine are misshapen in various ways, but he does not realize this when he asks Olorun, the sky god, to breathe life into them. When Obatala recognizes what he has done, he vows that he will never drink wine again and that he will forever serve as the protector of all people with deformities. Similarly, in one of the creation myths from ancient China, Nu Gua, the mother goddess, models human beings from the wet clay of the Yellow River. When she tires of her painstaking work, she finds a means to make people more quickly: the goddess drags a rope along the riverbed and then shakes free the clumps of clay that adhere to it. According to this tale, the people Nu Gua shapes by hand become China's aristocratic class, and those formed when she shakes the rope turn into the common people.

REASONS FOR CREATING HUMANKIND

The creator deities of myth tradition bring human beings to life for a variety of reasons. In the Hebrew account, Elohim desires to crown his creation by granting dominion over it to the beings he makes in his own image. The Babylonian deities, who make people from the blood and bones of their vanquished foe, create humankind to serve the gods and to honor them in rituals, ceremonies, and sacrificial offerings. The Mayan creator gods long to give life to beings who will praise them, love them, and call them by their names, and are therefore displeased when the original people made of clay or of wood are unable to do so. After the deities form people from corn, the food that can nourish them, they give life to beings who indeed praise their gods and who also celebrate the beauties of the world their creators have made. Finally, the myth told by Africa's Yoruba people offers yet another explanation of creators' purposes. After Obatala, who creates land upon the primal waters to add variety to the cosmos, finishes the task of making the world, he discovers that he is lonely. Desiring the companionship of beings similar to himself, he models human figures out of the earth's clay.

See also The Cosmic Egg; Deluge Motif; Earth-Diver Motif; Emergence Motif; Primal Parents; Separation of Earth and Sky; Ymir Motif

CULTURE HEROES

All myth traditions feature accounts of the extraordinary actions or memorable contributions of heroic figures. Agents of change within societies, culture heroes are the legendary characters who bestow great gifts, teach crucial skills, found social institutions, rescue people from peril, or otherwise serve humankind as important benefactors. Culture heroes can be creator deities or other gods, semidivine beings, animals, or heroic people; in many cultural traditions the wily trickster is also represented as a culture hero. Culture heroes often bring the gifts of light or fire to humanity, and in some accounts it is this figure that first provides people with their staple food. Sometimes culture heroes appear on earth to instruct societies in the arts of hunting, farming, or healing, and sometimes they impart sacred knowledge by teaching people how to perform rituals and ceremonies. In acts of bravery—and often self-sacrifice—culture heroes confront threatening monsters or dive into the dark depths of the primal waters to seek the soil needed for the creation of the earth. Occasionally culture heroes are the sole survivors of a deluge and thus the primal parents who repopulate the world. In many traditions culture heroes are the courageous warriors or bold adventurers whose mighty deeds reflect the values of a people.

GIVERS OF GIFTS

Fire

As the givers of gifts, culture heroes are widely celebrated for improving the conditions of human lives. Although stories from around the world enumerate a variety of gifts that serve people's welfare, it is the gift of fire that is most frequently acknowledged. Interestingly, in almost all accounts the hero who presents fire to the people does so only after stealing it, and it is perhaps because the culture hero in this instance is also a cunning thief that it is so frequently the trickster who performs this deed. In the story told by North America's Klamath people, the great trickster Coyote steals fire from Thunder by cheating him at dice, and in Polynesian tradition another trickster, Maui, descends to the underworld to steal the burning fingernails of Mahui-ike, keeper of the flames. In the tale recounted by the San of Africa's Kalahari Desert, Cagn, the praying mantis that is both creator deity and cunning trickster, steals the fire that is hidden beneath the wing of Ostrich—and thus causes Ostrich to keep his wings closed forever after and therefore to forgo his ability to fly. As the story goes, Cagn is consumed by the stolen fire and then later reemerges from his own ashes. Prometheus, the trickster-like Titan from Greek tradition, also pays a price for his theft of fire when the angry Zeus decides upon his punishment: lashed to a pinnacle, Prometheus is doomed to serve as prey to the mighty eagle that pecks at his liver throughout eternity. (According to some versions of the tale, Prometheus is finally freed when the hero Herakles slays the voracious eagle.)

Light, Water, Night, and Seasons

In addition to their gifts of fire, the trickster thieves of myth are also credited with providing many other treasures. The Native American trickster Coyote is particularly resourceful, and in a story recounted by the Miwok he brings light into the world of the people who live in the Village of Darkness when he journeys across the mountains to steal the sun and the moon. In a myth of the Kalapuya, Coyote is the culture hero who provides water for everyone by traveling to the land of the Frog People, who hoard all the water, and destroying their dam. The White Mountain Apache tell of how Coyote steals tobacco from the sun, and the Crow describe how he steals summer from the powerful Old Woman who keeps it in a bag. In this tale, Old Woman's children demand the return of the black bag and threaten Coyote with a fight to the death. The trickster, who relies on cunning rather than on strength, suggests a compromise, and thus all eventually agree that Coyote's people will keep summer for half of the year, and during the other half they will take possession of another bag, the white one that contains the winter.

In tales from Africa and Polynesia, tricksters are the culture heroes who present people with a very special gift when they successfully reorganize the passage of time. Although Anansi, the spider trickster of Africa's Ashanti people, often causes trouble for human beings, he does them a great service when he notices that their lives are filled with their unending labor in the fields. Determined to find some way of providing relief for the people, Anansi spins a thread and climbs up into the heavens to consult with Nyame, the powerful creator deity and ruler of the sky. Nyame listens sympathetically to the trickster's petition and agrees to create the dark interval of night as a time when people can set aside their work and rest from their daily chores. In the story told by Polynesia's Maori and Hawaiian peoples, the trickster Maui confronts a very different problem: because the fiery sun god travels so quickly across the sky each day, human beings do not have time to complete their tasks before the fall of night. Although he recognizes that the flaming sun god might prove to be a formidable adversary, Maui nevertheless resolves that he will try to force the fleet-footed deity to cross the sky more slowly. He therefore captures the god by ensnaring his sixteen rays in strong nooses made of coconut fiber. When the angry sun attempts to turn Maui into ashes, the brave trickster overcomes him with his magic axe. As in the story of Coyote's theft of summer, Maui and the sun god agree to settle their quarrel with a compromise, and thus during half the year the sun travels slowly across the sky and then moves much more quickly throughout the other half.

Food

In many traditions culture heroes first introduce the food that a society then comes to accept as a necessary staple. In most of these tales, those who bring the gift of food also teach the people how to plant and harvest it or how to hunt and kill it. Throughout North America, where maize is traditionally an important source of food, numerous myths portray the figure of the hauntingly mysterious Corn Mother as a great culture hero. In the stories told by both the Abenaki and the Penobscot peoples, the Corn Mother must sacrifice herself to bestow her gift, but in doing so she leaves her people with a legacy that never dies. The Abenaki account of the origin of corn begins when a young woman with long, light-colored hair appears before a lonely hermit who lies dreaming in the sun. Although he is reluctant to carry out her bidding, the hermit finally accedes to her strange requests, and, after burning clear a patch of earth, he takes hold of the maiden's hair and then drags her body to and fro over the scorched ground. In time, when graceful stalks grow from the earth and ears of corn appear, the hermit once again can see the young woman's silken hair in the plants' golden tassels.

According to the Penobscot, First Mother is the culture hero who saves her people from starvation in their time of need. In this origin myth, Kloskurbeh the Maker and his helper, a young man born from the foam of the sea, create the world together, and then the young man marries a maiden who is born from a plant and the morning dew. The young man and his wife, First Mother, have children, and as the people grow in number, the animals they hunt for food become increasingly scarce. First Mother weeps to see her people starving, and it is then that she tells her husband that her grief will never end until he has killed her. The sorrowful young man journeys far to consult with Kloskurbeh, but the great maker advises him that he must heed each one of First Mother's instructions. The deed is done, therefore, and two of the couple's sons take hold of their mother's hair and drag her body back and forth over the bare earth until her flesh is gone. They then burn her bones and bury them, and after seven moons have passed, they return to find the wonderful plants that are First Mother's enduring gifts. Throughout the years to come, the sweet corn, made from their mother's flesh, sustains the people, and from the leaves of the tobacco plant, which grows from her bones, comes First Mother's breath.

Knowledge

Fu Xi, the great culture hero of several Chinese myths, not only climbs the Tree of Heaven, Jianmu, to seek precious gifts for his people, but also, according to some ancient tales, survives a devastating flood. In stories from the peoples of southern

China, Fu Xi and his sister Nu Gua, two peasant children, escape drowning in the deluge created by Gong Gong, Spirit of the Waters, by shaping a sturdy boat from a gigantic calabash. Finding themselves the sole inhabitants of the world after the waters recede, brother and sister Fu Xi, who assume the name of the calabash, marry and give birth to a new race of people. In other accounts of the hero's adventures, Fu Xi is the only living being who is able to visit the celestial realm by climbing Jianmu, the tree that rises from the center of the world to link the heavens with the earth. Fu Xi acquires great wisdom during the course of his travels, and it is he who teaches the people to produce fire by rubbing sticks together, to use fire to cook, and to harvest fish and game with the use of a net. Yet another valuable gift, that of music, also comes from Fu Xi when he constructs a stringed instrument and shows his people how to play it.

After the first of China's culture heroes teaches his people to hunt and fish, a second figure, Shen Nong, introduces them to the art of agriculture. Because Shen Nong is recognized as the god of hot and fiery winds as well as the deity of husbandry, scholars speculate that China's early farmers might have practiced burning the land before seeding it with crops. Revered as the culture hero who teaches the people to plough and to plant the five grains, Shen Nong is represented as a man with the head of an ox, the animal that traditionally draws the plough. The Five Grains that Shen Nong introduces when people become too numerous to rely on hunting and fishing are not his only gifts, for the Lord of the Earth also shows his people how to cultivate and use restorative plants and healing herbs. As the culture hero who provides the Chinese people with knowledge of agriculture, Shen Nong plays a role similar to those of Sido in Melanesian tradition, Basajaun in the Basque culture, and Manco Capac in the myths of the Incas. Like Shen Nong, these deities live or travel among the people, instructing them in skills they need to improve their lives. Shen Nong, Sido, Basajaun, and Manco Capac are all culture heroes whose gifts transform hunting and gathering societies into ones that enjoy the benefits of husbandry.

Technology

Culture heroes, associated with such technological advancements as the ability to use fire or to cultivate crops, are also celebrated for supplying other forms of expertise, including the art of making iron. The Basque deity Basajaun, for example, not only protects herds and flocks and teaches the practice of agriculture, but also instructs his people in the craft of producing wrought iron. In Finnish tradition, Ilmarinen, the divine smith who forges the stars in the sky and shapes the heavenly vault, also shares his art with humankind, and the figure of the blacksmith serves as an especially important culture hero in the myths of several African peoples. Among the Fon of West Africa, the blacksmith Gu is brought to earth by the creator deity to teach people to make tools of iron, and in myths from the Sahara the first blacksmith makes a hoe so that he can show people how to plough the earth. In Dogon tradition the blacksmith is the divine ancestor who crosses from heaven to earth on the rainbow bridge and carries with him a hammer and anvil, the seeds of all plants for cultivation, and the gift of fire. Ogun is the divine smith in tales told by the Yoruba, and it is he who shows both gods and people how to forge tools and weapons that will not bend or break.

China's third great culture hero, the successor to Fu Xi and Shen Nong, is Huang Di, the mythic Yellow Emperor who is honored for inventing the wheel and the bow and arrow, and for teaching his people how to write. In Mayan tradition, where writing is also a significant cultural achievement, the god Itzamna first instructs his people in this art. In addition to his other contributions to Chinese culture, the Yellow Emperor shows his people how to construct houses and boats made of wood. Indeed, knowledge of building techniques is valued in other traditions as well, and the Kiwais people of New Guinea describe how human beings dwell in holes in the ground until their great culture hero, Marunogere, teaches them to build longhouses designed for communal living. It is Marunogere who also creates the pig, one of the people's staple foods, and he instructs the people to incorporate parts of the sacred pig in the architecture of their houses: a pig's jaw is placed beneath the entrance, its trotters are buried at the corners, and its ribs rest on the beams that support the roof.

Sacred Ceremonies

According to Chinese tradition, the Yellow Emperor establishes his people's religious ceremonies and thus performs another task frequently attributed to the culture hero. Among North Dakota's Lakota people, the sacred pipe rituals that symbolize the unity of all creation are first introduced by White Buffalo Woman, the holy woman who visits her people to show them the ways to practice expression of their humanity. In the version of the tale told by the Brule Sioux, two hunters encounter Ptesan-Wi, the White Buffalo Woman, as she journeys toward their camp. When one of the young men rudely reaches out to grasp her, a bolt of lightning turns him into ash. White Buffalo Woman sends the other hunter ahead to prepare a medicine lodge, and by the time she reaches the camp the people are ready to receive her precious gift. Holding its stem in her right hand and its bowl in her left, the holy woman presents the Lakota with the *chanunpa*, the sacred pipe whose smoke represents the breath of the creator. She then instructs the people in its proper use for prayer, for the marriage ceremony, and for the rituals that attend a death: she shows them how to approach the pipe by circling it four times in the direction followed by the sun and thus demonstrates for them the movements that symbolize the sacred hoop, the unending circle of all life.

White Buffalo Woman visits her people during a period of hardship, when many are threatened by the danger of starvation. When she has shared her wisdom and the time has come for her departure, she promises to return again during a time of need and then walks toward the setting sun. Before she disappears, however, she stops and rolls four times on the ground. The first time she rolls over she becomes a black buffalo, and the second time she turns she is changed into a brown one; when she rolls a third time she turns into the red buffalo, and, in her final transformation, she becomes the most sacred of animals, the white buffalo. Great herds of buffalo appear following the visit of the holy woman, and they provide food for the people, skins for their clothing, and bones for their tools. Thankful for their new knowledge, the Lakota practice their sacred rituals, rejoice in their bounty, and live in harmony with the creatures of the earth.

LEADERS, WARRIORS, AND ADVENTURERS

While many of myth's culture heroes are acknowledged for the wondrous gifts they bestow, others are recognized for their valiant deeds. These heroic figures, whose behavior expresses a society's ideals, can include warriors and adventurers, slayers of monsters, saviors of people, and the founders or defenders of cities and states. In some myth traditions, great spiritual leaders are also culture heroes. For example, Gautama Siddhartha, the Buddha, personifies the heroic quest for spiritual enlightenment, and in the story of his life, his followers in India and elsewhere find an exemplar of human aspiration. Whereas the culture heroes who bear extraordinary gifts or who impart knowledge of new technologies change the material conditions of people's lives, those who perform admirable feats serve their societies in other ways by providing people with models of behavior, by saving them from terrible danger, or by representing their highest values. Tales of these heroes' deeds preserve cultural traditions by reinforcing a society's sense of its communal identity.

Mighty warriors such as Achilles, Hector, and the other heroes of the Trojan War are often the central figures of the world's great epics, as also are such notable adventurers as Gilgamesh, Odysseus, or Jason, all of whom set forth on voyages or quests that require both courage and endurance. Beowulf, the Germanic hero of Britain's Anglo-Saxon epic, begins his career as the bold adventurer who voyages forth to slay the monstrous Grendel and concludes it as the dragon slayer who is the savior of his people. Like the culture heroes of other warrior societies, Beowulf embodies the strength, courage, resourcefulness, and spirit of adventure that are valued within the warrior traditions. Among the mythic heroes who also share these traits are such warriors as Dagda, Cuchulainn, and Finn, whose brave deeds on the battlefield are recounted in Ireland's epic cycles, and Gesar Khan, the legendary warrior-king of Tibeto-Mongolian tradition. Although heroic warriors are almost always men, exceptions can be found in the seventh-century ballad that tells the tale of Mulan, China's courageous woman-warrior, in the Greek accounts of the Amazons, and in the story of France's legendary hero, the great Joan of Arc.

Monster Slayers and Saviors

The monster slayers of myth save their societies from terrifying (and often supernatural) creatures that threaten to destroy them. In Greek tradition, for example, Perseus rids the world of the hideous Medusa, who turns people into stone, and Theseus slays the dreaded Minotaur that devours human beings. Herakles, the greatest of the Greek monster slayers, kills the ferocious Nemean Lion, the snake-headed Hydra, and an entire flock of the flesh-eating Stymphalian birds. In the myths of the Mayans, the Hero Twins Hunahpu and Xbalanque must destroy the monstrous bird Seven Macaw as well as the two giants that are his sons to make the world safe for human beings. When they also defeat the lords of the underworld and kill their leaders, the Hero Twins bring an end to the practice of human sacrifice. Like Beowulf, the Germanic hero Sigurd destroys a mighty dragon, the fire-breathing Fafnir, and, according to medieval lore, Saint George slays the terrible dragon that consumes young maidens for its daily meals.

Interestingly, Chinese tradition also offers an account of a maiden-devouring monster, and in this tale it is a young woman, Chi Li, who slays the gigantic serpent that preys upon her people. Although the maiden Chi Li is an unlikely monster slayer, one who does not possess the strength of a Herakles, she nonetheless shares that hero's courage as well as his sense of single-minded purpose. Determined that she will not become another of the Yung Serpent's victims, Chi Li first distracts the monster with a mound of sweetened rice balls and then unleashes the serpent hound that is her companion. When the dog sinks its teeth into its foe, Chi Li plunges her sword into the evil creature's head. In destroying the Yung Serpent, Chi Li not only saves her own life, but also the lives of other young maidens. Word of Chi Li's heroism spreads throughout the kingdom, and her deed is rewarded when she agrees to marry its prince and become its queen.

Monsters are not the only threats to societies, and in another myth from China, the great culture hero Yu labors for thirteen years to free his people from the dangers of devastating floods. Yu's story actually begins well before his birth, when his father, Gun, is asked to quell a tremendous flood that has forced people to seek refuge in the mountains. Gun attempts to dam up the waters, and to do this he steals from heaven a small portion of magical soil that absorbs the moisture. Yu's father, however, is unsuccessful and is eventually executed, perhaps for his failure or perhaps for his thievery, and years later his son is called upon to complete the task. Because the floodwaters rise from springs in the earth, Yu must burrow into the ground and dig trenches to divert the streams. As he works both day and night, without pausing to visit his family, he becomes increasingly calloused and lame—his skin shrivels in the sun and he wears his fingernails to the bone. After a confrontation with Gong Gong, the Spirit of the Waters, and after many years of toil, Yu finally finishes building channels that drain the flooded land while also providing water for its irrigation. The hero of his people, the great engineer is rewarded when he is named the new emperor of China.

FOUNDERS

Yet another group of culture heroes includes the mythic or legendary founders of states, dynasties, or empires. In Greek tradition, for example, the heroic Theseus is credited with founding the state of Attica in the region surrounding Athens, its most important city. Although Athens itself predates Theseus's reign as its king, he is known as the ruler who unifies its people and establishes its assemblies, its law courts, and its democratic ideals. Two important founders are celebrated in myths from the Roman tradition. On the one hand, Virgil describes Aeneas, the hero of his epic, as the founder of the dynasty that is destined to rule the mighty Roman Empire. Aeneas, therefore, is the culture hero who establishes the Roman state. On the other hand, however, tradition grants to Romulus the honor of founding the great city that carries his name. The legendary Arthur, whose exploits are first popularized in French medieval literature, is often regarded as Britain's national hero. While scholarship suggests that the original Arthur was probably a Welsh chieftain who fought invading Saxons during the fifth or sixth century, the Once-and-Future King of the medieval myths unifies his nation and founds the brotherhood of knights who practice the chivalric code.

See also Monsters; The Quest; Tricksters

DELUGE MOTIF

Accounts of a catastrophic flood appear in myths from every continent on earth. While some descriptions of a deluge resemble one another closely enough to indicate that an original version probably spread through cultural diffusion, diverse examples of this remarkably common motif suggest that the tale of a flood is a universal theme. There are, of course, several reasons why stories of floods play an important role in the myths of many cultures. From a practical perspective, the occurrence of a great flood, a sudden and disruptive event, is an especially memorable occasion, one that readily invites the act of storytelling. Furthermore, the destructive nature of a deluge, an event that transforms the landscape and changes the world into an unfamiliar place, necessarily introduces the idea of rebirth: when the flood that drowns and destroys the world finally recedes, life must begin anew.

Narratives of floods, then, frequently initiate a process of re-creation, a second stage of creation that follows an account of how the world first came into being. For this reason, many instances of the deluge motif occur in the context of a creation myth, a story that recounts the birth of the cosmos. When the tale of a flood is included in an account of creation, the cyclical pattern of birth, death, and regeneration emerges in the myth. The idea that new birth might arise from the destructive waters of the deluge is particularly appropriate, for in most creation myths it is the primal waters of chaos that first give birth to life. When floodwaters destroy the original creation, the world returns to a state of chaos, and, when the world is reborn, a new order is established. In re-creating the world, the waters of the deluge cleanse or transform it.

REASONS FOR THE DELUGE

While creation myths answer people's need to understand how the world came into existence, stories of a deluge serve to address other kinds of questions: in the aftermath of a tremendous calamity, people seek to understand how or why their world has been transformed. Myths offer numerous explanations for the occurrence of the flood, but the most common among them represents the deluge as a form of divine retribution, the means by which the gods cleanse the world of its wickedness, impiety, or folly. In most of the accounts where a deity unleashes a flood to punish evildoers, the righteous few who are spared repopulate the earth. Floods, however, are not always an expression of the anger of the gods. In some myths that incorporate the deluge motif, the creator gods are not satisfied with the world they have made and seek to eradicate its flaws before they complete the work of creation. In other tales that feature a flood, the reasons for its occurrence are more arbitrary: in some cases a trickster inadvertently unleashes the deluge, and, in some myths, floodwaters pour forth when the cosmic tree is chopped down. In a few instances, furthermore, the inhabitants of the earth are the hapless victims of a flood that is unleashed when deities engage in disputes with one another.

Whatever the cause of the flood, its effects are usually devastating, and in many myths only a few manage to survive its destructive force. Those who do escape either find safety in a seaworthy vessel or seek refuge on a mountaintop or high in the trees above the raging waters. Those who ride out the flood in an ark or some other form of boat frequently first come ashore on a mountain peak. Time passes, in many instances, before the floodwaters recede, so survivors use birds or other messengers to test the depth of the waters. In many stories of the deluge, only one couple is preserved, a man and a woman who become the primal parents of a new generation. Typically, cultural tradition honors a survivor of the catastrophe as its flood hero. Sometimes survivors of the flood rescue animals or plants, but occasionally the floodwaters themselves serve to spread the seeds of life all about the earth. While water is most frequently the medium of the deluge, in a few tales it is a river of blood that inundates the world.

DELUGE IN THE MIDDLE EAST

The account of the deluge that is most familiar within Western traditions appears in the biblical story of Noah and his ark. The tale that is recorded in Genesis, however, is remarkably similar to versions of a flood myth that circulated much earlier among the peoples of Mesopotamia, and scholars therefore regard it as derivative of those. Indeed, scholars have noted in particular the striking correspondences between the story of the deluge that is included in *Gilgamesh* (ca. 2000 B.C.E.), the Babylonian epic, and the later account that emerges from the Judeo-Christian Hebraic tradition. Although the two versions offer markedly different explanations of the cause of the flood, the details of the tale they unfold share a distinct narrative pattern. The differences in the ways the Babylonians and the Hebrews interpret the significance of the deluge reflect differences in the values and beliefs of the two cultures, but the parallels between their accounts suggest a common origin in a catastrophe that the peoples of the Middle East regard as an historical event. The tale, in its various versions, that is told by these traditions both records and explains the ancient occurrence of a mighty flood.

Whereas the deluge described in Genesis is unleashed to punish the wicked and to cleanse the world of its violence and corruption, in the Mesopotamian myths the gods more whimsically inundate the earth to suit their own convenience. In *Gilgamesh*, the story of the flood is recounted by Utnapishtim, one of the survivors, and he explains that the gods become annoyed when it seems to them that the people of the earth have become too numerous and noisy. Not all the gods agree, however, that human life should be utterly destroyed, and so Utnapishtim, like Noah, is instructed to gather up his family and to build a sturdy ark. It is while the floodwaters are raging and the gods must bear witness to the destruction they have wrought that they begin to regret their impulsive act. They therefore rejoice to discover that one of the gods has spared Utnapishtim and thus preserved human life. Utnapishtim's family repopulates the earth, and, in honor of their steadfastness, Utnapishtim and his wife are granted the gift of eternal life.

Although their deities call forth the floodwaters for different reasons, Utnapishtim and Noah share a common experience in surviving the deluge. Like Noah, Utnapishtim receives specific instructions as to the dimensions and the design of the ark he must build. Singled out because of their virtues, both Utnapishtim and Noah obey the commands they are given, and both preserve animals and plant seeds by taking them on board. The rains fall, in both *Gilgamesh* and Genesis, for a specific number of days and nights, and, after they have ceased, both Utnapishtim and Noah release three birds to discover whether dry land has yet emerged. In both accounts the arks bearing the survivors come at last to rest on mountain slopes. When they leave their vessels, both Utnapishtim and Noah immediately build altars and offer their thanks in the form of the burnt offering of animals. In both accounts a rainbow appears in the sky to symbolize the acceptance of the sacrifices. The rainbow in *Gilgamesh* is Ishtar's jeweled necklace, offered with the promise that she will never forget the flood. In the Hebraic version, the rainbow represents a covenant with Noah and his seed, a promise that the flood will never again recur. Unlike Utnapishtim, Noah is not granted immortality, but his lifespan is nevertheless a long one, at 950 years.

MYTH ASSIMILATION OF THE MIDDLE EASTERN FLOOD

If the account of the deluge recorded in Genesis can be traced to its source in the Middle East, the story of Noah has indeed in its turn influenced many other cultural traditions. Through the work of missionaries, the Hebrews' version of the flood has been spread around the world and assimilated by a variety of peoples. In Hawaii, for example, an indigenous flood myth tells how the sea once rose to cover all the land except the very top of Mauna Kea, where two human beings were saved from being drowned. After the arrival of Christian missionaries, however, the old version was expanded to include additional details: in the revised account the flood hero builds a houseboat for himself and his wife, and, when he eventually lands on the mountain peak, he makes offerings to a god who accepts them after descending on a rainbow. As is characteristic of myth assimilation, the Hawaiians embed features of the Genesis story in their own tradition.

In the *Leabhar Gabhala* (Book of invasions), the monks of twelfth-century Ireland recount a history of the island's settlement that begins with Noah's flood. The monastic scribes, in their tale of the deluge, assimilate elements from an earlier Celtic culture into Christian tradition. The *Book of Invasions*, which describes the six distinct ages of Ireland's ancient past, tells how the first age of colonization ends in a flood. To link the flooding of Ireland to the story of Noah, the account reports that Bith, the leader of the first wave of invaders, is in fact Noah's son. Bith is not mentioned in the Bible, and so the narrative explains that he is a son who was not allowed to go aboard the ark. Bith, therefore, builds a boat of his own, and, accompanied by two other men and fifty-one women, makes his way to Ireland. The first age of settlement does not last long, however, because the entire population drowns in the very flood that Bith's father survives. In their accounts of the second and third invasions, the Christian scribes again link Irish history to the story of Noah's flood, for the new groups of settlers are led by Partholon and Nemed, both of whom are said to be descendents of Japheth, another of Noah's sons.

The flood myth of the Greco-Roman tradition provides yet another example of a tale that was probably influenced by the earlier accounts of the Mesopotamians and Hebrews. In some versions of the Greek myth, Zeus inundates the earth to punish the Titan Prometheus for his insubordination. In these accounts the human beings who drown are the hapless victims of the immortals' dispute. In the best-known version of the story, however, the Roman poet Ovid explains that during the Age of Iron, Zeus, having grown tired of people's arrogance and wickedness, decides to destroy them. Deucalion, the son of Prometheus, and his wife, Pyrrha, are the only two mortal beings who are virtuous enough to escape the wrath of Zeus. After their small boat comes to rest on Mount Parnassus, the two make their way to a sacred cave. The world around them is desolate and empty, and, although they are grateful to be alive, they find that they must now seek some purpose for their lives. The purpose for which they search is provided when the oracle declares that they should throw behind them the bones of their great mother. Gaea, of course, is the great mother earth, and the rocks are her bones. When Deucalion and Pyrrha toss stones over their shoulders, the bones of mother earth become the men and the women who repopulate the world.

VARIATIONS WITHIN THE MOTIF

Roles of Animals

Although gods often use a deluge to cleanse the world of evil, in some traditions a flood is unleashed to punish people who fail to live in harmony with nature. The Chewong people of the Malayan forest, for example, tell of how the primeval snake causes the floodwaters to rise when someone mocks an animal. Respect for nature is also an important virtue within Native American traditions, as is demonstrated in the flood myth told by the people of Montana's Yellowstone Valley. In this story, the people at first obey the Great Spirit's command that they share their land with the buffalo and all other creatures. When they kill a buffalo for food and its hide, they do so with respect. Eventually, however, they forget the words of the Great Spirit and begin to kill for sport. Because the people no longer regard the animals as brothers, the Great Spirit sends a great flood to destroy them. The buffalo disappear, and many people drown, but a few move to higher ground and eventually make their way into the mountains. There the medicine men search for the buffalo, for they know that if they can find them and live once more at peace with nature, they will survive. In the end it is indeed a buffalo that saves the people from the flood. When they discover the drowned remains of the Great White Buffalo, the people stretch its hide from mountaintop to mountaintop to create a shelter in the Yellowstone Valley. The floodwaters then begin to recede, and when the sun shines upon the White Buffalo's hide, it gleams in all the colors of the rainbow.

The story of Manu, from Indian tradition, is another in which an animal protects human life when a flood occurs. Manu, the first man, scoops up a small fish one day while he is bathing. Fearful of being devoured by a larger fish, the small one requests Manu's protection. Manu keeps the fish in a jar, and, when it eventually grows into a *ghasha*, the largest of the fish, he moves it to the sea. As it so happens, the *ghasha* is Matsya, the first animal avatar of Vishnu. Incarnated first as a fish because all life originally arises from the water, Vishnu the Preserver makes his appearance in order to save humankind from a devastating deluge. Matsya therefore instructs Manu to build a boat and to stock it with all the seeds of life. When the floodwaters rise, the fish tows Manu's boat to a place of safety on a mountaintop. Manu slowly makes his way down the mountain as the waters subside, and the slope where he climbs down is named Manu's Descent to recognize and honor the hero of the flood.

The llama, an animal important to the people who live in the Andes, plays a special role in a flood myth from the Peruvian coast. The llama, it is said, is sometimes the reincarnation of a human soul and a creature that possesses the power to see into the future. The Peruvian myth tells of a time called Pachachama, when human beings had become wicked and cruel. Angered by the people who ignore them, the gods decide to exact their vengeance with a flood. Two virtuous shepherd brothers, however, learn of the impending disaster from their llamas, for the animals have read the portents in the stars. Acting upon the advice of their flock, the brothers and their families gather provisions and journey to the peak of the towering Villacota Mountain. From their lofty perch they watch the floodwater rise, and as it grows ever closer, it engulfs a fox's tail, leaving the tip forever blackened. The waters continue to rise, but so too does the mountain, and thus the families are spared. The survivors repopulate the earth, finding new homes all across its surface. The llamas, however, make their home only in the highlands, for they always carry with them the memory of the flood.

Eradicating Flaws

Unlike the gods in the Peruvian myth, the deities of the Mayan creation myth do not make use of a flood to punish evildoers. Rather, they invoke a deluge to correct various missteps they take in the process of creation. Desiring to create a being that will respect and honor them, they first try to fashion bodies out of mud. These figures, however, are too pliable and soft, and soon fall apart. For their next attempt, the creators carve bodies out of wood. Although the wooden people are solid, they are too stiff-jointed, wrinkled, and warped to satisfy their makers. Furthermore, the gods can clearly see that their minds and hearts are empty. Perceiving that the wooden figures also fall short of the being they long to create, the gods call forth a flood to correct their mistakes. Although most of the wooden creatures drown, those that survive can easily be recognized as the monkeys in the trees. In a similar tale, the Wyot people of California relate how Old Man uses a flood to destroy the furry people who were his first creation. And the Inuit of Greenland also tell a story in which the flood serves to correct a flaw in the original creation. Because people do not die when the world is first made, it is not long before the earth is teeming. A deluge destroys the First World, and the few who survive to repopulate the earth are thereafter all mortal beings.

In the Mayan creation myth, the deities seek to create people who will honor them with sacrifices and speak their names with respect. The Mayan gods are not alone in desiring the veneration of the people they create, and in some myths the deluge occurs when human beings fail to pay homage to their gods. In a myth recounted by the people of Laos, for example, three divine ancestors known as the Thens demand that all people living on the earth should offer the gods a portion of every meal as a gesture of respect. When the people refuse, the Thens inundate the earth. Although three great men and their families escape on a raft, their voyage takes them into the heavenly kingdom, far from their earthly home. Only after they have paid due homage to the king of the Thens are they permitted to return to the earth, the place where they prefer to live.

Theomachy

While the gods are wont to use the flood to punish impious, wicked, or annoying human beings, in some myths people are not held to blame for the deluge. When the gods invoke a flood to spite one another, people are the unfortunate victims of a cosmic disaster. In a tale told by the Araucanian people of Chile, for example, the deluge occurs when two great snakes, Caicai and Tenten, quarrel with one another. Each serpent claims to possess superior magical powers, and so the two engage in a contest that will measure their strength. While Caicai causes the ocean to rise, Tenten makes the mountain called Thegtheg grow taller and taller. Many people drown in the swelling sea, but a few manage to survive by making their way to Thegtheg, which rises high above the flood. Another South American flood myth, that of the Chibcha of Colombia, tells how the deluge arises from a marital dispute. When Chia, the wife of the sun god Bochica, grows resentful of the attentions her husband pays to human beings, she decides to do away with her rivals by conjuring up a flood. Once again a few survivors are able to find safety in the mountains, and Bochica, the sun, quickly dries the land. He then banishes Chia to the realm of darkness, and she becomes the moon.

Trickster Antics

Occasionally people are also the unfortunate victims of floods that are caused by the antics of tricksters. For example, in the Navajos' account of their emergence from the underworld, the fact that the people are forced to leave the bountiful fields of the Fourth World to seek a new home on the surface of the earth is the fault of Coyote, the mischief-making trickster. The trouble begins when Coyote cheats Water Monster out of his fur coat and then discovers the creature's babies sleeping in the pockets. Because Coyote neglects to restore the two children to their father, the furious Water Monster inundates the world, destroying its rich crops. Forced to abandon their harvest, the people flee to the Fifth World by climbing a bamboo stalk—and luckily for them, Turkey, the very last to emerge, carries with him the seeds of all their plants. As it happens, the raging water soaks Turkey's tail and leaves its mark forever on the tips of his feathers. When it appears that the new world too is endangered by the flood, the people finally become suspicious of Coyote, and, after the culprit is revealed, they quickly appease the Water Monster by returning his babies to him.

Rivers of Blood

Although recurring patterns of imagery and theme can be observed in flood myths from around the world, some accounts offer interesting variations in the details they provide. In tales from the Norse and Egyptians, for instance, blood rather than water inundates the earth. According to Norse tradition, all but two of the Frost Giants drown in the deluge of blood spilled by Ymir, and, in the Egyptian story, people who are not slaughtered by Hathor drown in the blood of her many victims. Only when Ra distracts Hathor by flooding the earth with beer do a few human beings manage to flee the bloodbath of her fury. Bergelmir and his wife, the Frost Giants who escape Ymir's rivers of blood, become the primal parents of a new generation, and the people who do not drown in Hathor's ocean of blood and beer repopulate the earth.

Survivors Punished

Like the story of the flood in Irish tradition, the deluge described by the Aztecs brings to a close one age of the world. Each of the five ages is governed by a sun, and it is the Sun of Water that shines during the Fourth World. Because the people are too greedy during this era, they are punished by a flood that brings their world to its end. Although most people are transformed into fish, Tlaloc, the god of the rains, spares Tata and Nena, the most honorable of all human beings. Tlaloc instructs the couple to hollow out a tree trunk and seek refuge there. He warns them, however, that they will only survive if they are able to master their greed—they must, he insists, take with them only one ear of corn apiece. Up to this point the Aztec myth follows the pattern of those tales wherein a man and a woman who survive the deluge become the primal parents of a new generation. As it happens, however, the two disregard the words of Tlaloc. After the floodwaters subside and they can see that fish are plentiful, they cannot resist the temptation to devour one. Thus Tata and Nena do not become the primal parents who repopulate the earth, and, as the price of their greed, they are changed into dogs.

Refuge from the Flood

People in the Aztec myth escape the floodwaters by hiding inside a tree. While many other myths describe flights to mountaintops or voyages on rafts or other kinds of boats, a few accounts diverge from these patterns. For example, the flood heroes in the Chinese tradition ride out the deluge in a type of gourd known as the calabash. Not only does their giant calabash keep the brother and sister safe from the flood, but it also preserves their lives when the waters suddenly retreat at a tremendous speed. The children's father, riding in the iron boat that he builds to save himself from the flood, is immediately killed when he crashes to the earth, but the gourd bearing the heroes bounces harmlessly on the ground. In honor of the calabash, the survivors in this tale take its name as their own. Brother and sister Fu Xi eventually marry and produce a new race of people to dwell upon the earth. In other variations, the Caddo people of the Great Plains say that a hollow reed provides survivors a refuge from the flood, and, in the story told by Arizona's Pimas, it is a floating gumball, a large, hollow sphere fashioned from spruce gum, which serves to shelter Suha and his wife until they finally come ashore on Superstition Mountain.

Welcoming the Deluge

In an unusual variation of the deluge motif, the Efik Ibibio people of Nigeria tell a charming tale about a friendly flood. This story portrays neither the punishment of wicked people nor the cleansing of the earth, but instead presents an amusing explanation of how the sun and the moon come to live in the sky. In addition to the etiological purpose it serves, the myth also offers wry commentary on the unforeseen consequences of a simple act of hospitality. Indeed, the trouble begins when the Sun and the Moon, who are husband and wife, encourage their good friend the Flood to pay them a visit in their home on the earth. Because Sun and Moon often call on Flood and are always well received, they quite naturally desire to return the favor. Flood, however, declines their invitation with his polite explanation that their house is too small. Sun and Moon therefore build a palatial abode, and then once again they ask their friend to join them. When Flood at last agrees to visit the new house, he carries with him the fish and other sea creatures that are his relations. Because he quickly rises to the rafters of their house, Sun and Moon seek refuge on the roof. When Flood continues to rise, and eventually engulfs their house, the gracious hosts are forced to ascend into the heavens.

Initiation Rites

Among the indigenous people of northern Australia, a story of the flood is linked to traditional initiation rites. In the myth of the Yolngu people, it is sexual transgression that causes the flood. When the two Wawilak Sisters mate with men who are members of their own clan, a monstrous serpent named Yurlunggur first swallows the sisters and then inundates the earth. After the floodwaters are gone, Yurlunggur spits up the two women and the sons they have borne. In an initiation ceremony for their young men, the Yolngu reenact the story of the deluge. Women play the role of the Wawilak Sisters and men take the part of the serpent that swallows them. When Yurlunggur symbolically swallows the boys who are being initiated, they retreat to a sacred site forbidden to women. At the initiation grounds, said to be the place where Yurlunggur rested on the earth, the young men learn which women are appropriate for marriage. With this knowledge, the initiates return from the sacred grounds, reborn as adults. In other traditions, rituals that feature purification by water echo those mythic narratives that represent the flood as a means whereby the world is cleansed before it is reborn. In the practice of baptism, for example, immersion in water represents a rebirth to a new life.

See also The Apocalypse; Changing Ages; Creation Myths; Culture Heroes; Primal Parents; The Rainbow

DESCENT MOTIF

The realm of the dead, often envisioned as an underworld, is depicted as a fearsome place in the myths of most cultural traditions. Not only is the netherworld represented as a site replete with dangers for the living, it is also a realm that is difficult to enter, for mountains or bodies of water usually serve as barriers, and sentries stand guard at the gates or bridges that characteristically lead to the land of the dead. In the myths of several traditions, however, the living do journey to the otherworld, despite the obstacles they must overcome and the dangers they must confront. The descent into the realm of the dead, also known as the harrowing of hell, is most commonly undertaken as a quest, either a search for knowledge, wisdom, or advice, or as an endeavor to rescue, visit, or avenge people who have died. Occasionally, as is the case when one of Herakles's Twelve Labors requires that he capture Cerberus, the three-headed hound of Hades, a descent to the underworld is an ordeal that serves to test the hero.

INANNA'S DESCENT

The oldest instance of the descent motif appears in Sumerian and Babylonian versions of the goddess Inanna's journey to the underworld. Inanna (or Ishtar) is the Mesopotamian people's powerful queen of the heavens, and her older sister Ereshkigal is queen of the underworld. Although extant versions of the myth do not fully explain Inanna's purpose in visiting the kingdom of the dead, because the two sisters are characterized as rivals, most interpretations suggest that Inanna undertakes a quest to usurp her sister's power. Before she departs for the Great Below, Inanna dresses in all her finery, her jewels and her crown, and then she instructs her servant, Ninshubur, to seek help from the gods should she not return to the Great Above after three days have passed. At the first of the seven gates along the Road of No Return, Inanna demands entry to the underworld and indeed threatens to break down its gate if she is not admitted. Namtar, the guardian of the lapis lazuli gate, first consults Ereshkigal and then allows the Queen of Heaven to pass into the netherworld.

Ereshkigal, who is displeased by the appearance of her sister, demands that Inanna be subjected to the laws that govern the underworld, where all the dead are equal. Accordingly, as she passes through each of the seven gates, Inanna is stripped of her clothing and her jewels. At the first gate her crown is taken from her head, and then her rod of lapis lazuli, her necklace, her breastplate, her golden ring, and her belt are all removed. At the seventh and the last gate, Inanna's garments are stripped off, and then the Queen of Heaven stands naked before her sister. In the Sumerian version of the myth, the Anunnaki, the seven judges of the underworld, pass sentence on Inanna, turning her into a corpse that hangs from a stake. In the Babylonian account, Ereshkigal inflicts the sixty miseries of death upon the body of her sister and then makes a water skin out of her remains.

When Inanna does not return from her journey within the allotted time, her loyal servant Ninshubur appeals to the gods for their assistance. In the Babylonian version of the myth, which emphasizes Inanna's role as a fertility goddess, the gods conspire to rescue the Queen of Heaven because on the earth all procreation ceases during the interval of her absence. In the Sumerian account, the god Enki (or Ea) at last agrees to help rescue Inanna. From the dirt under his fingernails, he creates two creatures that are able to pass like flies through the hinges of the gates to the underworld. The creatures, the *kurgarru* and the *kalaturru*, revive Inanna with the life-giving herb and restorative water that they carry with them, and then the goddess attempts to make good her escape. The Anunnaki, however, stop Inanna and demand that she provide a substitute to take her place among the dead. When Inanna discovers that her consort, the shepherd Dumuzi (or Tammuz) did not mourn for her while she was gone, she chooses him to take her place. In the Babylonian version of the story, Ea (Enki) carries out his rescue by creating a handsome young man for Ereshkigal's pleasure. When the queen of the underworld invites her lover to choose a reward, he asks for the water skin that is Inanna's corpse. Although she curses the young man, Ereshkigal must honor his request, and Inanna therefore returns to the world of the living in the Great Above.

BEREAVED LOVERS

Orpheus and Eurydice

Within Western tradition, the story of Orpheus and Eurydice is perhaps the best-known account of a journey to the underworld. In this Greek myth, Orpheus descends into Hades to rescue his beloved wife, but there he discovers, as does Inanna, that the living are subject to the laws of the netherworld when they presume to enter the realm of the dead. Orpheus, the son of a Thracian king and the Muse Calliope, is an extraordinary poet and musician, and when he plays his lyre, a gift from Apollo, all who hear his music are enchanted by its beauty. The story of the ill-fated lovers begins on their wedding day. Although Orpheus invites Hymen to bless the ceremony, the god of marriage is not joyful, but somber; furthermore, he does not sing his customary hymn to celebrate the nuptials. The significance of these unpropitious omens becomes apparent soon after the wedding, when Eurydice, bit by a poisonous serpent, joins the shades that dwell in Hades.

Desperate in his grief, Orpheus seizes upon the hope that by visiting their domain he might persuade Hades and Persephone to release his young bride. Carrying only his lyre, Orpheus passes through the netherworld's gate of Taenarus to reach the River Styx. There, Charon the ferryman is so transported by Orpheus's sad song that he grants him passage without collecting the fare. Cerberus, Tantalus, Sisyphus, and the other inhabitants of Hades all pause to listen too, and even the cruel Furies are moved when Orpheus sings the story of his sorrow. Hades and Persephone grant the grieving husband's request, requiring only that he not look upon the face of his beloved until the two emerge in the land of the living. Groping in the darkness, Orpheus and Eurydice make their way up the steep path that leads to the upper world. Finally, just as they reach their goal, Orpheus turns back to reach for his wife. Eurydice, however, is still in the underworld, and when her husband turns to look at her, that is where she must remain. Stricken, Orpheus returns to the River Styx, but this time Charon refuses to allow him to cross.

Hiku and Kawelu

Although those who rule the underworld require that its laws be obeyed, in some myths a visitor to the netherworld manages to evade the rules by means of trickery. A story from the Hawaiian Islands, for example, follows a plot similar to that of the tale of Orpheus and Eurydice with the notable difference that its hero's quest is indeed successful. Like Orpheus, Hiku, the son of the moon goddess, loses his beloved Queen Kawelu when she dies unexpectedly. He too descends to the underworld with the design of rescuing his lover's spirit. Hiku, however, covers his body with an ointment that smells like putrefying flesh and then sneaks into the realm of the dead. Through his guile, Hiku fools the ruler of the dark kingdom into thinking that he is nothing but another corpse. Free to roam the underworld, he discovers that Queen Kawelu's spirit has taken the form of a butterfly, which he manages to capture in a coconut shell. Hiku then returns to the world of the living, and when he releases her spirit in the presence of his beloved's corpse, Queen Kawelu, as though awakening from sleep, is restored to life.

HEROIC DESCENTS

Hermod's Journey to Hel

Bereaved lovers are not the only characters in myth who harrow hell in an attempt to rescue the dead. In the Norse tradition, the murder of Balder, the most virtuous of gods, necessitates a journey to the realm of the dead. Hermod the Bold, one of Odin's sons, volunteers to undertake the task of persuading Hel, the ruler of the netherworld, to accept a ransom for his brother's life. Riding Sleipnir, Odin's eight-legged horse, Hermod sets forth on his arduous journey. After nine days and nights of travel through swamps and dark valleys, over mountaintops and rivers, he finally reaches Gjall, the river that the dead must cross to enter into Hel. At the golden bridge called Gjallarbru, Hermod is stopped by its guardian, Modgud the skeleton, but when she learns of his mission, she allows him to pass, for even she grieves for Balder the Good. Hermod then passes through the Iron Wood, where trees have leaves of metal, and when he at last reaches the high walls of the city of Hel, he spurs Sleipnir to leap over the gate that is guarded by Garm, the ferocious hound of hell.

Like Orpheus, Hermod pleads with the ruler of the netherworld for the release of his brother, and after listening to his entreaties for an entire night, Hel at last relents. Like Hades, however, she requires that a condition be met before Balder can return to the land of the living: only if everything in the world, both living and lifeless, sheds tears for the murdered god will Hel set him free. Hermod hastens back to Asgard, the home of the gods, and soon messengers are dispatched throughout the world to spread the news of Hel's decision. All human beings, plants, animals, birds, serpents, and other living creatures weep for Balder, and so too do the mountains, the stones and metals, the sparks of fire, and the water. Just as it appears that everything in nature has tears to shed for the most beloved of the gods, the messengers encounter a withered old crone sitting in a cave—and she alone seals Balder's fate by refusing to weep. As the gods well know, the crone is Loki in disguise, and thus the one who first contrived Balder's murder also ensures his confinement in Hel.

Greco-Roman Heroes

Several heroes visit Hades in myths told by the ancient Greeks. The mighty Herakles, in fact, makes two journeys to the underworld. Although his purpose in the second of these adventures is to perform one of his Twelve Labors, when he goes to Hades to capture Cerberus, he also rescues Theseus from the Chair of Forgetfulness. Some years earlier, Theseus and Pirithous had tried to abduct Persephone and had been caught by her angry husband. Until Herakles rescues him, Theseus is tormented by the Furies and the serpents in the lower realm. Although Hades appears before Herakles can free the unfortunate Pirithous, the great hero is able to seize Cerberus and wrap him securely in the skin of the Nemean Lion. When Herakles first visits the underworld, his purpose is to rescue Alcestis, who had joined the shades in Hades to spare her husband's life. The Greek hero, who wrestles with Hades, is successful in this endeavor, for Persephone, who does not think that any woman should ever die for her husband, is sympathetic to Alcestis's plight.

Both Odysseus and Aeneas, the great heroes of the Greco-Roman epic tradition, experience encounters with the netherworld even though Odysseus does not actually descend into Hades. As recounted in the *Odyssey* (eighth century B.C.E.), Odysseus' meeting with the shades from the underworld occurs as he struggles to return home to Ithaca after the Trojan War. Acting upon the advice of the witch Circe, Odysseus endeavors to summon the ghost of Tiresias, the great seer, to learn what lies in his future. To accomplish this, he first travels to a cave near the Grove of Persephone, where three of the rivers of the underworld all flow together. At the mouth of the cave, he digs a trench and then pours into it the blood sacrifice of a ram and a black ewe. When the shades of the dead smell the fresh blood, they swarm from the cave in order to taste it. Odysseus does speak with Tiresias and thus gains the wisdom of his prophecies, but he also recognizes many others among the dead. He meets with Achilles, Ajax, and Patroclus, fallen heroes from the plains of Troy, and he is startled to discover that Agamemnon, the victim of his wife Clytemnestra, also numbers among the ghosts. He is surprised as well when his mother, Anticlea, steps forward to greet him. Three times Odysseus tries to embrace his mother, who died of grief while awaiting his return to Ithaca, but since she is a shade there is nothing he can touch.

Like Odysseus, Aeneas seeks knowledge of his future from a shade that dwells within the land of the dead. In Virgil's *Aeneid* (19 B.C.E.), however, the epic hero does indeed descend to the underworld to fulfill his quest. When Aeneas at last reaches Italy, years after his flight from Troy, he seeks out the cave of the Cumaean Sibyl. After hearing the oracle's prophecies, he asks to visit the shade of his father Anchises, and the Sibyl agrees to serve as his guide on the perilous journey through Pluto's domain. Before embarking, however, she advises him to collect the sacred golden bough that can serve to protect him in the realm of the dead. Aeneas offers a blood sacrifice of four black cattle, and then the Sibyl leads him toward Elysium, the region of the netherworld reserved for those favored by the gods. To reach Elysium and the shade of Anchises, however, Aeneas must pass through the other regions of the underworld, and there he witnesses all the horrors of Pluto's dark kingdom.

Near the entrance to the underworld, Aeneas encounters all the evils that beset human beings and all the monsters killed by famous heroes—he sees the Chimera, the Hydra of Lerna, the Gorgon Medusa, and the fearsome Harpies. He passes the Caves of Sleep and then comes to the River Acheron. Countless wailing shades wait there to cross the river, but when Charon sees the golden bough, he allows the Sibyl and Aeneas to cross aboard his ferry. Cerberus, too, is subdued by the sight of the golden bough, and, after safely passing him and the judges of the underworld, Aeneas finds himself in the midst of the shades of tragic lovers. Dido is there, and when Aeneas tries to explain why he had to leave her, she turns away in silence. Among the shades of the dead heroes, Aeneas recognizes many Trojan warriors, and, like Odysseus, he stops to speak with his old friends.

Eventually the Sibyl guides him to the path that leads to Elysium, the right fork of a crossroad. To the left, across the Phlegethon, a terrifying river of flames, Aeneas can see the triple-walled fortress where the dead are punished for their crimes. Sisyphus is there, as are Ixion and Tantalus and all the others condemned by Rhadamanthys to never-ending torment. At last, turning from this dreadful sight, Aeneas moves on to the arched gate where he must leave the golden bough, a gift for Pluto's queen. When in Elysium he finds Anchises's shade and tries three times to embrace it, there is, of course, nothing there for him to touch. The reunion of father and son is nevertheless a joyful one, and while he is in the underworld Aeneas learns his destiny: in time he will become the father of the mighty emperors of Rome.

Mayan Hero Twins

One of the most engaging accounts of the descent to the underworld comes from the *Popol Vuh* (ca. 1558), the epic of the Mayan people. The myth is actually a story in two parts and begins when the twin gods, One Hunahpu and Seven Hunahpu, are summoned to the land of the dead by the lords of Xibalba. As it happens, the twin deities receive the summons because their ball court lies directly above Xibalba, and One Death and Seven Death are disturbed by the noise of the ball as it ricochets overhead. Believing that they have been invited to a ballgame in the underworld, One Hunahpu and Seven Hunahpu make their descent. Four owls guide the twins into the depths of the earth, where they encounter treacherous obstacles. They leap great chasms, cross roaring rapids, traverse rivers of pus and blood, pass through barriers of spiked thorns, and battle armies of fierce scorpions.

Finally the twins come to a crossroads, with four paths of different colors. When they choose to take the black road, they make their first mistake, for it leads them not to the lords of Xibalba, but to wooden images of the lords. The choice at the crossroads is the first of three tests the twins must undergo, and when they mistakenly pay homage to the wooden statues, the lords of the underworld laugh at them in scorn. The twins also fail the second test, for when they accept an invitation to sit down, they find that their bench is a slab of heated stone. The twins squirm as they begin to sizzle, and the Xibalbans shriek with laughter when the two leap up from their hot seat. For their third ordeal, the twins are each given a burning torch and a lighted cigar and told that when the lords return in the morning, the torches and cigars must still be burning and yet must also remain whole. Once again the twins fail to pass their test, and therefore they do not play ball with the lords of the underworld. Instead, the brothers are sacrificed and then buried beneath the ball court in Xibalba.

The second part of the story begins when Hunahpu and Xbalanque, the twin sons of One Hunahpu, become ballplayers too. Like their father and uncle, the brothers answer a summons from the underworld when the messenger owls once again appear. The Hero Twins, however, are determined not only to play ball in Xibalba, but also to avenge the deaths of their father and his brother. They easily overcome the initial obstacles and then find themselves at the site of the crossroads. To discover the whereabouts of the death lords, the twins release a mosquito that lands first on the silent statues but then quickly discovers where the real Xibalbans are hiding. As the mosquito bites the lords, they call out the names of one another, and thus, when the twins approach their fearsome hosts, they enjoy the advantage of knowing all of their enemies' names. According to Mayan tradition, the lords of Xibalba lose some of their power when they are called by their names.

When the Hero Twins decline an invitation to rest on the hot seat, they are immediately taken to the House of Gloom and presented with the burning torches and cigars. The twins hastily extinguish these, but, knowing that the Xibalbans will check during the night to see if the fires are still glowing, they attach red macaw feathers to the tops of the torches and place fireflies on the ends of the cigars. Having passed these tests by means of trickery and guile, the Hero Twins are subjected to further ordeals. They survive a night in the House of Knives by granting to these cruel implements the flesh of all animals, and they also manage to outwit the death lords by successfully passing nights in the House of Cold, the House of Jaguars, and the House of Fire. Finally, they are sent to the House of Bats, and there they sleep inside their hollow blowguns to protect themselves from the sharp-nosed vampires that fly about the room. Near dawn, Hunahpu peers from his blowgun, and then Camazotz, the killer bat, cuts off his head.

Undaunted, Xbalanque affixes a pumpkin to the shoulders of his brother, and the two go to the ball court to play with the lords. The ball that the Xibalbans set in play is the head of Hunahpu, delivered to them by the killer bat, so Xbalanque contrives to hit the ball out of the court. When he retrieves it, he substitutes the pumpkin for the head—and thus his brother is made whole. Once again the Hero Twins outwit the death lords, who are forced to acknowledge defeat on their ball court when the pumpkin splits apart. After their victory on the court of sacrifice, it remains for the twins to avenge the deaths of the original ballplayers, and they accomplish this by further trickery. Through an elaborate ruse, they bring about the deaths of One Death and Seven Death, the leaders of the lords. Their power diminished, the other Xibalbans plead for mercy, and the brothers spare them in return for their promise that they will no longer practice human sacrifice. The Hero Twins fulfill their earthly mission when they humble the powerful lords of Xibalba, and, their task completed, they rise into the heavens to become the sun and the moon.

See also Culture Heroes; The Quest; Twins, Pairs, and Doubles; The Underworld

EARTH-DIVER MOTIF

Like other types of creation myths, narratives of the earth-diver provide an explanation of the world's transition from its original chaotic state to a condition of ordered existence. In these tales, which focus on the creation of the earth itself as landmass, chaos is represented by the primeval waters, and the world comes into being when a deity or creature dives into the depths of the watery void and returns with a particle of sand, clay, or mud. From this bit of earth, the entire world takes shape, born of the primal ocean that lies beneath it. The accounts typically describe the expansion of the earth's surface, which sometimes rests on the back of an animal or is supported by pillars or cords, and the stories often recount the means by which mountains and other terrestrial features assume their shapes. When the world is thus made ready for habitation, the process of creation continues to unfold.

The earth-diver motif is particularly common in the myths of North America's native peoples but also appears in accounts from Asia, Eastern Europe, and pre-Aryan India. Although versions of the story vary in their details, several recurring patterns emerge in the myths of Native Americans: earth-divers are usually animals; multiple descents (often three) are required before an earth-diver is successful; many earth-divers sacrifice their lives in the course of their quests; the earth-diver's descent requires a long passage of time; the successful earth-diver brings to the surface of the water only a few grains of earth clutched in its claws or embedded under its nails; and land grows from the particles of earth brought from the bottom of the primeval sea. In many of the Native American accounts, the grains of earth are placed on the back of a great turtle, the World Turtle, and in a version of the earth-diver myth that comes from central Asia, the bits of earth are cast onto the stomach of a frog that floats upon its back.

The earth-divers from many traditions are either aquatic birds or amphibious animals, creatures that inhabit the watery void before land appears. When they plunge into the depths, they usually serve as the emissaries of creators such as Raven, Eagle, Coyote, Old Man, or other creator deities. In some accounts the animals make their dives because they have grown tired of flying or swimming and long for a place where they can roost or rest, and in others they wish to help prepare a world where human beings can also live. Sometimes the diving is a contest wherein animals compete to succeed in their quests, and in these narratives it is occasionally a small and humble creature, such as the water bug or toad, that triumphs over larger and stronger swimmers. Within these myths even the successful earth-diver can suffer loss of life, and in these instances the particles of earth are removed from the beak, claws, or nails of the diver's corpse. As earth-divers, animals assist in the process of creation, and, in doing so, they sometimes sacrifice their lives.

CREATING A NEW WORLD

In the closely related creation myths of North America's Mohawk, Seneca, Huron, Iroquois, and Onondaga peoples, earth-divers help create a world where human beings can live. Although the earth, at the beginning of these tales, is a realm of darkness covered in water, the duck, loon, beaver, muskrat, toad, and other water animals live in this lower world. Above the watery void lies the land of the Great Spirit and his people, and, at the center of the upper world, a great tree grows. Interestingly, the creation myths of these traditions relate two occurrences of descent, for when the Great Spirit uproots the celestial tree and thus creates an opening where it stood, Sky Woman falls through the hole in the heavens. The animals below, who can see Sky Woman descending toward them, attempt to prepare a place where she can safely land. Indeed, in several of the accounts, helpful birds fly beneath her to cushion her fall.

In the Mohawk version of the tale, Beaver is the first to descend beneath the waters. A long time passes, and, when Beaver's dead body finally floats to the surface, Loon attempts the dive. Loon never reappears, and, after other unsuccessful dives, Muskrat takes his turn. Another long interval of time passes while Muskrat is gone, but when his corpse at last rises to the surface, the other animals discover a few grains of earth clutched in his claws. By placing the mud from Muskrat's nails on the back of a mighty turtle, the animals provide a place for Sky Woman to come to rest, and, when both the earth and the turtle then grow to great size, they also create a world where Sky Woman's progeny can continue the process of creation. In Mohawk tradition, the shaking or trembling of the earth is regarded as a sign that the World Turtle is stretching beneath the great weight she bears.

It is a diving bird that brings earth to the surface of the sea in the Seneca version of the tale, and, in the earth-diver creation myth of California's Mono people, a whole community of birds collaborates to create the earth. The Mono myth begins with a conversation between Prairie Falcon and Crow: although these birds do not possess the ability to dive, they nonetheless wonder what lies at the bottom of their watery world and therefore enlist the help of the aquatic birds that can descend into the depths. Duck, the first to dive, drowns in his attempt, and then Coot also fails to reach the bottom of the sea. When Grebe, the third earth-diver, eventually floats lifeless to the surface, Prairie Falcon uses his magical powers to restore the birds to life. Although his companions do not at first believe him, Grebe asserts that he was successful in his quest, and, indeed, the birds discover a few grains of sand embedded in his claws. In the Mono tale, birds create the earth when they scatter Grebe's sand upon the primal waters.

EXPANDING THE EARTH

While the Mohawk and Mono narratives simply state that the landmass of the world expands when earth is placed upon the turtle's back or sand is scattered on the primal sea, other earth-diver myths elaborate upon the means by which the world's growth occurs. In some accounts, including those of North America's Maidu and Blood peoples, the creator rolls the primordial mud into a ball and then stretches it across the water. Maheo, the great creator spirit of the Cheyenne people, kneads the bit of mud he takes from a coot's beak until it expands to such great size that only Old Grandmother Turtle can support it on her back. In variations of the myth told by California's Miwok and Yokut peoples, the creators make the world by mixing the earth-diver's bounty with seeds or tobacco, and in the version told by the Yauelmani Yokuts, Eagle mixes the primal dirt with seeds and water to produce a dough that swells into the shape of the earth. In the Crow creation myth, Old Man Coyote causes the earth to grow by blowing upon the bit of mud provided by an earth-diving duck, and in the tale of the Yuchi, Buzzard makes the earth spread out when he fans it with his wings.

Yet another example from central Asia offers an interesting variation, for in this tale the devil is responsible for the expansion of the earth. In the Asian story, two creator gods descend to the primal waters and turn a frog on its back to provide a place to sit. One of the gods then dives into the waters, and, after several attempts, returns with some earth to sprinkle on the stomach of the frog. Having thus created sufficient land where they can rest from their labors, the two gods are sleeping soundly when the devil chances upon them and decides to destroy them. Intending to hurl the creator deities into the sea, the devil seizes them and begins to run. As he runs, however, the earth keeps expanding, making it impossible for him to reach the water's edge. At last the devil gives up and releases the divinities—who are very pleased indeed to find themselves in the midst of an immense new world.

ACCOUNTING FOR EVIL

Although the devil's wicked intentions backfire in the Asian tale, other earth-diver myths include details that serve to explain the presence of evil in the world. In the Huron and Mohawk accounts, for example, Sky Woman gives birth to twin sons after she lands on the newly created earth, and these sons, one good twin and one evil one, compete in their efforts to complete the creation of the world. The good twin provides light for the sky, and the wicked son adds the darkness of night. The good twin makes beautiful trees, useful animals, and streams of pure water, and the evil twin responds by fashioning trees with thorns and poisonous fruit, by creating dangerous animals such as vipers, and by placing rocks in the rivers to turn streams into rapids. Eventually the brothers battle one another and the good son overcomes his malevolent twin, but by the time this occurs evil has already established its presence in the world. According to the Mohawks, this is why every person possesses both a good and a wicked heart. A Christian version of an earth-diver myth also addresses the problem of evil. This account, from central Europe, explains that creation becomes tainted when the devil, who is the earth-diver in the tale, first touches the primal mud from which the earth is then shaped.

SHAPING TERRESTRIAL FEATURES

Many earth-diver narratives include details that explain the formation of mountains, hills, and valleys on the surface of the earth. In the myths of both the Yuchi and the Cherokee people, features of the landscape are shaped when a great buzzard flaps its mighty wings. The earth, in the tale of the Yuchi, consists of only a mound of soft mud until Wind asks the birds to make it hard and dry. When Buzzard gently fans the moist mound, it spreads out in all directions, and when he then flaps his gigantic wings, the earth hardens in the shape of plains, hills, and gullies. In the Cherokee myth, the mud provided by Water Beetle is at first too soft to bear the weight of all the animals, who wait at the top of the rainbow for their new land to dry. The mud is just beginning to solidify when the animals send Grandfather Buzzard to scout the terrain, and as he flies over the empty landscape, its appearance starts to change: valleys are formed where Buzzard's wings touch down upon the earth, and when his wings rise up, the mountains are created. Because Grandfather Buzzard makes many mountains before the other animals realize what is happening and therefore call for his return, the traditional land of the Cherokees is a mountainous world.

In one of the versions of the Yokut people's creation myths, Eagle and Crow compete to build a new world out of the mud supplied by Duck, an earth-diver who repeatedly descends into the depths of the primal sea. Duck's labors make him hungry, and so Eagle and Crow reward his hard work with gifts of fish. Because Eagle presents Duck with twice as much food as does Crow, the earth-diver adds twice as much soil to the mound that rises on Eagle's side of the world. According to Yokut tradition, Eagle creates the towering Sierra Nevada Mountains from his mound of mud, and Crow, working with a lesser quantity of earth, shapes California's Coast Mountain Range on his half of the world. Duck is also the earth-diver in the Crow creation myth, and when Old Man Coyote, in the role of creator, asks red-eyed Duck to dive into the primal waters, he eventually returns with both mud and a root. From the mud, Old Man Coyote makes a new world, and from the root, he produces plants, grass, trees, and many kinds of food. When Coyote the Creator asks Duck's opinion of the land he has made, the earth-diver points out that the world is too flat. Old Man Coyote can see that this is true, and he therefore embellishes his creation by fashioning its many mountains, hills, valleys, lakes, rivers, and springs.

ANIMAL DIVERS

In addition to deities, the devil, and the red-eyed duck, the beaver, muskrat, mink, frog, and mudhen all serve as earth-divers in various creation myths. Water

Beetle is the earth-diver in Cherokee tradition, and in the tales of the Chickasaw, Tuskegee, and Yuchi peoples, the crawfish provides the primal mud from which the earth is made. In the Yuchi account, the crawfish named Lock-chew builds a mound of mud that reaches from the bottom of the primal sea to the surface of its waters, and in the Tuskegee myth, Crawfish spends four days underwater before he finally reappears with grains of dirt beneath his claws. According to the Huron earth-diver myth, a toad supplies the bits of earth that Sky Woman places upon the back of the Great Tortoise, and in the stories told by the Blood and Maidu peoples, the turtle does not support the world but serves instead as the earth-diver who bravely journeys to the bottom of the watery abyss. Turtle's journey, in the Maidu myth, is indeed a particularly arduous one, for in this account the successful earth-diver returns to the surface of the water six years after making his descent.

An interesting variation on the earth-diver motif appears in Indian tradition in the form of a tale that describes Vishnu's third incarnation as Varaha the boar. In this story, the divine Vishnu assumes the form of an animal that possesses the strength and the will required to rescue the earth from the depths of the primordial sea. As earth-diver, Varaha descends into the realm of chaos represented by the primal waters. At the bottom of the timeless ocean, the boar avatar confronts and slays Hiranyaksha, the vicious demon who has stolen the earth. Then, with his mighty tusks, Varaha carries the earth back to its proper place beneath the sun. Although Varaha's feat of earth-diving does not create the world, his achievement can be understood as an act of re-creation; by rescuing the earth from the timeless realm of chaos, Varaha restores the cycles of time that order the cosmos.

See also Animals in Myth; Creation Myths; Twins, Pairs, and Doubles

EMERGENCE MOTIF

Although an image of birth as the means by which the cosmos, earth, divinities, or mortal beings come into existence is present in all creation myths, the stories of people's emergence into the world focus explicitly on the birthing process, the passage from a dark and womb-like realm to the sunlit world that lies beyond it. These creation myths tell of a people's journey from a dim, enclosed, and often crowded place into a bright and spacious new land. In most of these narratives, the world that is left behind lies in the depths of the earth, and in some accounts people must ascend through several subterranean caverns or spheres before they finally emerge on the surface of the earth. The people, in this category of creation myths, symbolically emerge from the earth's womb, and it is particularly fitting that they do so, for emergence myths characteristically circulate among agricultural societies: just as the plants that sustain people's lives are rooted in the earth, so too are the origins of the people themselves.

ESCAPE

In many emergence myths, people seek a new world to escape the miserable conditions of their lives underground. The underworld caverns are often described as dark and dismal places where quarrels break out when populations increase within the constricted space of the subterranean realm. In Hopi tradition, for example, the chief of the underworld people searches for a means of escape when men and women feud with one another and then decide to live apart. In some accounts people ascend from the underworld to flee an encroaching deluge, and in others they return to the upper world after they have found sanctuary from a flood by retreating to the depths of the earth. In several tales the emergence occurs only when people have been taught the skills, customs, and ceremonies they need to establish a new life on the surface of the earth.

SIPAPU

Tales of people's emergence from the depths of the earth or from trees rooted in the earth come from North America's Southwest and Great Plains, from Mesoamerica, from Oceania, and from Southeast Asia. This form of creation myth is especially prevalent among the Navajo and the Pueblo peoples of Arizona and New Mexico, where the emergence story plays an important role in religious ceremonies and practices. The Navajo, for example, incorporate the narrative of their creation in curing ceremonies and in other rituals that celebrate a new beginning, and, in the middle of their kivas (sacred ceremonial chambers), the Hopi dig a small hole that represents the opening through which their ancestors passed when they first entered their new world. Among the Pueblos the opening to the subterranean realm is known as *sipapu*, and several groups believe that the dead pass through this hole on their journey to the underworld. According to Hopi tradition, *sipapu* can be found at the bottom of the Grand Canyon. Other groups of Pueblos, the Tewa and the Keresan peoples, say that *sipapu* is located beneath a lake or at the back of a deep cave.

MEANS OF EMERGENCE

In stories of the emergence, the people of the underworld make good their escape by a variety of means. Sometimes they climb up a creeper, root, or vine that hangs down from the world above, and sometimes they plant a tree or a reed that can serve them as a ladder. Often birds or insects are sent to search for a hole in the roof of their cavern, and in some tales burrowing animals are dispatched to dig a hole for the people. In several accounts the mole digs a hole and is then blinded by the sunlight when it looks out upon the surface of the earth. In other stories the badger burrows through the earth and its paws are then forever stained by the dirt it displaces. When the people are ready to leave their underground world, a leader or helper frequently appears to show them the way or to instruct them in knowledge they will need to live in their new land. In Native American tales, the emerging people are assisted in their journey by spirits, deities, animals, or heroes. In several narratives a female helper, Corn Mother, Spider Woman, or Thinking Woman, serves the role of midwife during the people's passage from the earth's womb.

HOPI EMERGENCE MYTHS

In one of the Hopi people's several versions of the emergence myth, the world creators are the primal parents, the earth goddess Spider Woman and the sun god Tawa. When Tawa thinks animals and people into being, Spider Woman shapes them from clay and brings them to life. At first the animals and people dwell deep in the underworld, in Spider Woman's realm. However, when crowding in the lower world causes men and women to quarrel and the subterranean cavern then begins to flood, the chief of the people offers a prayer stick to Spider Woman, calling upon her to help his people leave their original home. Spider Woman first plants a mighty spruce tree, but when it fails to grow tall enough to reach the land above, she plants the seeds of the lowly reed. The reed quickly shoots up into the heights, towering above the people and then finally piercing through the roof of their world.

After Spider Woman provides a means of escape, the chief of the underground people sends several animals to climb the reed ladder and scout the world that lies above it, and, finally, the flute-playing Locust successfully emerges into the land of the sun. There his courage is tested when the gods of the four directions hurl their thunderbolts upon him, but Locust, who calmly plays his flute throughout his ordeal, wins the gods' permission for the people of the underworld to enter the upper land and claim it for their own. The people's ascent requires a journey of eight days, but their labors are rewarded when they reach the top of their ladder and begin a new life in a world of great beauty. To prepare them to live in their new homeland, Spider Woman establishes the people's clans, shows them how to build kivas, and teaches them to hunt and grow corn.

The Hopi live in a world of four directions where four winds blow through their land, and the significance of this sacred number is suggested in other versions of their emergence myth. In one account, for example, Spider Woman leads the underground people through four caverns of the underworld before they finally emerge from the spider hole that opens into the floor of the Grand Canyon. In another version of the tale, the chief in the underworld seeks to lead his people from the depths when wicked beings appear in their midst. The chief first sends birds to search for a hole in the roof of the underworld. The eagle, hawk, and swallow all fail to fly high enough, but the fourth bird, the shrike, discovers the hole. The chief then uses seeds provided by a chipmunk to attempt to grow a ladder his people can use. The spruce, fir, and pine do not grow tall enough to reach the hole, but the fourth plant, the reed, extends into the upper world. As they ascend through the reed, the chief and his people are pursued by the evil ones. The chief, however, cuts down the reed before the wicked people can emerge, and thus the Hopi, whose name means peaceful ones, are free to establish a new and harmonious society on the surface of the earth.

In yet another version of the Hopi emergence story, the original creation consists of four worlds, three underground realms and the upper land. Until it becomes overcrowded and filthy, all the animals and people live in the lowest and blackest of the underworld caves. In this version of the myth, living beings are assisted by Two Brothers, the sun twins who come from the sky bearing all the plants of the world. Hoping to find a plant that will be strong enough and tall enough to serve as a ladder, Two Brothers grow a variety of trees. In this account it is the cane, jointed like a ladder, which provides the means for people and animals to ascend to the second cave. This world, however, is also dark and soon it too becomes overcrowded, and so the twins guide its inhabitants to the third of the caverns. There, Two Brothers provide the people with fire, and, for the first time, they can see their world and build houses within it. Life in the third cave world nevertheless becomes unbearable when all of the women fall under the spell of the dance and then neglect their families. To escape the social disorder caused by the women's frenzied dancing, the people make their last ascent, and, once again guided by Two Brothers, they at last emerge into the Fourth World.

NAVAJO EMERGENCE MYTH

North America's Navajo, neighbors of the Hopi, borrow elements of the Pueblo people's emergence myths in their creation stories. The Navajo, like the Pueblos, recount several versions of their emergence, but all of the tales describe the people's long and arduous journey as they ascend to their homeland. According to Navajo cosmology, the world consists of six domed lands that lie one atop another. The Navajo today live in the Fifth World, the land of the sun, and above it rests another world, a realm of perfect harmony. The Navajo emergence tales relate the story of a journey upward that begins in the small, dark realm of the First World, also called the Black World. The wingless insect people that inhabit the bottom world long for a brighter and more spacious land, and so they cleverly fabricate wings for themselves and follow Locust when he flies through a crack in the sky that opens into the Blue World. The Second World, the land of the bird people, is both lighter and larger than the Black World, but when the insects multiply and can no longer find food, the birds decide to drive them from their land. Led once again by Locust, the insect people fly through a hole in the dome of the Blue World and then find themselves in the Yellow World.

Although the insects soon discover that the Third World is the home of First People—all the members of the animal kingdom—it is larger and lighter than the lower worlds, and for many years all creatures there live comfortably and peacefully together. First Man and First Woman join the First People in the Yellow World when four gods appear and create them from white and yellow ears of corn. Eventually, when populations multiply and food becomes too scarce, the people of the Yellow World recognize that the time has come for them all to move to another world. First People divide into four groups and ascend into the Fourth World, the Black-and-White World, from four directions: from the east First Woman leads the people who will become the Navajo, and from the west First Man leads the animal people; the bird people enter from the south, and the insect people ascend from the north.

When First People reach the Fourth World, they find there the Hopi, the Zuni, and other Pueblo peoples. The Apache, the Ute, and the peoples of the Great Plains are also distant neighbors. In this world, with its white days and black nights, First Man and First Woman teach the Navajo the skills they need to cultivate the land. Crops flourish in this world and all its peoples live in harmony together until Coyote causes trouble. The sly trickster, who cheats when he gambles, plays games of chance with Water Monster and wins his fur coat. When Coyote discovers Water Monster's two babies in the pockets of the coat he has won, he foolishly decides that he will keep them too. Furious over the loss of his babies, Water Monster floods the entire world, forcing its inhabitants to seek sanctuary on a mountain peak. Most of the Navajo, Hopi, Apache, and other groups reach the mountaintop, but those who do not are transformed into fish, seals, and other water people. Turkey, dragging his tail feathers in the water, barely makes it to safety, and his feathers forever show the marks of the water.

High on the mountain, the Navajo plant the seeds of the bamboo, and, when a gigantic plant grows into the sky, they carve a door in its side. All the people of the Fourth World then climb into the bamboo and pass through its tunnel into the Fifth World. The thirty-two clans of the Navajo are the last to emerge, and it is therefore they who first understand that the danger has not passed. Indeed, when the floodwaters begin to pour forth from the top of the bamboo, First Woman and First Man recognize that Water Monster is displaying his anger. Suspecting that Coyote the trickster must somehow be responsible for the coming of the deluge, the two seize his fur coat and quickly discover the babies hidden in its pockets. Water Monster is finally appeased when First Man and First Woman return to him both the babies and the coat, and, according to Navajo tradition, he never again troubles the peoples who now dwell in the Fifth World.

APACHE EMERGENCE MYTH

The creation myth of the Jicarilla Apache, traditional neighbors of the Navajo and Pueblo peoples, offers yet another version of the emergence motif. In this story the living beings of the underworld at first live in darkness. Although some in the underworld, the panther, bear, and owl, prefer to move in darkness, other animals and people long for a light to illuminate their world. After presenting their different arguments, the animals and people agree to settle their dispute by playing games of chance, and when those who favor light prove to be victorious, the morning star and the sun suddenly appear. As the sun moves across the top of the underworld, he spots a hole in the roof, and when he then tells the people about the world that lies above, they immediately decide that they will try to move there.

In their efforts to reach the hole at the top of their world, the people make mounds that soon grow into mountains. The four mountains, however, are not tall enough, and so the people fashion a ladder made out of feathers. When the ladder of feathers cannot bear the weight of the people, they make another ladder out of larger feathers. This ladder is still not strong enough, and so they try again using eagle feathers. Although the eagle feathers are stronger than the others, they too collapse under the weight of all the people. On their fourth attempt, the people finally succeed in making a suitable ladder from the straight horns of the buffalo, and they are thus able to climb through the hole that leads to their new world. Although the horns of the buffalo do not break during the people's ascent, they do bend, and that is why, as the Apache explain, the buffalo's horns are thereafter curved. When the people leave the underworld, they take the sun and morning star along with them, attached to a spider's thread, and when they emerge, they then immediately release them into their new sky.

GREAT PLAINS EMERGENCE MYTHS

While emergence myths are widespread among the peoples of North America's Southwest, they also occur in regions within the Great Plains. The Mandan Sioux of North Dakota, for example, tell a tale that is strikingly similar to the emergence myth of the Mojave Apache. In both of these accounts, the people of the underworld discover the root of a grapevine dangling down into their village. When the people climb up the root, they find a wonderful new land, a sunlit world filled with animals and plants. In the Mandan version of the story, half of the underground people make their way to the new world before the root breaks, leaving the other half of the people stranded in the underworld. According to Mandan tradition, people rejoin their underground relatives after they die. The myth of the Mandan is not the only one in which relatives of emerging people remain in the underworld.

In the tale told by Oklahoma's Kiowa, a pregnant woman becomes lodged in the hollow log through which the people emerge, and those trapped behind the woman cannot pass through to the new world. As the Kiowa explain, this is the reason why their tribe has always been a small one.

EMERGENCE FROM TREES AND HOLES IN THE GROUND

In some tales of emergence, people come forth from trees that are rooted in the ground. The Ceram people of Indonesia's Molucca Islands, for example, tell in their creation myth how the nine original families of their agricultural society emerge from bunches of bananas. Similarly, in the creation story of the Papuan Keraki people of New Guinea, the first human beings emerge from a palm tree. For other peoples of Indonesia and Melanesia, emergence myths serve to explain the origins of their social orders. For example, in the tale told by the Carabaulo people of Timor, the first of their ancestors to climb up the creepers of a tree and emerge from a hole in the ground become aristocrats and owners of land, and those that follow become commoners or laborers. This pattern also appears in the emergence myth of the Melanesian Trobriand Islanders. In their account, the animals that originally emerge from a hole in the ground are associated with the islanders' four clans, and the first to emerge is the animal ancestor of the society's most prestigious clan.

See also Animals in Myth; Creation Myths; Deluge Motif; Tricksters

ETIOLOGICAL MYTHS

In the broadest sense all myth is etiological, offering as it does explanations for the nature of the world and for its origins. People's creation myths explain how the cosmos first came into being, and their accounts of the afterlife or underworld envision what might follow earthly existence. Fertility myths offer ways to understand the cycles of nature, and tales that recount the actions of heroes explain what people value as well as what they fear. In a narrower sense, however, the etiological myth concerns itself with the how and why of other commonplace details, accounting for how some feature of the landscape comes to take its shape, how some animal acquires its distinctive behavior or markings, or why it is that earthly life always ends in death. Some explanatory narratives describe the origins of traditional customs or cultural taboos, and others provide reasons for apparent differences in people's social status or physical appearance. In many cultural traditions these myths answer questions about where the sun goes at night or what meaning lies behind the sudden occurrence of an earthquake or eclipse. In other words, etiological myths address the practical questions of "how" and "why" that naturally arise when people seek to understand the workings of their world. Although these kinds of explanatory details are often embedded in accounts of creation or in other kinds of myths, they also take the form of independent narratives. Indeed, etiological myths are especially popular among Native American peoples and among the indigenous inhabitants of the Australian continent.

LANDSCAPE

Among several groups of Native American peoples, Devil's Tower, the massive basalt formation that rises above Wyoming's plains, is known as Bear Rock, and traditional tales recount the stories of its origin. In one version of the myth, the Sioux explain that two young boys, far from home and lost, find themselves in desperate peril when a gigantic grizzly bear picks up their scent and begins to pursue them. With nowhere to hide, the boys pray for deliverance, and the Great Spirit causes the earth beneath them to rise over a thousand feet into the sky. Enraged at the loss of its meal, the ferocious bear tries in vain to climb the sheer cliffs, and they forever after show the markings made by its monstrous claws. In another version of the tale, one told by the Kiowa people, the origins of two natural features are described, for this account also explains the formation of the constellation known as the Big Dipper. According to the myth, seven sisters seek the safety of a large stump when their brother suddenly assumes the form of a terrifying bear. The magical tree trunk rises as the bear grasps it with his claws, and when the tree turns to rock, the scratches left by the bear remain clearly visible. The bear's sisters, who are carried high into the heavens, become the seven stars that give shape to the Big Dipper. Astromorphosis, the transformation of living beings into celestial objects, is indeed a feature of numerous etiological myths.

Like the Native Americans, whose etiological myths provide a history for numerous features of the landscape, the original peoples of Australia tell stories that explain the landmarks of their world. In Australian cosmology, creation occurs during the Dreamtime, the era when people's ancestors roam about the earth shaping its valleys, hills, and plains and forming all its rivers and springs. Thus, in Australian tradition, every rock formation, spring, or other natural landmark tells a tale that serves to link the people with ancestral powers, and in rituals that reenact the wanderings of their ancestors, the people participate in Dreamtime's unfolding of creation. In one of the stories, an ancestor of the Buandik people, a giant named Craitbul, creates the four lakes of Mount Gambier during the course of his wanderings. Fleeing from an enemy, Craitbul and his wife and sons travel to the mountain with the hope of finding a new home there. However, when they dig into the earth to prepare a place to cook, their hole quickly fills with water that rises from below. After three more holes also become flooded, Craitbul decides that he and his family must resume their journey, and so they travel on until they find a home in a cave on Berrin's Peak.

NATURAL PHENOMENA

Not only do many traditional narratives account for the earth's geological features, they frequently offer explanations of other natural phenomena as well. Numerous myths, for example, offer ways to understand the occurrence of an earthquake. According to North America's Iroquois people, the world rests upon the back of a great turtle, and when the turtle stretches, the earth begins to tremble. The Wasco, another Native American people, explain that both earthquakes and volcanoes occur when war breaks out between the powerful mountain spirits that rule Mount Adams and Mount Hood; according to the Wasco, volcanoes erupt when the mountain spirits hurl hot stones at one another. The occurrence of an eclipse is another occasional event that often inspires explanatory narratives, and a tale told by the Dusun people of Borneo provides an example. Rice is the staple food of the Dusun, and their myth recounts a time when starvation threatens them because the winged serpent Terab, who also eats rice, steals all their food. Salvation comes when the creator deity tells the people of a magical spell that will cause Terab to eat the moon instead of their rice. However, when the immense serpent sometimes swallows the entire moon, then an eclipse takes place, and the people must recite another incantation to force him to spew it forth.

People's myths, of course, also address other celestial phenomena, accounting for the formation of patterns among the stars or explaining what happens to the sun at night. In a myth from ancient Greece, a story of unrequited love lies behind the creation of the constellations known as Orion and the Pleiades. According to the tale, the gigantic hunter Orion falls hopelessly in love with all the seven daughters of the nymph Pleione and devotes seven years to pursuit of the maidens. Zeus finally intervenes, however, and places the hunter's quarry high up in the heavens far beyond his reach. When Orion dies and is transformed into the constellation that lies behind the Pleiades, the two groups of stars form an eternal tableau of unrequited love. In a remarkably similar story, the Pitjandjara people of Australia tell of the ancestor Yoola's pursuit of seven sisters. When Old Man Yoola at last traps the maidens near a waterhole, they leap in and drown. Old Man Yoola follows them and thus drowns as well, and the spirits of the dead assume the heavenly form of the Seven Sisters of the Pleiades with Yoola forever in pursuit. Australian tradition also offers various accounts of the sun's nightly disappearance, and the Arunta people explain that during the night the sun goddess pays a visit to the people's ancestors, who live beneath the world. While the nightly absence of the sun signifies a time of peaceful rest in the Australian myths, in the tradition of ancient Egypt it heralds an interval of great peril, for each night Apophis, the monstrous serpent of the underworld, strives to destroy the sun, and the people can never know when he might succeed at last.

CHARACTERISTICS OF ANIMALS

Accounts of how animals assume their physical characteristics and temperaments appear in myths and animal fables from around the world. Tales from Africa, for example, explain how it happens that the leopard acquires its spots. In the story told by the Tumbuka people, Tortoise, who has been hoisted into a tree by the prankster Hyena, rewards Leopard for lifting him down by decorating him with his handsome black spots. Tortoise paints the stripes on Zebra's coat as well, but he naturally refuses Hyena's request that he also be painted, and thus the hyena remains undistinguished in appearance. According to the people of Sierra Leone, Leopard's spots are the result of his own folly, for, in a gesture of hospitality, he unwisely invites Fire to visit his home—and Fire, of course, consumes the house and singes Leopard's pelt. In yet another version of the tale, that of the Ashanti peoples, Leopard's spots are also caused by fire. The hero of this story, Half a Ball of Kenki, rescues Fly when Leopard ties him up. Leopard then fights with Half a Ball of Kenki, who is made of cornmeal mush, and it is during this altercation that his coat becomes spotted after being scorched.

Other explanatory myths account for features of animal behavior, and a story told by North America's Iroquois people focuses on the timid nature of the rabbit. According to this tale, during the process of creation, Rabbit asks that he be given long legs and ears and sharp claws and teeth. The creator Raweno agrees to this request and begins his work by fashioning long hind legs for Rabbit. Suddenly, however, Raweno is interrupted by Owl, who finds it hard to wait for his own turn to be formed. The creator reminds Owl that he is not allowed to watch the shaping of other animals and then places a pair of long ears atop Rabbit's head. When Owl interrupts again and defiantly declares that he will continue to watch the creator at work, Raweno finally becomes annoyed, and, seizing the unformed bird by the ears, he shakes him until his eyes grow large from fright. Rabbit, who witnesses Raweno's outburst of anger, runs away in fear before his creation is completed, and that is why his front legs are still short and why he lacks the sharp teeth and claws originally promised him. Furthermore, because Rabbit's first instinct is to scamper off in fear, he remains a timid creature, one who is frightened all too easily.

DIFFERENCES AMONG HUMAN BEINGS

Some creation myths include details that explain how it happens that differences exist among human beings. In the tale told by Africa's Yoruba people, for example, the creator god Obatala uses clay to fashion the first people. In time, Obatala pauses in his labors to seek some refreshment and drinks too much of the fermented juice that comes from the palm tree. Not realizing that he has become inebriated, the creator resumes his task of shaping human figures out of clay, but his hands are not steady and therefore his creations are no longer perfect. Only later, after Obatala has asked the sky god Olorun to breathe life into his figures, does he notice that some of the new people have legs or arms that are too short or spines that are curved. Deeply sorry for his unwitting mistake, Obatala proclaims himself the protector deity of all people affected by his actions, and he also firmly vows that never again will he drink wine. Differences in people's appearances and customs are also accounted for in the creation myth of South America's Tiahuanaco culture, where the creator god Viracocha shapes people out of stone. Viracocha painstakingly fashions men, women, pregnant women, and children before painting distinctive hairstyles and articles of clothing on each of the figures. Before bringing his creations to life, Viracocha divides the figures into separate groups, and for each of these new communities he supplies the different foods they will need, the customs they will practice, and the languages they will speak.

Creation myths from some other cultures address questions about differences in people's social status. In one of ancient China's accounts of creation, the mother goddess Nu Gua carefully shapes the first people from clay that she finds in the Yellow River's bed. Like Obatala, the goddess, however, eventually grows weary, and she then searches for a more efficient way to carry out her work. She soon discovers that she can give form to several people at once by dredging the riverbed with a twisted rope and then shaking free the clay that adheres to the rope. When Nu Gua at last breathes life into her figures, the differences between the two kinds of people are immediately apparent: those who are born from the figures shaped by hand become China's aristocrats, and those who are born from the droplets of clay become the country's common people. In Tibetan tradition, where the universe emerges from a cosmic egg, one creation myth tells how the different classes of people are hatched from different eggs. In this account, the ancestors of kings come from a golden egg while the ancestors of servants emerge from a turquoise one. Among Melanesia's Trobriand Islanders, creation begins when four animals that serve as the totems of the people's clans climb to the surface of the earth from a hole in the ground. According to tradition, the prestige of a clan depends upon the order in which the animal associated with it first emerges, and thus the people's ruling class is identified with the first animal to appear.

DEATH

Myth tradition includes a great number of tales that seek to explain the occurrence of death, and several recurring patterns emerge from these stories. In some myths death is conceived as a form of punishment, and in others it results from an act of vengeance; in many accounts death comes into existence because of an unfortunate mistake, and, in a few cultural traditions, mortality is justified as a useful means of keeping the world from becoming overcrowded. According to Hebrew and Christian accounts, death is a punishment that is exacted for their disobedience when Adam and Eve choose to eat of the forbidden fruit, and it is also represented as a punishment in the myths of the Luba people of Africa's Congo. In the story that the Luba tell, human beings and deities all live together until the gods can no longer bear the frequent disturbances caused by the people. As punishment for their behavior, the people are sent to dwell on the earth, the place where death eventually makes its claim to all living things.

In some explanatory myths, death is unleashed as retribution for an insult or injury. In the tale told by the Diegueños people of North America's Southwest, Frog gets revenge after people laugh at the sight of his squat and hairless body. Enraged by the mockery to which he is subjected, Frog spews poison into the drinking water of the creator god who gave him his strange shape. When the creator eventually discovers what Frog has done, he understands that he and all the children of his creation will henceforth be subject to mortality. Another tale of revenge comes from the myths of the Kalauna people of Papua, New Guinea. In this account, the snake god Honoyeta unleashes death into the world when he becomes angry with one of his wives. As the story goes, Honoyeta keeps a secret from his two wives, for each day, while they are preoccupied with their labors, he sheds his snakeskin and takes the form of an alluring young man. Eventually one of the wives discovers this subterfuge and burns her husband's snakeskin. Infuriated because he can no longer assume his snake identity, the wrathful Honoyeta brings death into the world.

According to the accounts offered by many cultural traditions, death comes into existence by accident rather than design. Several African peoples, for example, tell versions of a tale in which the messenger who is sent by the deities to inform human beings that they can live forever somehow fails to deliver the good news. In the Ibo people's version of the myth, the creator Chuku does not intend that people should die, and when they begin to do so, he immediately attempts to correct the problem. Chuku dispatches a dog to tell the people that if they gently sprinkle the ashes from a wood fire over a corpse, they can thereby restore the dead to life. The dog, however, becomes distracted when it finds a bone to gnaw, and Chuku therefore sends a sheep to carry his instructions. Unfortunately, the sheep becomes confused and mistakenly tells the people to bury all their dead, and, when the people obey these instructions, then death becomes permanent. In the story of the Zulu people, it is the chameleon that fails to deliver the news of people's immortality, and, in a variation of the myth related by the Kono of Sierra Leone, the dog is once again the culprit. In this tale, the deity sends to the people a bundle of new skins that they can use to restore themselves after they grow old. However, when the dog that is carrying the bundle is distracted, serpents steal the skins and then use them for themselves. Because of the dog's mistake, snakes can renew themselves, while human beings must all die.

The myths of some peoples account for death by acknowledging it as a necessary means of affording adequate space for earthly life to flourish. Stories told by the Inuit peoples describe a time when death does not exist, but during that era the world's inhabitants continue to multiply until the earth itself begins to sink into the sea. To save the earth from imminent disaster, a wise old woman uses the power of magic to bring death into the world. According to a similar myth that comes from South America's Caraja people, human beings originally dwell deep in the underworld, where death does not exist. When the people's underworld home becomes overly crowded, they decide to move to the surface of the earth, and, although they find ample space there, they also discover that mortality is its cost, for, as in the tale told by the Luba, death exists on earth. In the myths of many Native American peoples, it is the trickster Coyote who brings death into the world. In the account of the Shoshone people, Coyote persuades the creator deity, who is at first opposed to death, that indeed mortality offers an appropriate way to keep the world from ending up too crowded.

Myth tradition includes some other explanations of death in addition to those that most commonly recur. In another of the Coyote tales, the Maidu people explain that the trickster introduces death out of his boredom with a perfect world where little change occurs, and Africa's Dogon people tell of how their first ancestor requests death when, after many long years have passed, he at last grows tired of living. In the tradition of the Maori people, the story of the origin of death is linked to a cultural taboo, for the tale also indicates that incest is forbidden. According to the myth, Tane, the Polynesian god of the forests, first separates earth and sky and then creates his wife from the red clay that contains his parents' blood. Tane and his wife, the first woman in the world, give birth to a daughter, Hine Titama, and when Tane and Hine Titama also give birth to children, they become the ancestors of the Maori people. Death comes into existence when Hine Titama discovers that her husband is also her father, for knowledge of this truth brings her such shame that she can no longer bear to live in the world. Hine Titama therefore descends into the underworld, the realm of death, and there she awaits the arrival of her children, all of whom will eventually be reunited with their mother. In the Maori myth, the figure of Hine Titama thus represents both birth and death.

CUSTOMS

While some myths describe the origins of cultural taboos, others explain how traditional rituals and customs first come into being. Among the peoples of North America's Great Plains, for example, the smoking of the sacred pipe is an especially honored practice, and a story recounted by the Lakota people tells of its origins. For the Lakota Sioux, the red stone pipe delivered from heaven by White Buffalo Woman is central to several important ceremonies, and therefore when she brings the pipe, the goddess first explains its sacred significance and then shows the people how it should be used. Emblematic of the unity that lies at the heart of all creation, the pipe represents the connection between the heaven and all the forms of life on the earth below. So that the people's words might ascend with the pipe's smoke as it rises toward the sky, White Buffalo Woman teaches them the pipe-filling song and the prayers they should speak during their observance of the seven sacred rites. To remind them of these rituals, the goddess also leaves with them a small stone engraved with seven circles that represent the ceremonial uses of the sacred pipe. Her earthly mission fulfilled, White Buffalo Woman departs after bestowing a great gift that the people thereafter pass down through all succeeding generations.

ORIGINS OF FIRE

Explanatory myths include numerous accounts of how people first gain possession of fire or obtain knowledge that leads to other cultural achievements. In many traditions the fire bringer is a trickster or an animal that acquires fire by theft and then passes this gift on to human beings. Fire bringers of this kind include the Greek Titan Prometheus, the North American tricksters Coyote and Raven, and a variety of helpful animals including such humble creatures as the wasp, mouse, and water spider. In tales from Peru and Australia, however, a person discovers how to make fire by rubbing sticks together but tries to keep his knowledge secret. In the tale of Peru's Jivaro people, Takkea kills and cooks the animals that try to steal his fire until finally Himbui the hummingbird sneaks away with flames to share with Takkea's neighbors. According to the Djauan people of Australia, it is also a hummingbird that manages to steal the rubbing sticks that belong to Koimul, the first of the ancestors to make use of fire. In reward for giving Koimul's fire sticks to all of humankind, the hummingbird receives brightly shining feathers to wear in its tail. Some myths also explain how it happens that fire becomes embedded within sticks of wood, and an example of this motif can be found in a story told by South America's Makiritare people. In this tale, the two culture heroes who steal fire by killing its guardian, the toad Kawao, must hide their trophy to escape the vengeance of Kawao's jaguar husband. Because the heroes choose trees as hiding places, the fire concealed within them can always be extracted when sticks of wood are rubbed together.

CULTURAL ACHIEVEMENTS

While the many myths that explain the origins of fire reflect its importance to early people's lives, other narratives describe discoveries that also bring significant changes to human cultures. For example, a tale told by North America's Cherokee people offers an account of the origins of medicine. According to the Cherokee, in the earliest of times—the era when animals and people all live in harmony together—there is no sickness in the world. Disease, however, comes into existence when human beings begin to lose respect for the animals and sometimes even kill their fellow creatures merely for sport. When this happens, the animal kingdom rises up in protest and decides to wage war on its former friends. Sickness and pain are the weapons animals use against the people, and the animals also send terrifying visions to haunt people's dreams. When the plants of the world hear of the conflict, they offer their assistance to those human beings who promise to respect all forms of life. Accordingly, each herb, flower, bush, and tree provides a remedy to counter one of the forms of illness unleashed by the animals, and thus the science of medicine is born.

In a myth from another Native American tradition, the Zuni people tell of their acquisition of the flute, an instrument that is played during ceremonial dances. According to this tale, when the people proclaim their desire to find new ways to express themselves through the exquisite beauty of music and dance, the Zuni elders seek the help of Paíyatuma, the god of the dew. To realize their goal, the four elders must set forth on a quest, and thus they climb the sacred mountain to find the Cave of the Rainbow that lies near its peak. The wise elders bring with them gifts of prayer sticks and plumes, and after they have presented their offerings to the god of dew, he and his musicians and dancers perform in honor of their guests. The elders are amazed at the wonders they behold within the rainbow-colored cave, for the harmonious design of all creation is revealed in the rhythms of the dance and the songs of the flutes. When the elders at last descend from the cave, they carry with them the long, tapered flutes that are Paíyatuma's precious gifts for the people.

See also Animals in Myth; Creation Myths; Culture Heroes; Tricksters

THE FALL

According to the accounts of many cultural traditions, immediately after the process of creation ends, the world exists in a state of original perfection. In the Hebrew and Christian traditions, for example, the unfolding of creation is completed when the first human beings are brought to life within an earthly paradise, the Garden of Eden. Creation's primordial perfection is lost, however, when the world's original circumstances change, and in the story recounted by Hebrews and Christians, the world is utterly transformed by humankind's fall from grace. When Adam and Eve eat of the forbidden fruit and are then expelled from paradise, all humanity is made subject to a changed mode of being, for it is then that mortality, sexual regeneration, and the need to work all become conditions for living in the world. Moreover, misfortune, disease, hardship, and adversity all accompany the advent of death and hard work, and thus evil is introduced into people's lives. This story, like other accounts of a fall from paradise, therefore explains how it happens that an imperfect world comes into existence. When Adam and Eve commit their act of disobedience, their punishment is the loss of creation's original perfection.

In a similar story told by North America's Blackfoot people, it is also an act of disobedience that introduces death, disease, and sorrow into the world. After the creation of the cosmos, human beings peacefully inhabit the earth while the deities, or sky people, dwell in the heavens. The circumstances that bring change to people's earthly lives begin to unfurl when Feather Woman and Morning Star fall in love and marry. Although Feather Woman is one of the earth people, she ascends to the Sky Country when she marries the god, and there she is welcomed in the home of Morning Star's parents, Father Sun and Mother Moon. In time, Feather Woman gives birth to a son, Star Boy, and she lives happily with her family until curiosity overwhelms her and she performs the single act that is forbidden in the land of the sky people. Although Moon warns Feather Woman that the dislodging of the Great Turnip that grows in the sky will lead to terrible consequences, she nonetheless digs it up and thereby uncovers a hole in the heavens. Discontent is the first of the ramifications of Feather Woman's deed, for as she gazes down on her former home, she is filled with nostalgia for her life on the earth. The young woman's sorrow only grows deeper, however, as further consequences of her act unfold. Banished forever from her husband and the land of the sky people, Feather Woman carries with her the burdens of unhappiness and death when she returns to the earth, and it is not long after her fall from the heavens that she dies from grief.

Although Feather Woman's act of disobedience brings death and suffering to the earth, the conclusion of the Blackfoot tale provides some hope for the people, for, when the young mother falls from paradise, she is accompanied by her son, a boy who eventually becomes a great culture hero. At first Star Boy's lot is a miserable one, for not only is he orphaned by his mother's death, but he must also endure the ridicule of those who make fun of a deep scar that marks his face. Indeed, Poia ("scarface") becomes the new name that is given to Feather Woman's unfortunate son. When Poia asks a wise old medicine woman how his blemish might be healed, she advises him to journey to the land of the sky people to seek the help of Sun. Poia therefore sets forth on a dangerous quest that leads him to the edge of the Great Water in the west, and there he discovers a shining pathway that leads to the heavens. Because he proves himself to be both courageous and noble, Poia is welcomed in the house of his grandparents, where Sun removes his scar and instructs him in rituals for curing the diseases unleashed upon the earth by his mother's deed. When Poia finally climbs down the Milky Way and returns to the earth, he carries with him the gift of his grandfather's wisdom. Among his people, Poia is soon recognized as the culture hero who teaches them the Sun Dance, the ceremony that restores those who suffer from pain and disease.

RELATIONS WITH ANIMALS

According to the stories of many Native American peoples, animals and human beings live together and speak the same language during the earliest days that follow the creation of the world. Eventually, however, people and animals lose their ability to talk with one another, and when this occurs, the world they originally share is inevitably transformed. Usually it is humanity that is responsible for the transformation, and in a tale recounted by the Cherokee people, the change in the relationship between animals and human beings comes about when the people lose respect for their fellow creatures and wantonly kill them. The repercussions of the change in people's behavior are severe, for the animals respond by introducing many forms of sickness into the world. The deer cause painful rheumatism to strike any hunter who does not show proper respect for an animal that he kills for food, and the birds and insects begin to spread a variety of other afflictions and diseases. Indeed, the animals cause mental suffering as well as bodily injury, for the reptiles and fish send terrifying dreams of snakes to torment the people. By changing their relationship with animals, human beings not only lose the original unity with other living beings that exists at the time of creation, but they also bring disease and misfortune into their earthly lives. As does the Blackfoot myth, however, the Cherokee tale ends with a promise of restoration when all the plants of the world offer the people remedies to counter the afflictions unleashed by the animal kingdom.

SEPARATION FROM DEITIES

In a tale told by Africa's Luba people, human beings live with their creator deity after he first brings them to life, and, while sharing his celestial kingdom, they are immortal. According to this myth, however, it is once again the people themselves who are responsible for changes in their original circumstances, for when they become noisy and quarrelsome, Kalumba the creator sends them to lead earthly lives of hardship and toil that inevitably end in sickness and death—and thus these people, too, fall from a state of grace. In an effort to regain the immortality they have lost, the people construct a gigantic tower that reaches to the sky. However, when those at the top of the tower beat their drums to announce the success of their ambitious enterprise, the commotion they create disturbs their creator deity once more, and Kalumba angrily demolishes the people's ladder to his home in the heavens. In this myth, as in others from the African tradition, the conditions of human beings' lives undergo a change when the people become separated from their deities, and, with the building of their tower, they make an attempt to bridge the great distance. Indeed, the Luba people's story of a tower that promises a return to paradise is but one of several similar accounts from Africa's myth traditions.

The separation from their deities that transforms people's lives is not always the result of human beings' own malfeasance, and in a story told by Africa's Nuer people, an animal is responsible for the breach between the heavens and the earth. According to this tale, people live on earth after their creation, but a rope that hangs from heaven provides them ready means to visit paradise. Therefore, whenever people begin to grow old, they climb up to the heavens to have their youth restored. The people lose their connection with the sky, however, when the troublemaker Hyena cuts down their rope and thereby leaves them all subject to mortality. Whereas the people in this tale are the victims of the consequences of Hyena's action, in many other myths misfortune comes to human beings through the actions of the gods. For example, a story recounted in the *Mahabharata* (ca. 200 B.C.E. to A.D. 200), India's great epic, attributes the occurrence of sickness within the world to the anger of Shiva, who is displeased when the other gods do not invite him to participate in their ceremony of the sacrificial horse. Shiva disrupts the ceremony with a violent assault, and, while he is soaring through the sky in pursuit of the sacrifice, his fury assumes the form of a bead of sweat on his forehead. When the droplet falls to the earth below, it bursts into a terrible blaze from which the monstrous figure of Disease then emerges, and from that time on Disease brings misery and grief to all the earth's inhabitants.

Conflicts among the divinities also lead to problems for humanity in the myths of the Greeks, where Zeus's dispute with the Titan Prometheus ends up causing human beings to suffer all manner of misfortune. By some accounts Prometheus is the creator deity who shapes the first people from clay, and, as it happens, this first race of human beings includes only men. As the champion of humanity, Prometheus is determined to provide people with fire even though Zeus has forbidden them possession of this precious gift. The Titan therefore steals fire from the gods, hides it in a stalk of fennel, and violates Zeus's dictum by offering this great prize to the human race. Zeus then exacts his revenge by ordering Hephaistos, the god of smithery, to fashion the first human woman, the beautiful Pandora. When Pandora makes her appearance on the earth, she carries with her a jar sent by the gods, and, by opening this vessel, she releases the host of plagues sealed up within it, for hardship, famine, disease, greed, spite, and other forms of evil all escape the jar and thereafter haunt the lives of all human beings.

EMERGENCE OF EVIL

In some myth traditions, imperfection in the world is the result of events that occur during the process of creation, and thus evil already exists by the time human beings are finally brought to life. In the creation myth of North America's Iroquois people, for example, two worlds are said to exist immediately after time begins: the upper world is the home of the divine sky people, and the lower world, the home of those birds and animals that can swim, is the dark realm of the primordial waters upon which the earth will later come to rest. Although there are various accounts of what happens in the upper world before the earth is formed, the events that unfold there transform the original creation. In one version of the story, Atahensic, or Sky Woman, is the wife of the sky people's chief. When she becomes pregnant and the Northern Lights wickedly raise doubts about the identity of the father of her child, the angry chief of the sky people uproots the Great Tree of Heaven and hurls his wife and daughter into the gaping hole produced by the removal of the tree. According to another telling of the tale, Atahensic is the beloved daughter of the chief of the sky people, and, when she suddenly falls grievously ill, her doting father can think of nothing but discovering some means to restore his child. When one of the sky people dreams that Atahensic can be cured only by the uprooting of the heavenly tree that nourishes the people, the chief does not hesitate before seizing upon this drastic measure. The uprooting of the tree, however, so enrages the people that one of them pushes Atahensic through the hole in the sky.

It is, of course, Sky Woman's fall from her heavenly home that provokes an extraordinary change in the lower world, for when the birds and animals see that she needs a place to land on the surface of the primal sea, they all work together to create the earth. Turtle first provides a resting place for the sky goddess on the top of his great back, and then other creatures dive to the bottom of the primal waters in search of the sand from which the earth can grow. According to many accounts, Muskrat is the successful earth-diver, and the grains of sand he clutches in his claws are scattered on Turtle's back to form the goddess's new home. Evil first emerges within this new world when Sky Woman's daughter, Earth Woman, is made pregnant by the wind and gives birth to one noble son and another who is wicked. Because Good Twin and Evil Twin both contribute to the task of preparing the world for the creation of people, the earth's features ultimately reflect the handiwork of each of the brothers. Good Twin, for instance, creates meadows and woodlands, while Evil Twin constructs rocky terrain and precipitous cliffs. Good Twin provides rivers that people can travel, and, by giving the rivers strong currents, treacherous rapids, or troublesome waterfalls, Evil Twin then creates hardships for all travelers. Thus, when the time comes for Good Twin to fashion the first people from clay, both good and ill already await these human beings in their imperfect world. According to the Iroquois, the dual nature of the world is indeed expressed in human beings as well, for every person is said to possess both a good heart and a wicked one.

Evil also emerges during the process of creation in the tradition of ancient Persia's Zoroastrians, for when the creator Ahura Mazda first casts his pure light into the primordial abyss, Angra Mainyu, the demon of destruction, rises up to oppose the Wise Lord's creation. According to the Zoroastrians, the history of the world subsequently unfolds within the context of a cosmic struggle between Ahura Mazda, who is also called Ohrmazd, and Angra Mainyu, who is sometimes known as Ahriman. Although Ahura Mazda creates a universe that is perfect in both its spiritual and material forms, Angra Mainyu, assisted by his hordes of monsters and devils, constantly endeavors to corrupt its goodness. In his fury, therefore, he assails the perfect and unmarked surface of the earth, gouging deep crevasses in it and building barren ridges out of naked rock. He defiles the earth's pure waters by poisoning them with salt and brings disease and death to Gayomartan and his ox, the first living beings the Wise Lord creates. When Mashya and Mashyanag, the primal parents of the human race, then emerge from the rhubarb plant, Angra Mainyu also infects them with his wickedness through an act of deceit: by persuading the couple that it was he who shaped their world, he makes them blind to the essential goodness of Ahura Mazda's original creation, and, because they then believe that the world is imperfect, Mashya and Mashyanag are beset by the demons of evil. According to the Zoroastrians, the great battle between the forces of good and evil will only end when Angra Mainyu is finally defeated and all wickedness is at last expunged from the Wise Lord's good creation.

In Zoroastrian tradition, where it is a sacrilege to regard the original creation as imperfect in any way, Angra Mainyu's unrelenting attempts to destroy the Wise Lord's universe afford an explanation of the presence of evil in the world, and, in like fashion, numerous stories of a fall from paradise account for the existence of death, disease, hardship, and misfortune in people's lives. While Angra Mainyu's assault upon the earth and Feather Woman's descent from the heavens both bring sudden change to people's earthly lives, transformation can occur in other ways as well, for in some myth traditions, paradise is conceived as a golden age, and human beings' loss of their perfect world is represented as a gradual process that takes place over time. For example, in Indian tradition, where the cosmos is endlessly created and destroyed, each cycle of its existence is made up of a succession of four ages wherein the world's original perfection is steadily eroded. Thus the first age, Krita Yuga, is a time of earthly bliss when gift-giving trees supply people's every need. During the second age, Treta Yuga, the bountiful trees disappear and people must work hard to provide for their needs. Disease, suffering, and sorrow become widespread during Dvapara Yuga, the third age of the world, and at the dawning of the last age, Kali Yuga, the world becomes a place of wickedness and strife. The depleted earth is destroyed after the passing of these changing ages, and then, after it is cleansed by fire and by flood, paradise is once again created.

See also Animals in Myth; Changing Ages; Creation Myths; Culture Heroes; Earth-Diver Motif

FERTILITY MYTHS

Fertility gods are commonplace in the pantheons of ancient traditions, and are usually rain or storm deities or divinities associated with the earth. In some cultures particular gods of agriculture preside over the production of crops, and many myth traditions include accounts of the culture heroes who first instruct people in the arts of husbandry. Scholars speculate that prehistoric peoples found the source of fertility in the earth itself, and archaeologists' discoveries of numerous Stone Age statues of pregnant female figures support the theory that a mother goddess, or great goddess, once personified the earth. Indeed, hints of fertility rituals or cults associated with the earth mother can be found in many ancient myths. Although the peoples of a good number of cultural traditions practice fertility rites to ensure the success of their crops, narratives of the nature or origins of seasons and accounts of the restoration of fecundity to a barren world provide abundant examples of fertility myths.

In agricultural societies, where people are ever watchful of changes in the weather, the seasons are frequently personified as deities. Among the Inuit, for example, the seasons are Nipinouke and Pipounouke, two spirits who take turns ruling the world. In other cultures, changes in the seasons are seen as resulting from conflicts between the weather gods, and thus in ancient Persian tradition Tishtrya, god of the rain, endlessly struggles with Apaosha, the demon of drought. Each year Tishtrya travels to Vourukasha, the great cosmic sea, in the form of white horse, and there he encounters Apaosha, who appears as a black horse. The horses engage in battle, and when the black Apaosha prevails, Tishtrya is unable to gather the water he needs to shower the earth with rain. When the Wise Lord Ahura Mazda provides sacrifices that lend strength to the white horse, a victorious

Tishtrya saves the people from the ravages of drought. Another of the rain god's adversaries is Duzhyairya, the witch who spoils the harvest; indeed Tishtrya's ongoing battle with these demons of destruction mirrors ancient Persia's conception of the world as the place where the forces of good and evil are engaged in never-ending struggle.

THE DISAPPEARING GOD

The recurring theme of the "disappearing god" emerges in many fertility myths' representations of the conflicts between weather gods. According to the ancient Persians, Rapithwin, the divine ruler of the summer's heat, vanishes each year into the depths of the sea on the occasion of the winter demon's assault upon the land. During the time that he remains hidden in the ocean, Rapithwin keeps its deepest waters warm. In myths from the peoples of Hawaii, the rain god Lono also disappears each year at the end of the growing season, and while he is gone, Ku, his traditional foe and the god of both war and dry weather, reigns in the islands. When the constellation known as the Pleides once again appears in the heavens, Lono returns to Hawaii, bringing with him the promise of fertility. In one of the most ancient of fertility myths, the Hittite tale of Telepinu, the land becomes barren when the fertility god grows angry and then disappears. Telepinu's story exists only in fragments that do not explain the cause of his wrath, but the consequences of his absence are vividly described: all crops fail, and neither animals nor people are able to give birth. The gods too grow hungry, and they therefore send emissaries to search for the missing deity. Telepinu is finally discovered by a bee, and after the gods and the people have performed rituals of healing to assuage his anger, the god of fertility is carried back to his home by a mighty eagle. The pole draped with fleece that is erected in his honor is symbolic of the bounty that comes from Telepinu.

The fertility myths of several cultures represent the disappearing god as one who is abducted. In the tale told by the natives of a small island north of Australia, the rain god Bara is captured each autumn by Mamariga, the god of hot winds. All vegetation dies during the time when the rain god is imprisoned in a hollow tree, but when the people make offerings to Bara in the spring of the year, he comes forth again and causes new plants to sprout. In Norse tradition, Idunn is the goddess of spring as well as the guardian of the golden apples that preserve the youth of the gods, and when she too is abducted, the earth becomes a wasteland and the gods begin to age. Loki, the trouble-making trickster, plays a large role in this tale, for after first assisting the Frost Giant Thiassi in the kidnapping of the goddess and her precious apples, it is finally he who restores the earth's fertility—and the gods' longevity—by securing her release.

One of the best-known abduction tales, the Greek myth of Demeter and Persephone, offers an explanation for the changing of the seasons. In this story Persephone, the daughter of Zeus and the fertility goddess Demeter, is the disappearing goddess who vanishes when Hades seizes her and carries her to the underworld to become his wife. Bereft over the unexplained absence of her beloved daughter, Demeter ceases to nourish the earth and instead wanders throughout the world, searching for her child. While the goddess of the corn is thus distracted from her duties, the people of the earth suffer from famine. Although versions of the myth differ in their accounts of how Demeter comes to learn of Persephone's fate, when the mother at last discovers the whereabouts of her daughter, she travels to Olympus to seek the help of Zeus. Persephone's father approves of her marriage to the god of the underworld, but when he fails to persuade Demeter to accept the arrangement, he agrees that as long as Persephone has not eaten the food of the dead, she will be freed. When it is revealed that the unfortunate Persephone has indeed swallowed the seeds of a pomegranate, Zeus declares that she must marry Hades. In deference to Demeter, however, he decides that she will be allowed to spend half of each year in the company of her mother. During the months when Persephone walks upon the earth, Demeter provides great bounty for her people, but when it is time for her daughter to return to the underworld, the grieving goddess lets all her lands lie fallow.

RESURRECTION

In yet another category of fertility myths, the disappearing god is the dying god whose resurrection signifies earthly life's natural cycle of birth, death, and regeneration. In Mesopotamian tradition, the fertility goddess Inanna (or Ishtar) journeys to the underworld, and while she is there the earth becomes sterile when neither people nor animals are able to procreate. Inanna is slain after she confronts her sister Ereshkigal, the ruler of the underworld, but one of the gods contrives to send emissaries to revive her with life-restoring potions. The resurrected fertility goddess is then allowed to return to the upper world, but only on the condition that she choose a substitute to assume her place in the realm of the dead. Thus Inanna's husband Dumuzi, a god of vegetation, is sent to the underworld for half of the year while his sister Geshtinanna serves as his substitute for the other half. Dumuzi (or Tammuz) is therefore yet another example of the dying or disappearing god, for the earth's vegetation annually withers and dies during the months of his confinement in the land of the dead.

Additional examples of the dying vegetation god can be found in the Phrygian tale of Attis, the Greek myth of Dionysos, and the Greco-Roman story of Adonis. Like these other gods, the Egyptian god Osiris and his sister-wife Isis figure in the annual festivals or rituals of renewal that were once practiced by fertility cults. Son of the sky goddess Nut and the earth god Geb, Osiris is a vegetation god who becomes ruler of the earth when his father ascends to the heavens. In his role as culture hero, Osiris travels throughout Egypt instructing his people in the arts of agriculture. He also introduces them to the practice of religion, teaches them to build temples and cities, and establishes their legal codes. Beloved of his people, the helpful god of vegetation reigns until his many achievements evoke the envy of his brother Set, god of the arid desert. Then, in an act that symbolically represents the encroachment of the desert on cultivated lands, Set slays and dismembers his brother. Isis travels across Egypt in search of the fourteen parts of her husband's corpse, and in some versions of the story she buries these where she finds them, causing the desert to bloom. In other versions of the tale, the faithful wife reassembles Osiris's body, and after she embalms it, the vegetation god is resurrected as the ruler of death and the afterlife.

Within Egyptian culture the complex symbolism of Osiris's story functions on multiple levels. From the perspective of his role as vegetation god, Osiris's slaying and dismemberment represent the harvesting and threshing of life-sustaining crops, and when the god is resurrected as the ruler of Duat, the realm of the dead, he then becomes the emblem of regeneration—and thus the dead are customarily addressed by his name during their rites of internment. As a fertility myth, the tale emphasizes the cyclical patterns within nature, for it suggests that just as the crops that wither each year sprout anew in the spring, all who must die can look to the promise of renewal in the afterlife. For the ancient Egyptians, Osiris's resurrection is symbolized by the annual flooding of the Nile, whose life-restoring waters revive the desert's land. Indeed, symbols of renewal also appear in the stories of other dismembered gods: spring violets grow from the blood spilled by Attis, pomegranates arise from Dionysos's blood, and from that of Adonis springs the blood-red anemone.

Fertility myths' instances of the dying and dismembered god echo a pattern found in the many accounts of creation that include the Ymir motif. In these stories the parts of a primordial being's corpse are used as the materials from which the earth is formed. In the Norse story of creation, for example, Odin and his brothers use the hair from the body of the Frost Giant Ymir to produce the world's forests, and, in similar fashion, the hair from Pan Ku's corpse turns into flowers, plants, and trees in a creation myth from China. In these tales the sacrifice of life is required to initiate the cycle that leads to regeneration, and the theme of sacrifice is one that also appears in both fertility myths and in some people's rituals of renewal. In the many versions of Native Americans' accounts of the origin of maize, for example, the culture hero known as the Corn Mother sacrifices her life to provide a staple food for her people, the corn that grows from her dismembered body. In Japanese tradition, a bountiful harvest arises from the corpse of Ogetsuno, the goddess of food, after the moon god Tsukiyomi kills her with his sword. Rice grows from Ogetsuno's stomach, millet from her forehead, and wheat and beans from her lower body. Furthermore, her eyebrows become silkworms, and the ox and the horse emerge from her head. In this myth the death of the food goddess provides all that people need to establish a flourishing agricultural society.

DROUGHT AND FAMINE

In other kinds of fertility myths, ones in which the practice of agriculture is already well established, a cataclysmic event interrupts nature's cycles and causes drought and famine to ravage the land. In these stories societies depend upon the strength and courage of a hero who undertakes the task of restoring what is lost. For example, Indra, the mighty rain and fertility god whose weapon is the thunderbolt, is such a hero in a tale from ancient India. In this myth the famine occurs when the demon dragon Vritra steals the earth's seven rivers and hides them in a mountain. The only god who is willing to confront the terrible demon, Indra engages Vritra in a fiery exchange of thunderbolts and emerges as the dragon slayer. Before he can recover the waters, however, the god of rain must overcome one further obstacle, for Vritra's dragon mother seeks vengeance for his death. Once again Indra's aim is true when he unleashes his powerful thunderbolt, and by freeing the seven rivers he rescues his people and restores the ravaged land.

In some versions of Indra's story, Vritra steals the rain clouds rather than the rivers, and in a tale told by North America's Zuni people it is also the disappearance of the rain clouds that brings drought and famine to the land. According to this myth there are no longer clouds in the heavens because a monster named Cloud-Eater stands high on a mountain peak and devours them each day. Knowing that his people will surely starve if the monster is not killed, the courageous Ahaiyuta, whose father is the sun, sets forth on a quest to rid the world of the insatiable Cloud-Eater. The heroes of myth who undertake a quest are often lent assistance by others, and indeed Ahaiyuta's grandmother presents him with four magic feathers to carry with him on his journey. The red feather guides him to his destination, a hole in the ground, and when Ahaiyuta sees a gopher standing by the hole, he uses the yellow feather to make himself the gopher's size. The blue feather lets him speak with the animals, and he therefore uses it to tell the gopher of his mission. A willing helper, the gopher guides the hero through his underground passage to Cloud-Eater's mountain lair and then nibbles away the fur over the sleeping monster's heart. Using the black feather, the one that affords him the strength to achieve his task, Ahaiyuta shoots the arrow that destroys the greedy creature who has swallowed all the clouds. Almost immediately the rains begin to fall, and the fertility of the land is thereby restored.

SUN

While the water that is necessary for the production of crops is often a concern in fertility myths, the sun also plays its role, and two stories from Chinese tradition address problems with the sun. In one of these tales, the vegetation on the earth begins to shrivel up and burn when its ten suns all rise in succession on a single day. According to this myth the suns ordinarily take turns passing through the sky, and therefore when they inexplicably pass together as a group, the consequences are disastrous for the world and its people. The great god and hero Yi, the heaven's finest archer, is quickly called upon to save the smoldering world. From his perch high atop a tower, the celestial archer shoots and kills nine of the suns, and thus forever after only one remains to pass daily through the heavens. Although Yi is acclaimed by the earth's people as the hero who saves them from the drought and the famine, he pays a price for killing the nine suns that were the children of Di Jun, god of the eastern heavens, for that angry father banishes the divine bowman, forcing him to dwell on the earth as a mortal being.

Like the Zuni people's myth, the other tale from China offers an account of the brave hero's quest to restore fertility to his barren land. In this story a great famine occurs when the king of the demons and his ghostly army steal the earth's sun and hide it in a cave at the bottom of the sea. In time the young farmer Liu Chun decides to venture forth in search of the sun, but before he leaves his home he promises his wife that should he fail in his quest he will become a bright star to guide others who might search for the sun. When a new star indeed rises in the eastern sky, it falls to Bao Chu, son of the farmer, to complete his father's task. Like Ahaiyuta, Bao Chu is guided by an animal helper, the golden phoenix that accompanies him throughout his travels. He also makes use of the gifts with which he is presented, the warm jacket made from the coats of one hundred families and the bag of soil that he uses to cross the ocean safely. Bao Chu's journey is long and arduous, and he barely escapes death in the terrible place where his father was killed, the Village of Lost Souls. Finally, however, he reaches his destination in the middle of the eastern sea, and there he fights the demon king for possession of the sun. Liu Chun's courageous son defeats his enemy in their battle to the death, but the task of lifting the sun to the surface of the water demands all his remaining strength, and thus Bao Chu dies at the moment when his quest is completed. In this tale that celebrates the single-minded purpose of both father and son, the crops that grow again when fertility is restored serve as a fitting memorial for China's farmer-heroes.

WASTE LAND

Features of a fertility myth lie at the heart of yet another account of a quest, the legendary search for the Holy Grail. Extraordinarily popular throughout Europe during the Middle Ages, the Grail myth exists in many different versions, but recurring patterns emerge from these various tales. Significant among them is the location of the sacred relic, which can be found in the Grail Castle, home of the wounded Fisher King. The Fisher King, or Grail King, rules over the Waste Land, a barren kingdom that can only be restored to fertility when its maimed ruler is finally made whole—and the healing of the king can only occur when the knight who seeks the Grail is successful in his quest. To succeed in his mission, a knight must be virtuous, for the object he seeks is holy to his people. He must also be persistent, for the Grail Castle is difficult to find, and he must be courageous, for he will encounter many dangers throughout his perilous journey. Finally, there is one further quality the worthy knight must possess, for it is required that when he first beholds the wondrous object, he must be perspicacious enough to pose the appropriate question. Indeed, the asking of the question is crucial to the completion of the quest, for if a knight remains silent at the sight of the Grail, it vanishes immediately, and the hero's quest must begin anew. In the end, the restoration of the Waste Land depends upon the Grail seeker's wisdom and sympathy, for the search for the holy object is essentially a spiritual journey.

See also Culture Heroes; Gods; Goddesses; The Quest; Ymir Motif

GODS

The supernatural powers possessed by the divinities of myth fall into a wide range of categories. Creator deities, for example, are the shapers of the cosmos, while rain or fertility gods are invested with the power to nurture life in the world. In some myth traditions various tutelary gods oversee domestic or business affairs, and many cultural traditions feature a war god, a fire deity, or a lord of the underworld. Additionally, the figures of the dying god, the divine child, or the deity as culture hero frequently recur. Although both goddesses and gods number among the creators, the personal guardians, the fertility deities, the culture heroes, and the underworld rulers of the world's myth traditions, some divine functions are served primarily by male deities. For example, the trickster, the thunder god, and the blacksmith god are all almost universally represented as male, and many more gods than goddesses personify the sky and the sun. Furthermore, the supreme being or ruler of the gods—who is often a sun or a sky god—is most commonly a male deity.

CREATOR GODS

The creator gods of myth bring the universe into being in a variety of ways. When Bumba, the creator deity among Africa's Boshongo people, feels pains in his stomach, he produces the sun and the moon and then the plants and the animals by vomiting them up. Baiame, the creator in the myths of Australia's Wiradyuri people, first creates himself and then the rest of the cosmos, and Nareau, a Melanesian creator god, shapes the heavens and the earth from a mussel shell. According to the Bena Lulua people of Zaire, the sun is produced from the right cheek of the creator

Fidi Mukullu, and the moon comes from the left cheek of the god. In one version of the creation myths told by the Dogon people of Mali, the creator Amma is the artisan who crafts the sun and the moon on his potter's wheel. Kun-tu-bzan-po, the creator in Tibet's Bon tradition, forms the world from a ball of mud and creates the cosmic egg from which all living beings then come forth. In the accounts of the Bambuti people of the Congo, the creator Arebati molds the first man from clay, covers his creation with a skin, and then pours blood into the form he has shaped, and Imra, creator among the Kati people, churns people into being within the udder of a golden goat. Quat, another Melanesian creator god, decides to make stones, trees, pigs, and human beings simply because he grows bored with the emptiness around him.

In many myth traditions the creator deities are remote figures. Baiame, for example, is said to be an invisible god who dwells high in the heavens and whose presence can only be recognized in the sound of thunder. Cghene, the creator deity of Nigeria's Isoko people, is an even more remote being, one who is accessible only through the mediation of a pole carved from a tree. In some cultures the ancient creator deities seem to have grown distant because they have been superseded or in fact usurped by other gods or because they have passed the responsibility for completing the creation to a younger generation. Moreover, in the myths of certain traditions, the creator simply disappears when his work is finished. After Nareau shapes earth and heaven from a mussel shell, he is killed by his son, Nareau the Younger, who makes the sun and moon from his father's eyes and then uses his father's spine to create the Tree of Life that gives birth to human beings. Ometeotl, the Aztec creator god who dwells in the highest reaches of heaven, remains aloof from the process of creating the world and its people, for that task is undertaken by Quetzalcoatl, Tezcatlipoca, and Ometeotl's other offspring. The Native American tradition of the Iroquois offers an example of the creator who disappears in its tale of Good Twin—who vanishes after making people, the last of his creations.

With such notable exceptions as Odin, Zeus, and Marduk, gods from the Norse, Greek, and Babylonian traditions, the supreme deities of myth often resemble the numerous ancient creator gods who are depicted as remote and sometimes inaccessible figures. Indeed, in many cultures the ancient creator, the father of the cosmos, is also recognized as the supreme being. Like Odin, Zeus, and Marduk, the supreme deity is generally regarded as the king of the gods and is most commonly a celestial figure, a sky god or a sun god; in some instances, as in that of Ngai, chief god of East Africa's Masai people, the supreme being is the provider of rain. As the progenitor of living beings or the ruler of the pantheon, the supreme deity is invested with paternal authority, and thus "father" is the epithet that is frequently assigned to this figure. While characteristics of the natures and personalities of such gods as Zeus or Odin emerge in the many myths that recount their exploits, some other gods are more abstractly conceived and do not necessarily play a role in a culture's storytelling. Kitanitowit, the invisible supreme deity of North America's Algonquian peoples, is represented as an all-embracing circle, and Watauinewa, the supreme lord among the Yamana people of Tierra del Fuego, is not portrayed in the people's myths. Among Australia's Kulin people, it is customary to use the epithet "father" rather than to speak the name of Bunjil, the supreme creator.

SKY GODS

Just as the earth is most frequently personified in the form of a goddess through-out myth tradition, the sky is generally represented as a male deity. Geb, the Egyptian earth god, is a well-known exception to the pattern, and his consort, Nut, is one of a few goddesses who rule the sky. While other celestial deities indeed include many of the primal creators and supreme gods, the recurring pattern of sky father and earth mother is a widespread one. In Greek tradition Uranos, the original sky god and consort of the earth goddess Gaea, is succeeded first by Kronos and then later by Zeus as each of these sons in turn usurps his father's authority. Dyaus, India's ancient sky god, is mated with Prthivi, the embodiment of mother earth, and in the myths of the Maori people, the sky father Rangi and the earth mother Papa are the primal parents at the beginning of creation. Among West Africa's Krachi people, the sky god Wulbari at first dwells just above Asase Ya, the earth mother who is his consort, but eventually he retreats high into the heavens, leaving earthly beings space to move about more freely. Indeed, most of the myths that feature a sky father and earth mother describe their necessary separation: for example, Greek tradition includes an account of Uranos's separation from Gaea, and the Maori creation story recounts the efforts made by their sons to move Rangi and Papa apart from one another.

SUN AND MOON GODS

Deities associated with the sun and the moon commonly appear within myth traditions, and while the sun is frequently represented by a god and the moon by a goddess, many exceptions to this pattern also occur. The ibis-headed Thoth, for example, is the Egyptian lord of the moon, and in myths from ancient Phrygia, Syria, and India, the gods Men, Aglibol, and Candra are all moon deities. Like the moon gods, sun gods can include those divinities that personify the sun as well as those who oversee, rule, or represent the life-giving powers of the celestial orb. Inti, the Incan deity who embodies the sun, is described as crossing the heavens each day and then diving into the primal waters that lie beneath the earth before once again emerging in the eastern sky. Among the ancient Incas, the sacred emblem of Inti takes the form of the Punchao, a golden human face surrounded by shining solar rays. In many cultural traditions the sun and moon deities bear a close relationship to one another; in Incan myths, for example, Inti's consort is the moon goddess, Mama Kilya. Apollo and Artemis, the sun god and moon goddess of many myths from Greece, are twin deities, and Malakbel, the ancient Syrian sun god, is frequently depicted as accompanied by Aglibol, the god of the moon.

Like Inti, who is said to be the direct ancestor of the Incan people's rulers, the Egyptian sun god Ra is an especially important deity; indeed, not only is the pharaoh regarded as the son of Ra, but he is also considered to be the living incarnation of the sun god. In other words, the kings of the ancient Incan and Egyptian peoples possess an authority vested them through their identification with the sun deity who keeps his watchful eye on the earth as he travels daily through the sky. Whereas Ra crosses through the heavens riding in his barque, Helios and Surya, the all-seeing sun gods of Greek and Indian myths, both drive chariots through the sky. Marduk, another powerful sun god, rises to supremacy in the Babylonian pantheon after defeating the primordial goddess Tiamat, the embodiment of chaos. As the god of order and light, Marduk, the "bull calf of the sun," completes the creation of the world by constructing the heavens and the earth from the remains of Tiamat's dismembered corpse. Another watchful sun god, Marduk is represented as a double god, one whose powers are strengthened through his possession of four eyes and four ears.

WEATHER GODS

In addition to the sky and sun gods, other celestial deities include myth's many weather gods, the deities associated with rain, wind, or storms, or specifically with lightning or with thunder. In some traditions weather gods oversee multiple related functions: rain gods, for example, are sometimes also regarded as fertility gods, and thunder gods are often recognized and honored as the bringers of rain. Moreover, storm gods—particularly those deities who command the tremendous powers of lightning and thunder—are sometimes also war gods whose mighty thunderbolts are their weapons in battle. The sky god Zeus, for example, is not only the supreme deity within the Greek pantheon, but he is also the thunder god as well as the provider of rain. In Indian tradition, the sky god Indra is also a weather god and, as the wielder of thunderbolts, the god of war. Thor, the thunder god of Norse tradition, is both a god of war and a fertility deity who provides life-sustaining rain, and Enlil, the Mesopotamian god of air, wind, and storms, is a war god too. Although weather gods serve humankind when they cause the crops to grow, in some accounts they are also the agents of destruction, for both Enlil and Zeus use their powers to command the rainfall to completely flood the earth.

Whereas gods who rule the winds are particularly important to seafaring peoples (the Greek god Aiolos gives Odysseus a bag of winds to assist him in his voyage homeward), rain gods play an especially significant role in the traditions of such agricultural societies as those of the Aztecs and the Mayans. In Aztec myths, Tlaloc, the jaguar-toothed god of lightning and rain, rules the Third World until Quetzalcoatl destroys it in a rain of fire. As the provider of rain, Tlaloc produces the gentle showers for planting, the heavy, crop-nourishing rainfall, and sometimes the destructive hail. According to tradition, the tears shed by infants sacrificed to Tlaloc are symbolic of his gift of rain. Interestingly, the rain god assumes an unusual position within the Aztec conception of the afterlife, for, although most of the dead must make a grim journey to Mictlan, the terrifying underworld, those people who are struck by lightning or who die of drowning, leprosy, or a contagious disease are welcomed to Tlaloc's realm, an earthly paradise filled with butterflies, flowers, and rainbows. Although there are similarities between accounts of Tlaloc and Chac, the Mayan god of rain and fertility, Chac is conceived as an unambiguously benevolent deity who spouts forth the life-sustaining rain through his elongated nose.

FERTILITY AND AGRICULTURE GODS

While certain weather deities assume the role of fertility god, others father offspring whose task it is to oversee the earth's fecundity. One such example is that of

Njord, the Norse god of wind, sea, and fire whose children Freyr and Freyja are the god and goddess of fertility. Another instance is that of Teshub, the ancient Hittite storm god whose son is Telepinu, the vegetation deity whose disappearance causes the earth to become a barren realm until the fertility god can be found and restored to his duties. The figure of the disappearing god is related to that of another fertility deity, the dying god whose death and resurrection symbolize the annual agricultural cycle of harvesting and replanting. In the story of Osiris, Egypt's dying god, the resurrection of the vegetation deity signifies not only a renewal of the earth's fertility, but also the promise of an afterlife for ancient Egypt's people. Like the human sacrifices offered to the rain god Tlaloc, the dying god—who is often the consort of the earth mother—represents a sacrifice offered to the earth. Dionysos, the god of fertility and wine, is a dying god in the Greek tradition, and Dumuzi, vegetation deity and consort of the goddess Inanna, is the sacrificial victim in Mesopotamian myths.

Among yet other ancient cultures, the fertility god is associated with a particular staple food. Egres, for example, is the vegetation deity who provides turnips for the Finnish people, and Cinteotl and Yum Kaax, the Aztec and Mayan gods of maize, are the deified embodiments of Mesoamerica's most significant crop. In several traditions other nature deities preside over hunting, agriculture, or specific forms of plant or animal life. In Finnish tradition, the forest god Tapio is the patron of the hunt, while Hittavainen is the deity who particularly oversees the hunting of hares. In ancient Siberia, the animal master Hinkon is also the god of the hunt—and thus serves the welfare of both animals and people. Silvanus, the Roman deity of forests and fields, is a god of agriculture, and Faunus, another Roman nature god, is the protector of animal herds. In Greek tradition, Pan, the god of meadows, woodlands, pastures, and fields, is both a vegetation deity and the god of flocks and herds, and Dionysos, the dying fertility god, is also the divinity especially associated with the grapevine and the wine made from its fruit. Another deity of plant life, Abellio, an ancient Gallic tree god, is specifically regarded as the lord of apple trees.

Not only do myth's gods oversee forests and cultivated lands, they also rule mountains, rivers, and oceans. Tork, an ancient Armenian mountain god, protects mountain animals, and Baal-Karmelos, a Canaanite mountain deity, is revered as the oracle of Mount Carmel. In Indian tradition, Himavat is the god of the mighty Himalayan peaks and the father of Ganga, goddess of the Ganges River. Egypt's most important river, the Nile, is ruled by the benevolent god Hapi, and Sebek, another Egyptian water deity, assumes the form of the fearsome crocodile to rule the streams and lakes. In the myths from China, the monster god Gong Gong commands the subterranean rivers, while the divine He Bo rules those that flow on the surface of the earth. Rome's Tiber River bears the name of its presiding deity, the river god Tiberinus, and Asopos, a river god in Greek tradition, is, appropriately, the son of Poseidon, the ruler of the sea. Although Poseidon, the "earth-shaker" who is the deity of earthquakes as well, is the most important of the numerous sea gods of Greece, Glaukos, Nereus, Okeanos, Phorkys, Pontos, Proteus, and Triton also number among the ocean deities of that seafaring people. The sea gods Glaukos and Proteus are known for their gifts of prophecy; Proteus and Nereus are famous as shape-shifters; and Triton, a gigantic deity, is one of myth tradition's several fish-tailed sea gods.

SEA GODS

Sea gods are also especially important to the inhabitants of islands, and in Irish tradition, Manannan, the ocean deity who is the son of another Celtic sea god, Lir, is seen as the guardian of the islands that are encircled and protected by his watery domain. Furthermore, Manannan is also regarded as the ruler of the Otherworld, the land that some myths describe as a realm of blessed isles. Watatsumi-no-kami, another sea god of an island people, offers hospitality at his palace in the waters that surround Japan, and Ebisu, one of the seven Japanese gods of good fortune known as the Shichi Fukujin, serves as the patron deity of fishermen as he journeys in his treasure ship. Makemake, the chief deity on Easter Island, is a sea god who is credited with creating the first human beings. Makemake is also regarded as the source of all fertility, and, indeed, the god of the sea often represents the great bounty of the ocean—Olokun and Njord, the sea deities of the Yoruba and the Norse traditions, are also venerated as the gods of wealth.

BLACKSMITH GODS

The presence of blacksmith gods in many cultural traditions signifies the importance of metalworking within people's lives. In Finnish tradition, the weather god Ilmarinen is also the smith who forges the heavens and its stars and then brings knowledge of metallurgy to the world's people. Indeed, in teaching human beings to make use of iron, Ilmarinen also assumes the status of a great culture hero. Perkons, the Latvian god of thunder, rain, and fertility, is another weather god who is also a celestial smith, and Teljavelik, the Lithuanian god of smithery, is credited with creating the sun. Goibhniu and Gu, the divine smiths of the Celtic and of the African Fon peoples, are both culture heroes who teach human beings to make tools of iron. In some myth traditions, including those of the Greeks, Romans, and Slavs, the blacksmith deity is also regarded as the god of fire. Deities who are particularly associated with volcanic fire, Hephaistos and Vulcan, the Greek and Roman blacksmith gods, toil in smithies deep within the earth—according to Roman accounts, Vulcan's underworld forge lies beneath Sicily's fiery Mount Aetna. Svarog, the divine smith of the ancient Slavs, is also both a sky god and the god of fire.

FIRE GODS

Although it is often a culture hero, and frequently a trickster, who commonly provides human beings with the gift of fire, many cultures associate the awesome power of fire with a deity. In ancient China, the fire god Zhu Rong (or Li) becomes ruler of the universe when he defeats Gong Gong, the malicious water god. Agni, the fire god of India, oversees sacrificial offerings and purifies the dead when their bodies are burned. In performing these offices, Agni serves as a mediator between the realms of earth and heaven. Similarly, the Aztec fire god, Xiuhtecuhtli, links underworld, earth, and sky as he manifests himself in the subterranean flames of Mictlan, in the fires that flicker on earthly beings' hearths, and in the fiery Pole Star that burns high up in the heavens; as a psychopomp, a guide of the dead, the Aztec fire god lends help to the spirits that must be absorbed into the earth. Atar, the fire god of ancient Persia, serves his father, the creator Ahura Mazda, as a warrior who represents goodness and light in the cosmic battle with darkness and evil. Other deities who combat the wicked spells of demons include Nusku and Gibil, the father and son who are the ancient Mesopotamian gods of fire and light.

GODS OF DEATH

Myth's gods of death are sometimes also war gods, as in the examples of Black Tezcatlipoca, the powerful Aztec deity whose name means "Lord of the Smoking Mirror," or the Norse god Odin, ruler of the gods and leader of the dead heroes who gather in Valhalla, the "Hall of the Slain." Other deities of death preside over the underworld, the traditional land of the dead. For instance, Sulmanu, the Assyrian god of war and death, is also ruler of the underworld. In Greek tradition, Hades is named the king of the underworld when Zeus becomes the god of the sky and Poseidon the ruler of the sea. Because his underground realm contains precious metals, occasionally Hades is also known as Plutos, the deity of wealth. The underworld gods of many traditions are fearsome deities: Mictlantecuhtli, ruler of the Aztecs' land of the dead, is represented as a skeleton, and One Death and Seven Death, the chief lords of the Mayan underworld, are the malevolent and cunning foes of the Hero Twins who come to play ball with them in the depths of Xibalba. Yama, the lord of the underworld in Hindu tradition, carries a noose that he uses to wrench souls from the bodies of the dead.

Among other deities of death are the ferrymen of the underworld and the gods that sit in judgment on the souls of the dead. In the Egyptian underworld, where Osiris rules the dead, Cherti is the ferryman who transports the souls, and the jackal-headed god, Anubis, then weighs them on a scale. In Hades' kingdom, Charon ferries the souls whose fates are decided by Rhadamanthys or the other judges within the Greeks' underworld. In the epic *Gilgamesh* (ca. 2000 B.C.E.), Urshanabi is the ferryman who carries the hero across the Waters of Death, and in Mesopotamian accounts of Inanna's descent to the underworld, the seven judges who preside there refuse to let the goddess leave until she agrees to send a substitute to the realm of the dead. Yama, the king of the underworld, is also the judge of the dead in the myths of India, and in Japanese tradition, Emma-o, the judge and ruler of the underworld, perceives the misdeeds of the dead reflected in his enormous mirror. Another frightening deity, Emma-o carries a flag that bears the image of a human head.

GODS OF WAR

Although thunder gods or gods of death are sometimes gods of war, these deities are by no means myth's only representatives of the martial arts. Indeed, in some cultural traditions—particularly those of the warrior societies—multiple significant war gods frequently emerge. Ares, one of several war gods from the Greek tradition, is the father of the queen of the Amazons, a tribe of fierce women warriors, and Mars, the war god of the Romans, is the father of Romulus, the founder of Rome. In the myths of the Norse, another warrior people, the one-handed deity Tyr is honored along with Odin as a battle god. Together, Odin and Tyr choose from among the fallen heroes those who are worthy of admittance to Valhalla.

According to tradition, Tyr loses one of his hands to the monstrous wolf Fenrir, enemy of the gods. The animal double of Huitzilopochtli, another Aztec war god, is the hummingbird, a symbol of the sun and a creature that is said to represent the spirit of a warrior. While most war deities are depicted as ferocious figures, Guan Di, ancient China's warrior god, is an unusual exception: a patron of the arts and trades, Guan Di is a reluctant war god whose greatest satisfaction comes during times of peace. The war gods of myth greatly outnumber those deities—most often goddesses—who protect the peace, but in the Polynesian cultures, Rongo is revered as the god of peace.

Just as war gods such as Odin, Tyr, or Guan Di are regarded as heroic figures, so too are the divine monster slayers and culture heroes of myth tradition. Although many of myth's heroes are mortal beings, others are either deities or demigods. In Greek tradition, for example, Prometheus, the Titan who endures cruel punishment for his great service to the human race, is an immortal deity, and the mighty monster slayer, Herakles, is a semidivine hero whose strength and courage are eventually rewarded with Zeus's gift of immortality. In a number of traditions, the hero-god is represented as *puer aeternus*, the divine child whose miraculous conception or birth presages his heroic deeds. Horus, the divine child who relentlessly battles to reclaim Egypt's throne from the usurper, Set, is miraculously conceived when Isis temporarily restores her murdered husband Osiris to life, and Kutoyis, a hero-god of North America's Blackfoot people, is wondrously born from the blood clot of a dying buffalo. According to Indian tradition, Gautama, the great spiritual hero who in time becomes the Buddha, is miraculously conceived when a majestic white elephant enters his mother's womb.

TRICKSTER GODS

Many of myth's trickster gods are also culture heroes. Maui, the Polynesian trickster-hero, provides fire for human beings and uses his fishing hook to raise islands for people to inhabit. A helpful figure in other ways, he also slows the passage of the sun as it moves across the sky and uses a poker to lift the heavens high above the earth. The trickster, however, is an unpredictable deity whose antics can sometimes create trouble for people. Although the Micronesian trickster Olofat is another culture hero who gives the gift of fire, he also causes problems when he provides the shark with its sharp teeth. Moreover, Olofat instigates a war among the gods that resembles the trouble caused by Loki, the Germanic trickster who brings about the final battle between the giants and the gods in the Norse tradition. Both hero and troublemaker, the trickster is also a messenger god in the myths of several cultures. Eshu and Legba, trickster deities from West African traditions, relay messages between earth and heaven, and Hermes, the trickster god of ancient Greece, is both the messenger of the gods and the psychopomp, the guide of the dead.

GUARDIAN GODS

The deities of myth include numerous tutelary gods (guardians) who oversee the welfare of animals or human beings. Keyeme, an important divinity among South America's Taulipang people, is an example of the animal master, the protector of wild creatures. Tutelary gods who preside over the affairs of human beings protect domestic life as well as the interests of the community or state. Although it is most commonly a goddess who oversees childbirth, Sabazios is the ancient Phrygian god of midwifery, and, in Japanese tradition, the god Jizo protects pregnant women. Examples of deities who guard the hearth and home include Nang Lha, the Tibetan house god, and Zao Jun, the kitchen god of China. Grannus is the god of healing in myths from ancient Gaul, and, while Hymen presides over marriage rites in the Greek tradition, Eros is the god of love. The Chinese god of luck, Fu Shen, is one of the many deities who oversee good fortune and prosperity, and the Mayan god Ekchuah serves as an example of those who govern commerce. Local divinities are often the protectors or patron gods of particular towns or cities, and, in the myths of Mesopotamia, the powerful deity Marduk is represented as the tutelary god of the ancient Babylonian Empire.

GODS OF WISDOM AND THE ARTS

Gods who are the patrons of the crafts and arts or other cultural achievements belong to yet another category of myth's divinities. Like the blacksmith gods, deities associated with handicrafts are significant figures in many ancient cultures. In Hindu tradition, Tvashtar, the patron god of craftsmen, fashions the thunderbolt carried by the war god Indra and shapes the soma cup that holds the nectar of the gods. Among the patrons of the arts are deities associated with literature, poetry, music, and dance. Wen-Chang is China's god of literature, and Bragi is the god of poetry in the Norse tradition. Both Apollo and Orpheus serve as gods of music in myths from ancient Greece, and, in Egyptian tradition, Ihi is the master of the *sistrum*, a musical instrument used to dispel the power of evil forces. Among the peoples of ancient Syria, Baal-Marqod is both a god of healing and the lord of the dance. In addition to those deities that represent aesthetic achievement are those that serve as the patrons of justice or knowledge. Forseti is the god of justice and law in the Norse tradition, and, in Irish myths Dagda is the deity who presides over contracts and pledges. The Japanese god Fudo Myoo and the Armenian deity Tir are both revered as divinities of wisdom and knowledge.

See also Creation Myths; Culture Heroes; Fertility Myths; Goddesses; Primal Parents; Separation of Earth and Sky; Tricksters; The Underworld

GODDESSES

The earliest images of a goddess-like figure appear in human culture in the form of cave paintings, rock carvings, and small statues that date from Upper Paleolithic times, the period between 30,000 and 7000 B.C.E. Although the artifacts are the products of preliterate peoples, many of their features suggest connections to the representation of the goddess in the most ancient of myths as the earth mother or the embodiment of the natural world itself—and thus the source of life. That the paintings and figurines, which depict pregnant women or emphasize female breasts and genitalia, possess ritual significance is indicated in a variety of ways. For example, unlike contemporaneous images of animals, the female figures are rendered in a stylized rather than a naturalistic manner; indeed, in obviously focusing on the reproductive function of the female body, the images draw attention to the roles of the goddess as giver of birth and nurturer of life. Furthermore, many of the artifacts are inscribed with symbolic markings—chevrons, horns, crescent moons, or notches that signify the thirteen lunar months—and some are colored with red ocher to suggest a connection to menstrual cycles or life-sustaining blood. Use of the figurines as ritual objects is further suggested by the fact that many are pointed at the base and could therefore be fixed in the ground to stand upright. In *The Language of the Goddess*, an encyclopedic study of Neolithic images of female figures, Marija Gimbutas thoroughly explores the symbolic significance of artifacts that date from 7000 to 3500 B.C.E., a slightly later period.

Although scholars can only hypothesize about the significance of ritual objects that date from the Stone Ages, many speculate that they represent early peoples' conception of a "great goddess" who is venerated as the personification of the mysteries of birth, life, and death. Interestingly, this supposition is supported by ancient myths in which the goddess is the primal being, the original creator, the source of all fecundity, or the deity of death and regeneration. With the emergence of patriarchal cultures, the goddess as earth mother and her consort, often the sky father, give birth to the pantheons of many cultural traditions. Within these families of deities, a plethora of fertility goddesses, especially divinities who represent the corn or the crops, appear to be vestiges of the prehistoric goddess. Characteristics of the great goddess also appear in myth's goddesses of death, destruction, or war and in the many goddesses who rule or personify the moon, whose waxing and waning are traditionally linked to agricultural cycles. Other important deities include goddesses of love or peace, divinities that oversee the unfolding of fate, and tutelary figures, including numerous goddesses who protect children and watch over pregnant women.

CREATOR GODDESSES

In the tradition of the Pelasgians, ancient inhabitants of Greece, the divine creator is the goddess Eurynome, the first being to emerge from chaos. Eurynome lifts the sky above the sea and begins the process of creation by dancing on the primal waters. With her dancing she creates a wind that she uses to give form to her consort, the great serpent Ophion. After mating with Ophion, the goddess assumes the form of a dove and lays the cosmic egg that hatches to produce the sun, moon, stars, and earth. When Ophion threatens to usurp her power, the creator goddess banishes him to the dark depths of the earth and then completes the process of creation by making human beings to live in her world. Whereas Eurynome is the mother goddess who dances creation into being, Thinking Woman, the original being and creator goddess among North America's Pueblo peoples, gives shape to the cosmos when she sings the world and all it contains into existence. Yet another primal goddess, Coadidop, begins the process of creation by smoking the first male being into existence. The creator deity of South America's Tariana people, Coadidop draws tobacco from her body to fashion a cigar whose smoke turns into the body of Enu. Coadidop's creation is completed when she makes the earth from the milk of her breasts, creates two female beings to live in the world, and commands Enu to make additional male beings. According to the Tariana, these female and male beings are the ancestors of their people.

Other creator goddesses include Bulaing, the celestial deity of Australia's Karadjeri people, and Laima, the Latvian goddess who is also the tutelary divinity who oversees people's births, marriages, and deaths. In some versions of China's creation myth, Nu Gua is the creator goddess who shapes human beings out of yellow clay. Like Laima, Nu Gua protects the people who are her creations, for it is she who saves the world from flood and fire when the water monster Gong Gong knocks down the pillars that hold the sky above the earth. In many myths of the Fon people of West Africa, the moon goddess Mawu creates the earth, sun, and all living beings while riding on the rainbow serpent. In other accounts, however, the creator is the dual deity Mawu-Lisa, the female moon divinity conjoined with the male sun god, Lisa. Indeed, androgynous creators are not unusual and can be found in various myth traditions. Awonawilona, the androgynous primal deity of North America's Zuni people, creates the earth mother and sky father who produce all living things, and among the Aztecs, the original god and goddess

Tonacatecuhtli and Tonacacihuatl are together regarded as Ometeotl, the dual creator deity.

EARTH GODDESSES

With some exceptions, the deities of myth who represent the earth are characteristically goddesses. In Greek tradition, Gaea is the embodiment of the earth itself, and Demeter is the earth goddess who oversees its fertility. Indeed, many earth goddesses are, like Demeter, also fertility deities, or, like Gaea, they are also earth mothers. The Celtic-Irish goddess Ana, for example, is an earth and fertility deity as well as the mother of the gods. In many myth traditions, creation arises from the union of an earth goddess and a sky god. According to the myths of the Jicarilla people of the North American Southwest, the primal deities Earth Mother and Black Sky give birth to the progenitors of human beings deep within the womb of the earth—and in their emergence myths, the Jicarilla describe how the people eventually leave the earth's womb by ascending to the surface of the earth. In Japanese tradition, the union of the earth mother Izanami and the sky father Izanagi produces the islands of Japan as well as several deities. Izanami dies, however, while giving birth to the god of fire, and she then enters the underworld and becomes its ruler.

MOTHER GODDESSES

The mother goddesses of myth include not only earth deities, but also numerous instances of the fertility goddess who is known both as the great mother and the great goddess. In the Middle East, the several names of this figure include those of Inanna, the Sumerian "Queen of the Heavens" and goddess of fecundity; Ishtar, the Babylonian goddess of fertility and the morning star; Astarte, the Syrian fertility and moon goddess; and Ashera, the Canaanite fertility and love goddess who is the mother of the gods. Isis, yet another deity who is related to these figures, is the Egyptian goddess of heaven, earth, and the underworld. In Anatolian tradition, the mother of the gods is Cybele, the great goddess who oversees the world's fertility from her throne on the peak of Mount Ida, and in myths from India the figure of the mother goddess is represented by several deities. Among the Dravidian Telugu people, the primordial goddess Ammavaru exists before the creation of the world, and it is she who lays the cosmic egg from which the creator god emerges. Aditi, another primordial Indian goddess, is the embodiment of infinity and the source of all existence. Mother of the sun gods known as the Adityas, by some accounts she is also the mother of Agni, fire god and mediator between the heavens and the earth. Other manifestations of the goddess are aspects of Devi ("goddess"), and Devi-Shakti personifies all female creative powers.

TRIPLE GODDESS

Because the great mother goddess commonly oversees the entire cycle of existence, that of birth, death, and regeneration, she is sometimes also known as the triple goddess. In Indian tradition, where Shakti represents the goddess as provider, other aspects of Devi assume the form of the destroyer. For example, in her warrior aspect, the great goddess Parvati takes the form of Durga, slayer of demons, and as the goddess of death she assumes the fearsome form of Kali, destroyer of life. As the destroyer goddess, Kali dances when the dead are cremated, but her dancing signifies rebirth as well as death, for in the cosmic cycle, from the act of destruction comes the renewal of creation. The goddess of the underworld and its promise of resurrection, Isis too is linked with death, and one of the goddess Cybele's roles is guardian of the dead. Like Kali and Eurynome, Oya, the mother goddess of Africa's Yoruba people, is an embodiment of the dance of creation. In her benign aspect, Oya is the goddess of the dance and of fertility, but she is also the destroyer who can command the power of violent storms and control the spirits of the dead.

SUN GODDESSES

Although the sun deities of myth are usually gods—and most of the great mother goddesses are associated with the moon—a sun goddess does appear in some cultural traditions. Saule, for example, is the sun goddess of the Latvian and Lithuanian peoples. In Latvian tradition, the "Mother Sun" oversees the earth's fertility from her garden high atop heaven's mountain. Saule is the wife of the moon god Meness, and thus she is part of a mythic pattern wherein the sun and moon are paired. In the Lithuanian accounts, where the divine blacksmith positions the sun in the sky, Saule's role is not as fully defined; however, she too is mated to the moon god Menulis. In ancient Celtic tradition, Sul is the sun goddess revered in southern England, and in Norse myths, the goddess Sol personifies the sun. Like many other sun deities, Sol travels across the heavens each day in her carriage drawn by horses. Among Australia's Arunta people, the goddess Sun Woman daily crosses the sky carrying a flaming torch. When evening comes, Sun Woman joins the ancestors who dwell beneath the world, and, when it is time for her to travel through the sky again, it is they who light her torch.

Amaterasu, perhaps the best known of myth tradition's sun goddesses, is Shintoism's most revered deity and the ancestor of Japan's royal family. Sister of the moon god Tsukiyomi, the ruler of the night, and Susano, the god of sea and storms, Amaterasu rules the Great Plain of Heaven. The bounty of the earth depends upon Amaterasu's radiant presence, so when she is threatened by Susano and hides in heaven's cave, the world becomes a dark, barren realm where demons run amok and living things begin to die. Determined to entice the sun goddess to leave her hiding place, hundreds of deities gather outside her cave with an assembly of roosters to herald her return. Uzume, the joyful goddess of the dawn, creates such hilarity with her lascivious dancing that Amaterasu, curious about the source of the laughter, is tempted to peek out at the throng. When she does so and sees her own shining beauty reflected in the mirror provided by the gods, the world is saved from desolation and its fertility is restored.

SUPREME GODDESSES

As in the case of Eurynome, whose powers are challenged by her consort, Ophion, the story of Amaterasu offers an example of a male deity's efforts to usurp the authority of the supreme goddess. Although neither Ophion nor Susano is successful, in the myths of some cultural traditions the usurping god overthrows the goddess. In Babylonian accounts, for example, the sun god Marduk becomes ruler of the cosmos when he defeats and dismembers Tiamat, the primordial, universal mother goddess. Although the myth represents the shift in power as a movement from chaos to order, to scholars it reveals the emergence of a patriarchal culture whose own construction of order supplants earlier beliefs. Interestingly, tales told by several South American peoples directly address the circumstances of similar changes in social order. In one version of several related myths, the Tupi people of Brazil describe a time when women are earth's rulers. Desiring to find a wife who is less powerful than he, the sun decides to bring changes to the people's culture. He therefore causes the virgin Ceucy to become impregnated by the sap of the cucara tree, and Jurupari, the son that she bears, passes sacred knowledge to men, overthrows the women's authority, kills his own mother, and searches for an appropriate woman to wed the sun. According to the Tupi, Jurupari still searches for that woman.

Among the Inuit peoples of the Arctic regions, Sedna, the sea goddess and the mother of the animals, is the supreme divinity. Along with Sila, the god of air and weather, and Tarqeq, the moon god who oversees fertility, Sedna controls the welfare of a people who make their living by hunting. The most important of the three principal deities, Sedna, who is also known by many other names, is the animal master who provides the creatures that the people hunt. According to tradition, Sedna lives on the land until she is cast into the sea that then becomes her kingdom. Although there are several versions of this occurrence, in most accounts she is a young woman who is thrown from a boat by her parents or her father. When she attempts to save herself by clinging to the boat, her fingers are chopped off, and the fingers of the goddess then assume the forms of the seals, whales, walruses, and fish. As master of the animals, Sedna can give or withhold the ocean's gifts. Indeed, the powerful sea goddess controls both the living and dead, for her kingdom at the bottom of the ocean is also conceived as the underworld. As it happens, in Inuit tradition the sun is also a goddess, the sister of the moon god.

MOON GODDESSES

Because the cycles of the moon correspond so obviously to the earth's agricultural seasons, fertility and mother goddesses such as Inanna, Astarte, and Isis are often closely associated with that celestial orb, and another fertility deity, Tanit, is the Canaanite moon goddess. Tanit also appears in Carthage, where, as Tinnit, she is regarded as the supreme deity who reigns over heaven and bestows fertility on the earth. In southern Ghana, Nyame is the supreme deity whose female nature appears as the moon and whose male aspect takes the form of the sun. As the moon goddess, Nyame is the mother of the cosmos. Other moon goddesses are the consorts of sun gods: the Incan moon goddess, Mama Kilya, is both sister and wife of the sun god Inti, and in the tradition of North America's Pawnee people, the moon goddess is also married to the sun god. According to Pawnee myths, the moon gives birth to the first male human being, and the first female is born of the stars. Two lunar deities preside in ancient Syrian tradition, and thus the moon goddess Nikkal is the wife of the moon god.

In the classical myth traditions of both Greece and Rome, several different goddesses are associated with the moon. Selene, an early Greek moon goddess, is the sister of Helios, the sun deity. Like her brother, Selene drives a chariot as she travels through the sky. In time, Selene becomes closely linked to Artemis, the Greek goddess of the hunt and master of wild animals, and when Artemis assumes the role of moon deity, the relationship between moon and sun indeed remains unchanged, for her twin brother Apollo takes on the role of sun god. During the Hellenistic era, the early moon goddess also becomes identified with Hekate, said to be the cousin of Artemis and Apollo. Goddess of magic, the crossroads, and the nocturnal world, Hekate is sometimes also depicted as a guardian of the underworld. As moon goddess, she represents the dark phase of the lunar cycle. Perse, the wife of Helios, and their daughter Pasiphae are two other Greek goddesses who are also associated with the moon. Like Hekate, Perse is connected with the dark moon, and Pasiphae, whose name means "all-shining," appears to represent the bright moon. In Greek myths, Pasiphae is best known as the mother of the Minotaur. The Roman moon goddesses, Luna and Diana, bear close resemblance to Selene and Artemis; Luna, the heavenly embodiment of the moon, is characteristically represented as the full moon, and Diana, goddess of fertility, wildlife, and the hunt, is often associated with the crescent moon.

FERTILITY GODDESSES

Myth tradition's great mother goddesses and moon deities are not the only divinities who serve as emblems of fertility. In the ancient Egyptian culture, for example, Hathor, Sopdet, Bastet, and Taweret are all revered along with Isis as fertility goddesses. The sky deity Hathor, goddess of love, music, and dancing, is associated with the fecund cow, a symbol of the sky that surrounds and protects the earth; Hathor is also the "Queen of the Date Palm" and the goddess who provides nourishment for the dead. Sopdet, the embodiment of the star Sirius, signals the beginning of the fertile season when she appears on the horizon in July, the time of the annual flooding of the Nile. Bastet, goddess of cats, fertility, and love, is also associated with the moon—perhaps because the eyes of the cat resemble the changing phases of the moon. Yet another fertility deity, Taweret is the pregnant hippopotamus-goddess who, as an embodiment of fecund maternity, serves as the protector of childbearing women. Anat, an important Canaanite fertility deity and the goddess of dew, is also assimilated into Egyptian tradition, and there she takes the form of a protective warrior goddess.

In Greek and Roman myths, fertility goddesses include nature deities who oversee the earth's fruitfulness and the production of its crops as well as the goddesses of love. Demeter, the Greek earth goddess who provides all bounty from the soil, becomes the disappearing fertility deity when she neglects her responsibilities while searching for Persephone, the beloved daughter who is abducted by Hades. According to some myths, Demeter is also the mother of Plutos, the god of wealth whose largesse represents the riches of the earth. The Roman goddess of grain, Ceres performs a service similar to that of Demeter as she presides over the planting and harvesting of crops. Like Demeter, who is the granddaughter of the earth goddess Gaea, Ceres is closely related to Tellus, the Roman goddess who personifies the earth. In Greek tradition, lesser deities called Nymphs are the fertility deities of the mountains, ponds, and woodlands. The Dryads, for example, are tree Nymphs, and the Naiads are water Nymphs who live in pools and springs. As figures that embody female beauty and sexuality, the Greek and Roman love goddesses, Aphrodite and Venus, are also considered fertility deities. Originally the Italic goddess of springtime's flowers and gardens, Venus eventually assumes Aphrodite's attributes as deity of love. Known as the goddess of gardens in ancient Athens, Aphrodite too is associated with the nurturing of plants.

In Norse tradition, where the pantheon includes two groups of divinities, the Aesir are warlike sky deities while the Vanir are ancient Germanic fertility deities who govern the earth and sea. According to myth scholars, the Vanir embody the values of an early agricultural society, and the Aesir represent the emergence of a warrior culture. Together, the two divine races oppose their common enemy, the evil giants. Freyja, goddess of love, fertility, and sexuality, is the daughter of Njord, chief god of the Vanir. Traveling in a chariot drawn by cats, Freyja assists women in labor and helps protect the dead. Like some other fertility goddesses, she is also associated with wealth from the earth and possesses a fabulous necklace constructed by the dwarves who dwell underground. Rosmerta, a Gallic fertility goddess who is also a deity of wealth, is frequently depicted with a cornucopia. In Celtic-Irish tradition, the fertility goddess Brigit oversees the ritual fires of purification that signify renewal. Indeed, she also represents the process of renewal by presiding over childbirth and serving as the goddess of healing. Brigit's festival, held when ewes begin to give forth their milk, appropriately takes place during the season of renewal.

GODDESSES OF THE HUNT

In addition to Artemis and Diana, the Greek and Roman divinities, myth tradition offers numerous other instances of the hunter goddess. In Germanic myths, for example, Skadi, wife of Njord and mother of Freyja, is the goddess of the hunt. As tradition has it, Skadi and Njord do not live together, for the goddess cannot bear to leave her mountain home, and neither will her husband, the sea god, abandon his domain. In Celtic traditions, Abnoba is the hunter goddess of the Black Forest region, and Artio, accompanied by a bear, serves as goddess of the hunt among the ancient people of Switzerland. To Arduinna, a Gallic hunting goddess, the boar is a sacred companion, and in the myths of early inhabitants of the Balkans, the hunter goddess Zana is traditionally accompanied by goats with golden horns. The "Mother of the Forest," the Latvian goddess Meza Mate is both the master of wild animals and the goddess of the hunt; as the deity who both protects animals and helps human hunters, the goddess's role is similar to that of Sedna, the Inuit master of animals and goddess of the sea. Neith, an Egyptian goddess who is associated with the hunt, is also a warrior deity.

GODDESSES OF WAR AND DEATH

In many myth traditions, goddesses of war or death represent the destroyer aspect of the great mother goddess. Ishtar, the Babylonian goddess of love and fertility, is also a war deity, as is Nanaja, an ancient Mesopotamian fertility goddess. In Indian culture, Durga, Kali, and Minakshi all embody the warlike or destructive aspect of the Devi, and, in Egypt, the Middle Eastern fertility goddesses Anat and Astarte are assimilated as warrior deities. Moreover, Egyptian tradition includes native war goddesses as well: Neith, a great mother deity and hunter goddess, is also associated with warfare, and the fierce lioness deity Sekhmet is goddess of the battlefield. Like Egypt's myth tradition, that of ancient Ireland includes multiple goddesses of war; interestingly, however, rather than engaging in the fighting, these goddesses all wreak havoc on the battlefield by dint of their presence. Nemhain, the battle goddess whose name means "frenzy," causes panic among warriors or frightens them to death with her eerie wailing. Badb, another Irish war goddess, appears on the battlefield in the form of the raven, omen of death, and Morrigan, the war goddess who washes the armor of those who are destined to die, is also a deity of the underworld. In somewhat similar fashion, the Valkyries of Norse tradition hover about the battlefield and then guide the fallen heroes to the great hall of the dead.

PEACE GODDESSES

The goddesses of myth also include champions of peace, and in the Greek tradition, wise Athena is both a war deity and a guardian of the peace. As warrior goddess, Athena carries into battle the frightful aegis (the shield that bears Medusa's head), but she is also the goddess of wisdom, the protector deity of Athens, and the benevolent provider of gifts greatly valued in her culture. Indeed, the many gifts bestowed by the goddess are said to include the potter's wheel and the loom and plough, the vase, the flute, and the olive tree, the finest gift of all. Known as Pallas Athena in her role as protector of the peace, the goddess of war assumes the epithet "champion" (Promachos) on the field of battle. Another Greek divinity, Eirene, is also a goddess of peace, and in Roman culture, where the goddess Bellona is the personification of warfare, the goddess Pax—depicted with an olive branch—personifies the times of peace. Just as the olive branch serves the Romans as a symbol of peace, the peace pipe fulfills that purpose among North America's Sioux people. According to tradition, the goddess Whope, daughter of the sun god, is the emissary of peace who brings the pipe to the people and then instructs them in its use.

GODDESSES OF FATE

Although a few male deities are portrayed as the rulers of destiny, goddesses characteristically oversee the unfolding of fate. In many myth traditions a group of deities presides over destiny, and, in a striking number of different cultures, a triad of goddesses performs that important office. The Moirai, for example, are the three goddesses of fate in Greek tradition, where destiny is envisioned through the metaphor of spinning. Thus, in Greek myths, Klotho spins life's thread, Lachesis weaves the thread into a pattern, and then finally Atropos cuts off the thread of life. Similarly, three goddesses collectively known as the Parcae control destiny in Roman tradition, and in the myths of Slavic Gypsies, the Urme are the three goddesses of fate. In Norse tradition, the three Norns possess all knowledge of the past, present, and future, and, along with the Valkyries, who control the destiny of warriors, these Norse goddesses of fate are known as the Disir. According to Albanian tradition, the Fatit—three goddesses carried by butterflies—determine the fate of every newborn infant, and, in myths from ancient Egypt, fate goddesses known as the Hemuset also attend upon the births of all children. Solitary goddesses of fate or fortune include the Greek and Roman deities Tyche and Fortuna, who both dispense luck, and the Siberian goddess Kaltes, who oversees childbirth and governs people's fates.

GODDESSES OF THE UNDERWORLD

Because the life that is born of the earth returns to it in death, many mother goddesses and fertility deities are associated with death or the underworld. The Japanese earth goddess Izanami, for example, receives the dead in her underworld domain, and in ancient Persian tradition, the fertility goddess Armaiti protects the dead who are buried in the earth. Isis, the queen of the underworld, Selket, the tutelary goddess of the dead, and Amentet, the guardian of the necropolis, are among the several deities who provide for the dead in Egyptian myths. Other goddesses of myth bring death to the living. The Lithuanian goddess Giltine, for example, suffocates the sick, and the Greek goddesses known as the Erinyes (the Furies) rise from the underworld to pursue evildoers. Of course, goddesses of death also include rulers of the underworld. In Mesopotamian tradition, the goddess who governs the underworld is Ereshkigal, the older sister of Inanna/Ishtar, Queen of the Heavens. According to ancient myths, the world becomes barren when Inanna visits her sister's kingdom, and thus scholars suggest that the figure of the death goddess might well represent the destroyer aspect of the great fertility goddess. The goddess Hel, daughter of Loki, is ruler of the underworld in Norse tradition, and all those who do not die in battle pass to her domain in icy Niflheim. Among the Navajo of North America, the benevolent goddess Estanatlehi presides over the Land of the Setting Sun, realm of the dead.

GUARDIAN GODDESSES

Like the many male deities that are recognized as tutelary gods or patrons of the arts, the goddesses of myth include both guardians of domestic life and divinities that represent cultural achievements. Among the ancient Greeks, for example, the goddess Hestia protects the home and the fire in its hearth, and the nine goddesses known as the Muses are revered as patrons of music, drama, literature, dance, and other intellectual pursuits. Goddesses also serve as representatives of justice, and in Greek tradition both Themis and Nemesis embody that role: Themis is the goddess of morality and justice, and Nemesis personifies the fair retribution that justice demands. Moreover, in some cultural traditions, goddesses assume roles that are more commonly served by male deities. In myths from China, for example, Lei Zu is a thunder goddess, and both the Lithuanian goddess Gabija and the Aztec deity Itzpapalotl are fire divinities. Brigit, the Irish fertility goddess, is also the tutelary deity of blacksmiths, and among North America's Pueblo peoples, the coyote trickster who is sometimes known as Old Man Coyote also frequently appears as Coyote Woman.

See also The Cosmic Egg; Creation Myths; Emergence Motif; Fertility Myths; Gods; Guardians; The Underworld

GUARDIANS

Numerous figures in the world of myth serve as guardians, watchmen, gatekeepers, or protective spirits. Deities, monsters, animals, or demons, the guardians stand sentry at the entrance of the underworld or watch over great treasures. They guard roads, bridges, doorways, and cemeteries, or protect gods, emperors, and wild creatures. They keep a watchful eye on kingdoms, sacred places, and the world of nature, and they stand guard at the portals of heaven. They also lend their protection to human beings, often in the form of spirits or animal helpers. Divinities, too, watch over people, but because the great celestial gods attend to other duties, the domestic gods are usually lesser deities, often familiar to a particular region. These lesser deities oversee kitchen, hearth and home, women in childbirth, and even the professional occupations. Unlike the fierce guardians of the underworld or the treasure hoards, the domestic deities are generally benign and, indeed, sometimes comic figures.

GUARDIANS OF THE UNDERWORLD

Among the guardians of the underworld are two fearsome dogs, Cerberus in Greek tradition and Garm in the myths of the Norse. The ferocious Cerberus, whose three snarling heads are adorned with writhing snakes, stands sentry at Hades' gate. There he turns away the living, frightens the souls that must pass through the gate, and prevents the dead from leaving the underworld. Garm of the bloody breast plays a similar role at the gate to Hel, the Norse underworld. His name means "barking," and he is the hellhound that ceaselessly howls as he strains at his fetters. Unlike Cerberus, Garm does not stop the dead from leaving the underworld, and when Hel's gate is occasionally left open, the dead emerge and roam about the earth. Originally a demon of death that took the form of a dog, Charon, the ferryman of the Greek underworld, is another guardian of the realm of the dead. But for the rare exceptions recorded in legend, he does not allow the living to cross the River Styx.

In Chinese tradition, two gods, Shen Tu and Yu Lu, guard the gates of hell to prevent the dead from leaving the domain of the Lords of Death, the ten Yama kings. Standing beside a massive door on the mountain that serves as barrier between the land of the living and that of the dead, the two gods capture and punish ghosts that try to escape their fate. When they seize the fleeing souls of the dead, the guardians of the hell's door imprison them with two vicious tigers. In Native American tradition, another gatekeeper, Tokonaka, also oversees the punishment of the dead. To enter the town of the dead, the Hopi must pass by a guardian who waits in the Grand Canyon at the place where the first people emerged into the world. Tokonaka allows good spirits to take a straight path to their destination, but the spirits that require purification must take a fork in the trail that leads to four pits of fire. Those who are cleansed when they pass through the first, second, or third fire pit return to the path that leads to the community of the dead, but the evil spirits that enter the fourth pit are consumed by its flames.

GUARDIANS OF TREASURE

In myth, monsters characteristically guard the great treasures that heroes seek as the objects of their quests—and the heroes who trick or slay the monsters earn fame for their deeds. Many of the monstrous guardians of Western tradition are, like Ladon of Greek lore, fire-breathing dragons. Ladon is the hundred-headed dragon with many voices that guards the golden apples in the garden of the Hesperides. By some accounts Herakles, who gathers the golden apples as one of his Twelve Labors, slays Ladon himself, and in other versions he asks Atlas to steal the treasure for him. Another venomous dragon guards the Golden Fleece in the sacred grove of Ares, and the hero Jason steals this great prize when his lover Medea uses the power of her magic to enchant the fearsome beast. The treasure that the Greek hero Cadmus claims by killing yet another guardian dragon is the sacred spring at the site of Thebes, the city that he founds there. In Germanic tradition, terrible dragons guard fabulous hoards of gold. Beowulf kills one such dragon in the last of his heroic adventures, and Sigurd, the hero of the *Volsung Saga* (A.D. 1300), slays Fafnir, the dragon that guards the golden treasures of Andvari the dwarf.

Python, the gigantic serpent, is another of the monstrous guardians from Greek tradition. A guardian of oracular knowledge, Python oversees the oracle at Delphi until the sun god Apollo slays the mighty serpent and triumphantly claims the most sacred of the oracles as his prize. In another Greek myth, Zeus's son Hermes kills Argos, the giant with one hundred eyes, on behalf of his father. As the story goes, Zeus transforms the lovely Io into a heifer to hide from Hera his dalliance with the maiden. Zeus's suspicious wife, however, demands possession of the heifer and chooses the giant that never sleeps to stand guard over her. Before he can kill the guardian of his father's treasure, Hermes must make sure that all one hundred of the giant's eyes are closed in sleep. The clever trickster, therefore, lulls Argos into slumber by patiently recounting numerous tedious tales. Another monstrous guardian,

Humbaba, is also a giant, and the treasure that he protects is a stand of mighty trees. In *Gilgamesh* (ca. 2000 B.C.E.), the Mesopotamian epic, the fire-breathing giant with dragon's teeth watches over the Cedar Forest of Lebanon until Gilgamesh and Enkidu, in search of adventure, slay the forest's evil guardian and take possession of the trees.

GUARDIANS OF PLACES

In addition to the guardians of the underworld and those that watch over treasures are those associated with other important places. In the Greek tale of Oedipus, the monstrous Sphinx that guards the narrow pass on the road to Thebes devours all travelers who cannot provide the answer to her riddle. The Norse god Heimdall is guardian of the rainbow bridge called Bifrost, and he stands ready to blow his horn when the gods' enemies begin to cross the bridge. In several traditions, guardians watch over cemeteries. In Egypt, the jackal-headed Anubis guards the necropolis, and in Japan Jizo, the god of mercy, protects souls in the graveyard from evil demons. Accompanied by her hellhounds, Hekate, the Greek death goddess, watches over tombs and stands sentry at crossroads. In Japanese tradition, five gods created from the jewels of the sun goddess Amaterasu guard the celestial realm, the High Plain of Heaven, and three gods created from the sword of Susano, god of thunder, watch over the earth, the Central Reed Plain.

Chinese tradition offers several myths about a Western Paradise found on the slopes of Mount Kunlun, one of six sacred mountains. The mountain has doors on each of its sides, and, in one account, the eastern door of light is guarded by a creature with nine human heads and the body of a tiger. In another story about Kunlun, the great Yellow Emperor, Huang Di, builds his palatial city high on its slopes. The main gate to this city of white jade faces east, where the dawn appears, and its guardian is the tiger god Hu Wu, another fabulous beast with a human face, immense claws, and nine tails. Indeed, the tiger often serves the role of protector in Chinese lore and is also the traditional guardian of the afterlife. Dragons, too, are guardians of places in Chinese myths, and because the Asian dragon is associated with fertility and rain, dragons are the guardians of rivers and lakes. Nu Gua, the nurturing creator goddess with a dragon's tail, provides protection for the world when her work on earth is finished. In an interesting variation on the Ymir motif, ten gods arise from the intestines of the dragon goddess's corpse to act as the guardians of the earth and its creatures.

GUARDIANS OF VIRTUE

The Zoroastrians of early Persia incorporate deities that date from even earlier eras into their own tradition by assigning these ancient Indo-Iranian gods new roles as the guardians of virtues or sacred objects. According to the Zoroastrians, these figures, who are known as the *yazata* (the "Worshipful Ones"), are the creations of the six Holy Immortals who themselves stand guard over distinct features of Ahura Mazda's perfect creation. In their service to the Holy Immortals, the *yazata* perform as warriors who defend the perfection of Ahura Mazda's creation throughout the cosmic struggle between good and evil. Mithra, the *yazata* of loyalty, protects truth and justice by serving as the overseer of all contracts and agreements, and the mace that he carries is the weapon he characteristically uses to battle injustice and dishonesty. Apam Napat, the *yazata* of oaths, is another guardian of honesty, and Atar is the protector of the sacred fire that signifies purity and truth. Obedience is also a highly valued virtue in Zoroastrian tradition, and this form of goodness is associated with Sraosha, the *yazata* who oversees the prayers of the faithful. As a warrior in the never-ending battle with evil, Sraosha ventures forth in his chariot each night to protect the earth from the powerful demons that roam the darkened world.

According to Zoroastrian tradition, the Holy Immortals who are served by the *yazata* are also guardians of the good creation. Along with Ahura Mazda, these divine beings preside over the seven stages of the creation of the universe and then protect its varied features. Vohu Manah, first among the Immortals, is the protector of creation's benign animals—especially the cow and the ox—and Asha Vahista, guardian of the sacred fire, protects the living from sickness and death. Spenta Armaiti is the immortal goddess who guards the earth, and Khshathra Vairya is protector of the sky. Haurvatat, the guardian of water, also oversees the resurrection of the dead, and Ameretat, the guardian of all plants, rewards the virtuous in the afterlife. Ahura Mazda, the supreme creator, is the protector of all humankind. As guardians of the good creation, Ahura Mazda and the Holy Immortals defend the righteous in their great battle against Angra Mainyu's evil powers of destruction.

GUARDIANS OF THE HOUSEHOLD

A variety of figures in myth tradition serve as guardians of the household. In ancient Egypt, Bes, a bandy-legged dwarf with protruding eyes, protects women in childbirth and wards off the demons and dangerous animals that prowl in the night. The Lares are the tutelary gods of the families and households of ancient Rome, and the Penates are the divine protectors of the larder or cupboard. The Roman goddess Vesta is guardian of the fire in the hearth, and Janus, the two-faced god of thresholds, drives evil spirits from the door. In China, numerous domestic deities oversee the functioning of both households and professions. The Men Shen, the two gods of gates and doors, guard the entrances of houses and temples, and Zao Jun, the Kitchen God, watches over households. As guardian of the hearth, Zao Jun is well positioned to observe life within the household, and, indeed, he insists that all family members fulfill their domestic duties—each year he travels to the heavens to report to the gods the behavior of all family members. Sun Pin, the god of cobblers, and Lu Ban, the guardian of carpenters, are among the many deities who oversee the occupations of China's workers. Lu Ban, also a gifted inventor, is said to have constructed a wooden falcon that could fly and to have discovered the ball-and-socket joint.

In many cultures, protective spirits watch over people, animals, or deities. The *nahual*, for example, is the personal tutelary spirit in Mesoamerican tradition. A particular animal or plant that serves as each person's spirit double, the *nahual* is an individual's constant companion. Deities, too, are attended by a *nahual* and sometimes assume the form of the animal that protects them. Huitzilopochtli, the Aztec god of war, is associated with the hummingbird, and the *nahual* of Tezcatlipoca, the dark god of mirrors, is the spotted jaguar. Similarly, the manitou is the spirit guardian among the Algonquian peoples of North America, and the tuunraq is the helper spirit of the Inuit. In both of these cultures, young people seek the protection of a particular animal's soul when they undergo their initiation rites. While the spirits of animals protect human beings, other powerful spirits, the animal masters, watch over the animal kingdom. Throughout the Americas, the guardians of animals ensure that human beings respect the wild creatures they hunt. Animal masters therefore punish people who injure animals, kill them needlessly, or fail to be thankful for the food they provide.

IMAGES OF THE GUARDIAN

Images, statues, or monuments that represent the figure of the guardian are commonplace throughout the world and express the importance of the role of protector. In China, portraits of the Men Shen are affixed to doorways and gates, and the life-sized statues of thousands of warriors form the Terracotta Army that guards the tomb of Shi Huangdi, the First Emperor of the land. The Egyptian sphinx—which eventually evolved into the monster of Greek lore—is the traditional protector of kings, and thus monumental sphinxes stand guard at the temples and tombs of many of Egypt's pharaohs. The image of Egypt's domestic god, Bes, is often carved on the headboards of beds, and, in Roman tradition, statues of the Lares and Penates serve as the household shrines to which families make small offerings of food. Other images of the guardian can be found in the statues of angels or saints, in the Hindu shrines to the Grami Devi, the local fertility goddess, or in the totem poles of the native peoples of North America's Pacific Coast. Near North America's eastern shore another figure of the guardian, the Statue of Liberty, stands as a modern emblem of a protective spirit.

See also Animals in Myth; Monsters; The Underworld

MESSENGERS

The messenger or guide is a recurring figure in tales from around the world and plays a variety of roles in myth tradition. Sometimes this character relays messages among the gods or serves a particular god, and other messengers move between deities and mortal beings. Messengers frequently serve as guides to the afterlife or underworld, leading the dead on the journey they must make. In some traditions they carry messages back and forth between the world of the living and the spiritual domain. Sometimes the role of messenger is assigned to one of the gods, as is the case of the Greek god Hermes, and frequently the messenger is an animal, often a bird. Birds, of course, are particularly swift messengers because they can fly, and Hermes, with his winged sandals and cap, shares this attribute. Hermes is a trickster as well as a messenger, and he is not the only character in myth that serves both these functions. As one who fearlessly crosses all boundaries, the trickster performs well in the role of messenger.

HERMES

Perhaps the best known of the messenger gods, Hermes wears a traveler's brimmed hat and carries the caduceus, the traditional staff or wand borne by a herald. Legend has it that Apollo presented him the staff in return for Hermes' gift to him of the first lyre, an instrument that he constructed from a tortoise shell when he was still a child. The caduceus, a symbol in miniature of the World Tree, is an especially appropriate emblem for the messenger, who, like the tree, links the realms of sky, earth, and underworld. One of the sons of Zeus, Hermes often serves as messenger for him. Indeed, in several tales his father enlists him to help deceive Hera during those numerous occasions when Zeus is unfaithful to her. Hermes, called Mercury by the Romans, is a guide to the underworld in both traditions. In fact, he is the only one of the Olympians to whom Zeus grants the power to travel freely to and from the home of the gods, the earthly home of mortal beings, and the underworld home of the dead.

The god of travelers, boundaries, and roads, Hermes is named for the herms, or stone pillars, that mark paths, crossroads, and frontiers throughout the landscape of Greece. It is perhaps as the god of roads that his responsibilities include that of psychopomp, the one who conducts souls along the road of the dead. A crosser of boundaries himself, he assists those who must cross from earthly life into the netherworld. Also the patron of traders and thieves, Hermes oversees the commerce that traffics on his roads. His sympathy for thieves is longstanding in Greek tradition, for it is said that as a cunning child he stole fifty of Apollo's cattle and hid them in his mother's cave. As trickster, he is not bound by convention—and therefore sometimes serves as the messenger of lies and deceit. His winged sandals, the *talaria*, were made for him by Hephaistos, the blacksmith of the gods, and when Perseus goes to kill the Gorgon Medusa, Hermes lends him a similar pair to speed him on his way.

TRICKSTER MESSENGERS

Like Hermes, tricksters from two West African traditions also serve the role of messenger. Legba, the messenger god of the Fon people, is the interpreter for the gods, who all began to use different languages when they established their separate kingdoms. He also carries messages between the deities and mortal beings, particularly the prognostications of Fa, the god of divination. The youngest son of the creator goddess Mawu, Legba is the translator through whom both deities and mortals must pass in order to address her, and, like Hermes, he sometimes carries messages that serve his own trickster's purposes. As trickster, he not only transcends boundaries, but also creates them. He is, for example, the Fon deity who separates the earth and sky, making the boundary between them. To force his mother, Mawu the sky, to move away from the earth, he conspires with an old woman. Every day, when she cleans her pots and pans, the old woman throws her dirty dishwater into the air and thus drenches Mawu—eventually the disgusted creator finds a new home far above the earth.

Eshu, the trickster god of the Yoruba people, is also a messenger who acts as mediator between deities and mortal beings. According to Yoruba tradition, it is Eshu who brought the art of divination to the people of the earth, and it is therefore Eshu's face that is always pictured on the divination board. As the instrument of prognostication, Eshu crosses the boundary between the heavens, where fate is decreed, and the earth, where it is revealed. As go-between, he serves the purposes of the gods by ensuring that people offer them sacrifices, but he also serves mortal beings by bringing them the power of prophecy. Like those of Hermes and Legba, however, his messages cannot always be trusted, for the trickster is wont to make trouble when an opportunity arises. It is said that the gods forced Eshu to live on the earth rather than in heaven because of his incessant mischief making, and legend has it that he acquired the sixteen palm nuts used for divination by tricking the monkeys into giving them to him.

ANIMAL MESSENGERS

In other narratives from Africa, animals serve as the gods' messengers. The python, for example, is the messenger of Olokun, the god of the sea, and when the Yoruba people see a python, they address it as though it were a king. Two stories about animal messengers offer explanations for the occurrence of death. In a tale of the Ibo, the creator god Chuku sends a dog to the earth to inform people that should someone die, ashes sprinkled on the body would quickly restore it. Although the dog is the trickster Legba's sacred animal and serves as his faithful messenger, the dog in the Ibo myth is too slow in delivering its message. Chuku therefore sends a sheep to carry his instructions, but the sheep becomes confused, and when it tells the people to bury their dead in the ground, death is then made permanent. A similar tale comes from the Zulu people of southern Africa. In their account, the gods send a chameleon to earth to tell the people that they will live forever. When the chameleon lingers to eat fruit, the gods change their minds and send the swift-moving lizard to tell people that they will die. Death comes into the world when the people believe the words of the lizard and therefore accept the idea that they are mortal.

Olokun and Legba are by no means the only gods associated with particular animal messengers. The two ravens, Huginn (thought) and Munnin (memory) are the Norse god Odin's traditional companions, and every day the two birds fly across the world gathering news to deliver to the leader of the gods. In Greek tradition, the raven is the special messenger bird of the sun god, Apollo, and also the messenger of Athena, the goddess of wisdom. In myths from Japan, a white fox carries messages for Inari, the god of rice, and therefore a statue of a fox is always present at the Shinto shrines that honor the rice god. The pigeon is the messenger for Hachiman, the Japanese god of war, and although Japan's great goddess of the sun, Amaterasu, often uses the brightly colored pheasant as her messenger bird, she is also associated with another divine messenger, the three-clawed crow. In the story of Jimmu, said to be the first emperor of Japan, she sends Yatagarasu, the red crow of the sun, to guide the emperor's army. Birds are also messengers in Mayan tradition: the death lords who rule the Mayan underworld, the dark kingdom of Xibalba, use four owls to send their messages to the land of the living.

In ancient Egyptian tradition, where particular animals represent certain gods, people send animal messengers to those gods by means of the practice of mummification. Mummified cats, for example, carry messages to the goddess Bastet, guardian and protector of homes, and falcons deliver them to Horus, god of the sky. Amun-Ra, the great sun god, receives messages from the goose or the ram, and a mummified ibis or baboon carries messages to Thoth, god of the moon. Not only do animals carry messages to the realm of the gods, but, serving as oracles, they bring messages from the deities to mortal beings. The sacred bull, for example, is said to be able to foretell the future. In many tales the goose is a messenger bird, and, among the Egyptian gods, Thoth plays the role of messenger as well as guide to the underworld. Indeed, the Greeks who conquered Egypt in the fourth century B.C.E. remarked on Thoth's similarity to Hermes, their own messenger god, and therefore gave the name Hermopolis to Thoth's traditional cult city.

WINGED MESSENGERS

Creatures of the sky carry messages throughout myth tradition. In the story of Noah's flood, it is a dove that carries to the ark the message that the flood has receded. In many cultures swallows are the traditional heralds of the arrival of spring and are thus regarded as emblems of rebirth. In both India and Mesoamerica, the parrot, a talkative bird, is said to carry messages between the spirit world and mortal beings. The high-flying eagle is messenger for Zeus, and sometimes Zeus transforms himself into his messenger bird. Iris, the Greek goddess of the rainbow, is another creature of the sky who serves as messenger. Iris is a winged goddess, and, like Hermes, she carries the traditional staff of the herald as she assists both gods and mortals. In Greek myths winds also carry messages, and in Japanese tradition clouds often serve as messengers from the gods. Another celestial messenger, the winged angel, appears in Zoroastrian, Judeo-Christian, and Islamic traditions. In Christian tradition, Gabriel is the messenger angel who announces to Mary that she will give birth to Jesus.

MESSENGERS AS INTERMEDIARIES

The Valkyries of Norse tradition are among the messengers of myth who do not travel by wing. Instead, these golden-haired warrior maidens ride white horses onto the field of battle in the service of Odin. Guides as well as messengers, they lead slain heroes over the rainbow bridge to Valhalla, Odin's great mead hall in the home of the gods. Ratatosk the squirrel, another messenger from Norse myth, scampers up and down Yggdrasil as he delivers the insults exchanged between the serpent that lives at the roots of the World Tree and the eagle that roosts at its crown. The messengers of Baal, storm god of the people of West Syria, are particularly interesting. The storm god represents the power of fertility, and to assert this power in the face of death, he sends Gapan the Vine and Ugar the Ploughed Field into the underworld to confront Mot, the god of death, with their message of fecundity and regeneration. In ancient Mesopotamia, genii, fabulous creatures that are part human and part animal, act as messengers for the gods, and in many cultures, including those of Africa, the Americas, and the Arctic regions, the shaman is the go-between who carries messages to and from the spiritual domain.

Although the figure of the shaman appears in many cultural traditions, the term itself has been borrowed from the Mongolian language of Siberia's Tungus peoples. According to the Tungus, the Inuits, and other nomadic tribes of the Arctic regions, the cosmos includes realms that lie beyond the physical realities that are manifest within the visible world. Spirits are said to inhabit these unseen planes of existence, and shamans are the messengers who travel to the domain of the spirits through the experience of a trance. Spiritual guides as well as intermediaries, shamans characteristically seek spiritual knowledge and power on behalf of their communities. Under the guidance of the spirits, shamans acquire the power to heal the sick, for example, or the wisdom to foresee the outcome of a hunt or another communal venture. Shamans also visit the spirits to seek pardon when members of the community have committed offenses or broken taboos, and it is they who help the people maintain a harmonious relationship with the spirit world.

See also Animals in Myth; Tricksters

MONSTERS

The multitudes of mythical creatures that populate stories from almost all cultural traditions include monsters, demons, and fabulous beasts of every imaginable description. Indeed, some of these extraordinary creatures are said to be too terrifying to be described at all, and others use their shape-shifting powers to appear in a variety of guises. While not all fabulous creatures are evil or fearsome, most of them bedevil human beings in various ways or represent whatever it is that people greatly fear. Gigantism is one of several different features that lend these figures their nightmarish characteristics, and thus many of myth's monsters are immense and ferocious creatures with supernatural strength. Others are frighteningly eerie and elusive beings that employ their remarkable powers with malicious cunning, and still others are hideously grotesque and therefore tremendously unsettling to behold. Many of myth's monstrous creatures, in fact, are instances of the chimera, the fabulous hybrid beast that is composed of parts from different animals or that is part animal and part human being. Indeed, the chimera is perhaps a particularly disarming monster, for it is at once both familiar and strange.

MONSTERS' ROLES IN MYTH

The monsters of myth and folklore traditions serve a variety of purposes in the tales told about them. In a great number of stories, the monster is, of course, the evil or disruptive force that great heroes must overcome. Characteristically, heroes either slay monsters that pose an immediate threat to their community's well-being, or they journey forth in search of adventure, looking for monsters that will test their courage, ingenuity, and skill. In other accounts, as in the story of the

Greek tradition's Herakles, heroes are assigned the task of ridding the world of particular monsters and are therefore obliged to prove themselves worthy by accomplishing this mission. More generally, monstrous beings serve the purposes of storytelling by offering a useful means of embodying that which is malicious, evil, terrifying, or threatening to human societies; by recognizing wicked forces through the act of granting them a body and a name, people can clearly define the evils or dangers that must be exorcised from their communities. Furthermore, the embodiment of the monstrous provides people with a figure to blame when adversity strikes or the unexpected occurs. Indeed, in some tales the presence of a monster functions to afford a name for the unknown, for that which is unfathomably mysterious and cannot be otherwise explained.

Among Australia's indigenous peoples, tales of the ancestral giants and monsters that inhabit the world during its primordial Dreamtime explain the existence of landmarks on the earth, for it is said that during the course of their wanderings, these creatures shape the hills, valleys, rivers, and springs of Australia's landscape. And, in myths from the ancient Babylonian, Chinese, and Norse traditions, the dead bodies of the monster Tiamat and the giants Pan Ku and Ymir are all used in the creation of the world. In folklore traditions, stories of monsters are often instructive, offering moral lessons, bits of sage advice, or warnings of danger in narrative form. As in those stories of the bogeyman that are commonplace in some Western cultures, these cautionary tales employ the threat of a monster to alert people, particularly children, to lurking dangers. For example, North America's Paiute people recount several cautionary tales that feature the Water Babies, eerie beings that dwell in Pyramid Lake or its surrounding springs. By some accounts the Water Babies steal unprotected children, and thus elders tell these stories to warn the young of the water's dangers. According to other accounts, however, the Water Babies watch for wicked people, and when they have an opportunity to seize them, they drag them down into the depths of the lake. The admonition implicit in this version of the tale is readily apparent, for the people captured by the Water Babies are never seen again.

ORIGINS OF MONSTERS

In some instances, features of mythic monsters appear to suggest the possibility of their origins in natural phenomena. For example, the Chimera, a hybrid beast that comes to Greek tradition from Anatolia, possesses a lion's head, a goat's body, and a serpent's tail. Interestingly, however, this monster consumes its victims with its fiery breath, and thus scholars speculate that the conception of a fire-vomiting beast might well have been inspired by the flames of natural gas that sometimes shoot from the earth in the monster's homeland. The venomous Hydra, another Greek monster, is said to have nine heads atop its serpent's body, and, whenever one head is chopped off, two more grow back in its place. This monster, whose name means "water serpent," lives in the swampy marshes of Lake Lerna, and it has therefore been suggested that its watery habitation might have inspired its original conception, for, like the Hydra's heads, when flowing water is dammed up, two streams emerge in the place of one. As for other traditions, including that of ancient China, it is commonly supposed that people's discovery of the bones of gigantic, prehistoric animals might have suggested to them images of such creatures as the dragon.

The characteristics of monsters can also take on a symbolic significance or assume a metaphorical meaning within a particular culture. The Windigo, an icy, cannibalistic giant that haunts North America's Ojibwa people during harsh winter seasons, represents the peril of starvation as well as the madness that can overwhelm a person who is driven to desperation. An emblem of insatiable hunger, the voracious Windigo devours human flesh, and, in keeping with its monstrous nature, the more it consumes, the hungrier it gets. According to tradition, a person who is maddened by hunger can become a Windigo that will then mercilessly stalk its family and friends. By extension, therefore, among the Ojibwa the concept of the Windigo also denotes a person who is crazy or one who is utterly consumed by a monstrous need. Another monster that symbolically represents people's sense of vulnerability is the hideous Flying Head of North America's Iroquois tradition. Particularly insidious because of its ability to fly, this gigantic, bodiless head swoops down from the sky when dark storm clouds obscure its approach. A flesh-eating monster, the Flying Head seizes people with its enormous fangs and then tears them to shreds. Like the Windigo, the Flying Head symbolizes monstrous greed and hunger—indeed, this monster is nothing more than a ravenous, gaping mouth.

The relationship between monsters and other beings takes several forms in myth tradition. While monsters are generally the enemy of people or the gods, in the Chinese culture the dragon is usually regarded as a benevolent creature that can use its supernatural powers to bestow the gifts of rain, fertility, good fortune, and even immortality. In contrast, the dragons of Germanic myths are evil, fire-breathing monsters that often serve as the guardians of a treasure hoard. Indeed, terrifying monsters frequently function as the guardians of treasures or of gateways: in the myths of the ancient Greeks, the monstrous serpent Python guards the precious oracle at Delphi, a dragon that never sleeps watches over the Golden Fleece, and Cerberus, the ferocious three-headed hellhound, stands sentinel at the entrance to the underworld. By some accounts, deities occasionally give birth to monstrous beings, and in the myths of the Greeks, for example, the sea god Poseidon is the father of the one-eyed giant Polyphemus as well as several sea monsters, while the goddess Pasiphae is the mother of the dreaded, flesh-eating Minotaur. As in the tradition of the Ojibwa people's Windigo, human beings can sometimes turn into monsters, and tales from Eastern Europe tell of people's transformation into both werewolves and vampires. Doctor Faustus, the legendary scholar in other European myths, makes himself into a monster when he bargains with the demonic Mephistopheles, and, according to more recent traditions, people like Victor Frankenstein create new monsters in the pursuit of their scientific investigations.

MONSTERS OVERCOME BY TRICKERY

While people are obviously vulnerable to monsters that descend upon them from the skies, they are also susceptible when they are asleep, and the people of the Arabian desert tell stories of the Palis, a monster that appears at night to suck blood from the soles of sleeping people's feet. Perhaps it is a nocturnal monster, or perhaps because its sleeping victims never wake to see the stealthy creature that drains them of their blood, the Palis is one of the mythic monsters that cannot be described. Although monsters like the Flying Head or the mysterious Palis are difficult to overcome, human beings can sometimes thwart them through use of trickery. In a story told by the Iroquois, for example, a young woman who is alone with her baby when the Flying Head descends, pretends to eat the heated rocks that surround her cooking fire. By signaling her satisfaction with each bite she takes, the brave mother persuades the Flying Head that she is relishing a delicious meal, and naturally the greedy monster cannot resist swallowing all the red-hot stones in one tremendous gulp. According to the Iroquois, the people see the last of that monstrous being when it hastily flies away screeching in its agony. As it happens, in a story that is told about a caravan that passes through the desert, the Palis too is foiled by an act of deception. When night falls, an experienced traveler suggests that all members of the party rest with the soles of their feet touching the soles of someone else's feet. Fortunately, this ruse is entirely successful, for when the Palis steals upon the sleeping forms, it is astonished to discover two-headed people with no feet to suck.

MONSTERS SLAIN BY HEROES

While stories of heroic monster slayers appear in many cultural traditions, the myths of ancient Greece are a particularly rich source of tales that feature heroes' encounters with fabulous beasts. Bellerophon, for example, is the hero who is given the task of slaying the fire-breathing Chimera, and he fulfills his mission by first taming the winged horse Pegasus in order to make his assault upon the beast from the sky above it. Bellerophon is not able to kill the monster with the arrows that he shoots, but when he hurls a lead-tipped spear into its open mouth, the Chimera's own flaming breath melts the lead into a molten mass that then consumes the creature's inner organs. The Gorgon Medusa, one of the monsters slain by Perseus, is a female being whose hair is a swarming nest of writhing serpents and whose power lies in her ability to change into stone anyone who dares to look upon her face. To achieve his task of slaying the Gorgon, Perseus dons the magic helmet of invisibility and then, using a mirror to avoid gazing directly at Medusa, he slices off her head with a magic sword. Theseus is the hero who slays the Minotaur, the flesh-eating beast that is part man and part bull, and Oedipus rescues the people of Thebes from the tyranny of the Sphinx when he correctly answers the riddle that she poses. The Sphinx, a winged beast with a woman's head and a lion's body, is another of the monsters that devours people, but Oedipus overcomes her power with his sagacity, and the defeated creature leaps from the cliffs to her death when she hears the hero's answer to her riddle.

Herakles, perhaps the greatest of ancient Greece's many heroes, slays or captures several monsters while performing the labors assigned to him by his cousin Eurystheus, the king of Mycenae. For the first of his tasks, Herakles takes on the ferocious Nemean Lion, a monster whose skin is impervious to any kind of weapon. Thus forced to use his brute strength against his mighty foe, Herakles wrestles with the gigantic beast until at last he strangles it. The nine-headed Hydra is the next of his adversaries, and strength alone is not sufficient to overcome this venom-spewing monster, for each time Herakles crushes one of its heads with his huge club, two new heads immediately grow back. Undaunted, the hero uses a flaming torch to sear the wounds from which new heads emerge, and in this fashion he is able to defeat another fearsome beast. To kill the Stymphalian birds, flesh-eating monsters with claws, beaks, and wings of iron, Herakles creates a great uproar that causes the flock to take flight, and while the creatures are in the air, he shoots them all with his arrows. For another of his labors, Herakles must steal the cattle that belong to Geryon, a fierce three-headed ogre, and when the monster fights for possession of his herd, the hero slays him by shooting arrows through each of his three necks. In the course of his travels, Herakles also rescues a young maiden by slaying the terrible sea monster that threatens her, and he captures the monstrous Erymanthian Boar, the flesh-eating horses of Diomedes, the great Cretan Bull that is the father of the Minotaur, and Cerberus, the snarling three-headed hound of Hades.

In Native American tradition, the great Blackfoot hero Kutoyis is the monster slayer who, like Herakles, rids the world of several dangerous creatures. Kutoyis resembles Herakles in another way as well, for both of these heroes prove their amazing strength just after they are born. According to Greek tradition, Herakles strangles two monstrous vipers while still an infant in his crib, and in the Blackfoot tale, Kutoyis, who is miraculously born from a clot of buffalo blood, grows fully into manhood within four days of his birth. Kutoyis's mission in life is to destroy the evil beings that torment and oppress his people, and thus he journeys about the world in search of various kinds of monsters. He slays a tribe of cruel bears that have enslaved people and a community of huge rattlesnakes that savor human flesh. He also enters the gaping jaws of the hideous Wind Sucker and rescues the people he finds still alive in its stomach by stabbing the monster in its heart. In killing this creature from inside its own body, Kutoyis performs a feat that is also undertaken by Herakles, who only succeeds in slaying the sea monster by climbing in its mouth and then hacking its intestines to pieces. The Blackfoot hero then goes on to encounter other monstrous figures, and, in all, he rids the world of seven kinds of vicious beings during the course of his travels.

Whereas Kutoyis searches out the monstrous beings that endanger his people, the heroes of some myths seek to make a name for themselves by slaying famous monsters. Gilgamesh, the hero of the ancient Mesopotamian epic, longs for both adventure and fame, and therefore he and his companion Enkidu set forth on the long journey that takes them to the land of the cedar forest and the home of Humbaba, the terrifying giant. Humbaba is one of the monsters that guard a precious treasure, and the adventuresome young heroes know that if they can slay the powerful giant, then the mighty trees he protects will be theirs to cut down. A fearsome creature whose face is a mass of coiled intestines, Humbaba is a fire-spewing demon with dragon's teeth and venomous breath. Furthermore, when the giant roars, the earth begins to tremble. Although Humbaba is a most formidable opponent, Gilgamesh is armed with his great ax, the Might of Heroism, and he and Enkidu are protected by Shamash, the god of the sun. Shamash causes eight winds to batter the ferocious monster, and while Humbaba is immobilized by this assault, Gilgamesh strikes the giant with his ax, and Enkidu slices off his hideous head. Gilgamesh and Enkidu then cut down the mighty cedar forest, and when they bring their trophy home to the city of Uruk, they are welcomed there as heroic monster slayers.

PHENOMENA ATTRIBUTED TO MONSTERS

In many cultural traditions the presence of monsters serves to explain the occurrence of particular events. In Russia, for example, the Vodyanoi is said to be the creature responsible for all freshwater drownings. Part man and part fish with scales and a long, green beard, the monster lives in the ponds where it claims its victims. Among the Hausa people of West Africa, a species of creature known as the Bori causes all diseases and misfortunes among human beings. A shape-shifter, the Bori can appear without a head, assume a human shape, or take the form of a giant python. Similarly, the Oni is the monster responsible for disaster and disease in the folklore of Japan, and in the myths of ancient Babylonia, the fabulous hybrid beast Pazuzu is the embodiment of pestilence and plague. Both of these monsters are grotesque in appearance, although the pink or blue Oni is a colorful creature. The flat-faced Oni has a gigantic mouth that extends from ear to ear and horns atop its shaggy head. Pazuzu, a chimera with a dog's head, a scorpion's tail, a lion's paws, and an eagle's feet, has four wings that symbolize the flight of disease that is carried by the wind. The Patupairehe, human-like beings that guard the mountain peaks in the tales of New Zealand's Maori people, sometimes take human lovers, and thus the Maori explain that all albino children are the offspring of these pairings. In Islamic tradition, the invisible Djinn are the creatures responsible for desert whirlwinds and sandstorms, and also for the shooting stars that flash in the heavens.

UNUSUAL FEATURES OF MONSTERS

The monsters of folklore and myth are often interestingly peculiar in their features or behavior. The shape-shifting Ghoul, for instance, can be killed with one mighty blow, but if the Ghoul is struck a second time, it will come back to life. A monster that haunts the Arabian deserts, the Ghoul assumes a variety of shapes as it searches for people to devour; even though it readily takes the form of human beings or animals, its feet are nonetheless always shaped as hooves. The Kuru-Pira, an ogre that lives in the forests of Brazil, is distinctive in that its feet point backward. According to the Desana people, the Kuru-Pira is the animal master, or guardian of all wildlife, and therefore this creature punishes hunters who kill too many animals or fail to show them due respect. Because its footprints are deceiving, the ogre can sneak up on unsuspecting hunters and kill them with its poisonous urine. The Kishi, a monster in myths from Angola, appears at first to be a man. However, the face of a hyena is hidden under the thick hair on the back of its head, and when the Kishi traps a woman, it simply turns its head around and then devours its victim. The Kappa, a water monster from Japanese tradition, is another interesting creature. A chimera with a frog's legs, a monkey's head, and a turtle's shell, the Kappa draws people into the water and then sucks out and consumes their internal organs. The top of the Kappa's head is indented in the shape of a bowl, and the water that the creature carries in this depression provides it with its supernatural strength. To escape the Kappa, a person must bow to the creature, and, when it returns the bow in accordance with Japanese tradition, the source of its strength spills from its head.

VORACIOUS MONSTERS

The large numbers of flesh-eating monsters within myth tradition give expression to people's atavistic fear of being consumed by a wild creature. A particularly insidious example of a monster that preys on human beings can be found in tales told by South Africa's Zulu people. Isitwalangcengce, a beast that resembles a hyena, especially delights in eating human brains. Like the Kappa, Isitwalangcengce has a basket-shaped indentation in its head, and the creature uses this to carry off the young children that it snatches from their mothers. The Al, another monster that stalks women and children, appears in stories from the Armenian tradition. Part human and part animal, the one-eyed Al has brass fingernails, iron teeth, and the tusks of a boar. This creature uses its power to make itself invisible to sneak into houses and attack pregnant women or tiny, helpless infants. The monstrous Al strangles its victims and then removes their livers. Some monsters consume people's spirits rather than their bodies, and stories of vampires or other creatures that take possession of human beings can be found in many cultural traditions. The word *nightmare*, for example, comes from the Germanic tales that recount the exploits of the Mare, a shape-shifting female monster that prowls for its victims during the night. The Mare takes possession of a person's sleep, causing restlessness, pain, and terrifying dreams. Sometimes the creature also visits animals at night, and when a cow has been possessed by the Mare, it produces sour milk.

See also Animals in Myth; Culture Heroes; Etiological Myths; Guardians; Ymir Motif

PRIMAL PARENTS

In the broadest sense, primal parents, or first parents, are the figures throughout myth who give birth to the earliest generation of gods or whose progeny are the first primordial beings, animals, or people to inhabit the world. Furthermore, in the many narratives where a catastrophic flood or similar disaster almost entirely eradicates the earth's population, primal parents are the survivors who give birth to the new race of people who then repopulate the world. As beings that appear near the beginnings of time, primal parents frequently play a significant role in creation myths, and, indeed, in one category of such myths, world parents are the source of the creation of the cosmos. In some myths primal parents are presented as natural elements or forces that give birth to life. For example, in the ancient Mesopotamians' account of creation, primal parents are the very waters from which all life arises. According to this myth, a pantheon of gods is produced by the commingling of primordial waters that take the form of father Apsu, the embodiment of all fresh water, and mother Tiamat, the personification of the salty seas. Similarly, the interactions of other natural forces, in the form of the primal parents yin and yang, are said to be the source of the universe and all it contains in a creation myth that comes from ancient China.

FORMING THE FIRST PARENTS

The primal parents of the people who inhabit the earth are often created by deities who commonly shape them from a natural substance that carries a symbolic significance. In the Hebrew account of creation, for example, Adam and Eve are formed from the clay that represents the fecund earth that is their home, and in

Navajo tradition First Man and First Woman are made from the white and yellow ears of corn that provide people with their staple food. In the myths of some cultures, however, the primal parents are not shaped from a natural substance, but simply grow from it instead. Indeed, in the tale recounted by the ancient Persians, Mashya and Mashyanag, the primal parents of the human race, emerge from a rhubarb plant. In this creation tale the primal parents are not the first living beings to inhabit the earth, for Ahura Mazda, the Wise Lord, originally peoples it with Gayomartan, a perfect being whose metallic body gleams in the sun. When Gayomartan is slain by the evil Angra Mainyu, his shining body becomes the gold and the silver that can be found buried in the ground, and from his semen sprouts a large rhubarb plant whose bifurcated stalks and leaves assume the shapes of the primal parents' bodies. Interestingly, the substance from which Mashya and Mashyanag take their human form is a plant that is often used as a medicinal balm.

EARTH MOTHER AND SKY FATHER

Myths from many cultures posit the original existence of another order of primal parents, or world parents, that most commonly take the forms of earth mother and sky father, and in these narratives the primal parents are indeed the source of all creation. Complementary figures, these primal parents serve to embody a conception of the fertile union of the earth and the sky, the realm of the material and that of the ethereal. In their initial state of primordial unity, the world parents generally represent the presence of chaos, but when earth and sky are differentiated, through the separation of the primal parents, the creation of the world can then fully unfold. In many of the creation myths that feature the motif of the world parents, the task of separating mother earth and father sky falls to the children of their union, but in some myths deities or animals also perform this necessary task. All creation myths symbolically depict the emergence of order from a state of chaos, which is characteristically conceived as the undifferentiated oneness of the primal void, and it is thus when the original parents have been separated and are no longer one that form arises from formlessness and the multiplicity of the cosmos comes fully into being.

In most accounts of the world parents, although by no means in all of them, the earth serves to personify the principles of maternity. As an emblem of the mother, the earth represents the fertile matter that first gives birth to life and that then nurtures and nourishes the fruit of the womb. Perhaps obviously, the representations of earth mother as primal parent suggest a relationship between this mythic figure and the archetypal goddess that has come to be known as the great goddess or the triple goddess. Although theories about the great goddess and her role in early and preliterate agricultural societies are largely based on interpretations of artifacts, primarily the many Paleolithic and Neolithic figurines that depict the female body as a symbol of fertility, students of myth have also discovered vestiges of this prehistoric, archetypal figure, particularly in accounts of the earth mother as world parent. One significant instance, for example, can be found in classical Greek tradition, in the creation myth Hesiod recounts in his *Theogony*. In Hesiod's tale, Gaea, the earth mother, and Uranos, the sky father, are indeed primal parents, but, interestingly, it is Gaea who first emerges from the yawning void that Hesiod calls Chaos, and who then, without partner, gives birth to the sky father who becomes her consort. Gaea, then, is both world mother and mother to the father of the world.

Just as the material earth that gives birth to life and then nurtures it frequently serves as an apt metaphor for the role of primal mother, the sky that surrounds the earth and is the source of energy and light typically symbolizes the role of the world father. On one hand, representations of the primal father as the embodiment of the ethereal serve the necessary purpose of distinguishing the parents; if the power of the mother can be seen in the germinating earth, the power of the father can be expressed by the rays of the sun or by the bolts of lightning that flash across the sky. On the other hand, however, the association of the father with the sky also signifies the ascendancy of the male that occurs with the emergence of patriarchal culture. The sky, after all, transcends the earth and envelopes it in its vast immensity. Furthermore, the sky is the realm of light, whereas the womb of the earth is the realm of darkness. As agricultural communities are supplanted by warrior societies, the primal parent known as the sky father is readily transformed into another familiar figure, the omnipotent sky god who can also take the form of the sun god or the god of storms.

While it is usually the male parent whose power is associated with celestial energy, the Egyptian creation myth that is recorded in the *Pyramid Texts* (ca. 2800 B.C.E.) offers an interesting exception. A complex tale, wherein creation unfolds through a series of stages, the *Pyramid Texts* describe the union and subsequent separation of a sky mother and earth father. Characteristically, chaos (in the form of the Ogdoad, the eight principles of disorder) exists before the time of creation. Creation begins when a primal mound appears on the surface of Nun, the primordial waters of the void. Ra, the sun god, comes into being on the primal mound and then expectorates Shu, the god of the air, and Tefnut, the goddess of moisture. Shu and Tefnut then give birth to Nut, the goddess of the sky, and to Geb, the god of the earth—who themselves eventually become the parents of two pairs of divine twins, Osiris and Isis and Set and Nephthys. As the parents of the twins Osiris, Egypt's first pharaoh, and his sister-wife Isis, Nut and Geb are generally regarded as the primal parents of the Egyptian people.

SEPARATION OF EARTH AND SKY

Before the sky mother and the earth father can give birth to their children, however, they must be separated, for there is no space between them where others could exist. Therefore, their father Shu, assisted by the Ogdoad, hoists Nut to a position where she arches high above Geb, and it is in this pose that the two deities are characteristically represented in Egyptian art. In effecting the separation of the primal parents, the god of the atmosphere provides both the space necessary for his daughter to give birth as well as the air required for all earth's living creatures to breathe. While Nut and Geb are united as one in their loving embrace, the process of creation is interrupted and comes to a stasis. Only when earth and sky are differentiated one from another are these world parents able to participate in the unfolding of creation through the act of bringing forth new life.

Geb, as an earth deity, personifies the impulse to procreate, and Nut, goddess of the heavens, contains within herself all celestial bodies. According to Egyptian tradition, each morning Nut gives birth anew to Ra, and each evening she swallows up the sun again. At night she takes the form of the sacred cow, clothed in the stars of the Milky Way. She plays a significant role in the Egyptian cult of the dead, both as the mother of Osiris, the resurrection god, and also as an emblem herself of a rebirth to a new life. Indeed, the ancient Egyptian coffin is seen as the symbol of heaven, and is thus also regarded as symbolic of the sky goddess herself. In the figure of Nut, as in that of Gaea, myth scholars can also find traces of the great goddess archetype. Just as Gaea exists before she bears the father of their children, Nut also exists before she gives birth to her grandfather, the sun. Scholars therefore speculate that accounts of the sky goddess as mother of the sun long predate the *Pyramid Texts'* depiction of her role as primal parent.

In the Egyptian creation myth, it is the father of the earth and the sky who makes the space between them, but more typically the children of primal parents must find a way to separate them. In the Greek myth, for example, the Titan Kronos, son of Gaea and Uranos, uses a sickle to emasculate the father who has forced his progeny to return to their mother's womb and whose suffocating presence weighs heavily on mother earth. After the maimed sky father has retreated to the outermost edges of the heavens, there is finally space for a second generation to emerge, and Kronos quickly claims his father's place as sky god, marries his sister Rhea, and in time becomes the father of Zeus and Greece's other immortal gods.

A myth from Polynesia offers a particularly fine example of world-parent creation and its link to the separation motif. In the Maori creation myth, existence first emerges from chaos in the form of father Rangi, who represents the sky, and mother Papa, who personifies the earth. These primal parents, however, are joined so tightly together in the primal void of their united existence that their bodies are in fact connected by tendrils and sinews. Trapped in the suffocating darkness between their parents, the six sons that Rangi and Papa engender must find some way to establish a space where they can lead their lives. The sons debate the problem, and Tu, the god of war, argues that their parents should be killed. When Tane, the god of the forest, proposes that Rangi and Papa might be separated rather than needlessly slaughtered, five of the sons attempt in turn to push the sky and earth apart.

Rongo, god of cultivated plants, lacks the strength necessary to succeed in his task. Tangaroa, god of the sea and its animals, and Haumia, god of wild vegetables and plants, also fail in their efforts to detach the sky from the earth. When it is Tu's turn, the ferocious god of war hacks with his ax at the tendons that bind Rangi and Papa together, and the blood that he spills through his efforts becomes the sacred red clay that the Maori people take from the earth. Tu, however, cannot separate his parents either, and therefore Tane steps forward to take the next turn. Planting his shoulders upon the earth and placing his feet up against the sky, Tane, like the trees of his forest realm, slowly and patiently presses upward until finally all of the tendons are torn, and sky and earth lie far apart. Light then appears in the world, freeing Tane and his brothers from the dark void that had once enclosed them. Among the six brothers, only Tawhiri, the god of the winds and storms, fails to rejoice when Tane succeeds in breaking the bonds that have tied Rangi and Papa together. Tawhiri, whose own nature is best suited to a state of chaos, resents the new order that has come into the world along with the emergence of light and space. In his fury he therefore joins his father in the sky and unleashes winds, rains, and hurricanes to batter the earthly realms of his mother and his brothers.

The Maori creation myth is fascinating in yet another respect, for it also presents an interesting variation of the deluge motif. After their separation father sky and mother earth naturally grieve for one another. Father Rangi, in fact, weeps copiously, and soon his tears begin to inundate the earth. Fearing that all of the world will in time be swallowed up by their parents' tears, the sons decide that they will turn their mother over so that she and her beloved can no longer see the sorrow in each other's face. The plan is successful, and the floodwaters eventually subside. Of course Rangi and Papa nevertheless continue to mourn their separation, and from time to time they gently weep: Rangi's tears are said to be the morning dew, while Papa's are the morning mist. And the primal parents' seventh son, nursing at mother Papa's breast when her other children change the position of her body, tumbles into the underworld and then makes that realm his home. Whenever Ruaumoko moves, therefore, the earth begins to quake.

REBIRTH AND REPOPULATION

In many traditions the world is reborn when a second set of primal parents, the survivors of the deluge, reestablish human life after the catastrophe. As in the original creation, order emerges from formlessness when the chaotic waters recede and the primal parents populate the earth. Particularly in those tales where the flood cleanses the world of its corruption, those who are spared by the gods while others are punished represent the promise of a new beginning in a better world. Noah and his family, the flood heroes of Hebrew tradition, number among myth's virtuous survivors, as do Deucalion and Pyrrha in the Greco-Roman story of the deluge. And, in the Mesopotamian account recorded in *Gilgamesh* (ca. 2000 B.C.E.), the wise Utnapishtim and his wife are the only people deemed worthy to be saved from drowning. As the reward for their righteousness or wisdom, the flood heroes of these myths become the primal parents of all succeeding generations. In fact, the Mesopotamian gods' pleasure in discovering that Utnapishtim saves the seeds of all earthly life is such that they not only honor him as the founder of the new race of people, but they also grant him the great gift of immortality.

Interestingly, the primal parents who survive a flood sometimes repopulate the world by unusual means. Deucalion and Pyrrha, for example, create a new race of people by paying homage to their mother earth through a ceremonial ritual: after veiling their eyes, the two throw behind them stones they have gathered, and from these rocks, the bones of mother Gaea, new men and women soon begin to emerge. Born of earth's stones, this race makes claims to be a particularly hardy people. Another remarkable means of producing a new race of human beings appears in the Chinese tale of the flood heroes named after the calabash that saves them. In this story, brother and sister Fu Xi marry after the waters recede, and, when it is time for the primal mother to give birth, a great meatball comes forth from her womb. The husband and wife chop the meatball into numerous pieces and then wrap the portions in bits of paper. When a great wind scatters the papers about the earth, the portions of meatball they contain become the new inhabitants of the world.

See also Creation Myths; Deluge Motif; Separation of Earth and Sky

THE QUEST

The quest motif is central to countless tales of heroic action, and therefore stories of perilous journeys undertaken in pursuit of an important goal recur throughout myth and folklore traditions. The objective of a quest can be either symbolic or actual, but in either case a hero's strength, courage, and spirit are all put to the test during the course of a series of ordeals. In folktales, the quester—who is often an unproven youngest brother—commonly completes a set of tasks that others fail to complete and thereby wins the hand of a beautiful princess, finds the answer to a puzzling riddle, or succeeds in uncovering a rare or hidden treasure. In the accounts of mythic quests, where heroes also often seek a person, an answer, or an object, the journey undertaken is characteristically both an arduous venture and a spiritual voyage that leads to wisdom, self-knowledge, or the hero's redemption. Whereas the heroic questers of fairytales are generally successful in their missions, those of myth tradition do not always achieve the goals they strive toward even though the journeys they embark upon inevitably provide rich experience and enlightenment. In some instances, in fact, the hero's journey is more meaningful or instructive than the actual outcome of the quest. In tales from both myth and folklore, heroic adventurers sometimes receive assistance from animals or other helpers during the course of a quest, and sometimes they use magic in pursuit of their goals.

GILGAMESH

The quest motif lies at the heart of the Mesopotamian epic *Gilgamesh* (ca. 2000 B.C.E.), the world's earliest extended heroic narrative. Indeed, *Gilgamesh* recounts the adventures of a hero who embarks on two related quests whose objectives and outcomes are strikingly different from one another. For the first of his quests, Gilgamesh, the young king of Uruk, journeys to the distant land of the cedar forest because he desires to make a name for himself as a bold monster slayer. Accompanied by Enkidu, his faithful companion, and assisted by Shamash, the god of the sun, Gilgamesh succeeds in killing the giant Humbaba, guardian of the cedar forest, and when he and Enkidu return in triumph from their quest, their fame is assured. Gilgamesh's first journey, in pursuit of adventure and renown, tests the young king's courage and resolve, and, by meeting these tests, Gilgamesh both gains a reputation and acquires the spoils of his victory, the magnificent cedar trees. This first quest, however, is the youthful adventure that serves as the overture to another journey, for, as the epic unfolds, Gilgamesh discovers that he must acknowledge the consequences of his actions.

Soon after Gilgamesh returns to his kingdom, his newly won fame attracts the attention of Ishtar, the great goddess of fertility, and she asks the brave hero to become her husband. Gilgamesh, however, offends the great goddess by refusing her request, and in an act of vengeance Ishtar unleashes the fearsome Bull of Heaven upon the people of Uruk. Of course Gilgamesh and Enkidu, the heroic monster slayers, are called upon to protect their people from this monstrous beast, and, after a fierce battle, they are once again victorious. However, because the two heroes have angered the gods by killing both Humbaba and the Bull of Heaven, the deities demand retribution for these insults, and thus Enkidu, the king's beloved companion, becomes sick and dies. Grief-stricken over the loss of his friend and haunted by his great fears of his own mortality, Gilgamesh sets forth alone on a second quest, this time in search of the secret of eternal life. To find the knowledge that he seeks, Gilgamesh must undertake a dangerous journey to reach the home of his ancestors Utnapishtim and his wife, the immortal survivors of the great flood that was earlier sent by the gods to destroy humankind. During this second venture, therefore, the hero is seeking both a person and the wisdom that he possesses.

After wandering for many days through grass-filled plains and searing deserts, Gilgamesh finally reaches mountainous terrain and meets with his first obstacle, a pair of ferocious lions. The hero gathers his strength, slays the wild beasts, and then makes clothing from their skins. Although Gilgamesh's strength and determination are tested throughout the course of his travels, he also encounters figures that offer him advice or lend him assistance. For example, when he comes to Mount Mashu, Shamash's home, he finds that its entrance is guarded by the terrifying scorpion people who possess the power to kill with their gaze, but instead of striking him dead, these demons praise the courage that has brought him to a place no other mortal has ever visited and then allow him to enter the dark cavern that passes through the mountain. Gilgamesh gropes his way through twelve leagues of utter, suffocating blackness before he finally emerges, haggard, in a garden where sparkling fruits gleam in the colors of all jewels. A glittering sea lies beyond the beautiful garden, and when Gilgamesh travels to its shores, he meets another helpful assistant: Siduri, the ale mistress who lives beside the sea, wisely counsels the weary traveler to return to his kingdom and take joy in his mortal life, but when Gilgamesh insists on continuing his journey, Siduri advises him to seek the help of the boatman Urshanabi. Gilgamesh must complete an arduous task before the ferryman will guide him across the perilous waters of death, for Urshanabi demands that he cut down 120 immense trees to use as punting poles to propel their boat.

Using these poles, Gilgamesh and Urshanabi are able to cross the sea without touching its deadly waters, and thus they finally make their way to Utnapishtim's home.

Gilgamesh is one of the heroic questers who does not achieve his original goal, for after he tells Utnapishtim that his purpose is to restore Enkidu to life and to find immortality for himself, he fails the single test that the old man asks him to perform. To prove that he has the strength of a god and is not subject to mortal weakness, Gilgamesh must remain awake for the duration of a week; however, no sooner does the weary traveler accept this challenge than he indeed succumbs to a deep, unbroken sleep. When Utnapishtim at last wakes him on his seventh day of slumber and Gilgamesh then learns that the gift of immortality cannot be granted him, his kindly host reminds him of the great gifts of youth, strength, and friendship that he already possesses. Utnapishtim echoes the sage words of Siduri by encouraging the brave hero to savor the life that he has been granted and then sends him home to his kingdom with another precious gift, a magical plant that can restore youth and vitality. Yet Gilgamesh is also denied the consolation of this treasure, for a serpent steals the wonderful plant during the hero's homeward journey and thereafter all snakes use its magical power to renew themselves and shed their old skins. Although Gilgamesh possesses neither immortality nor the restorative plant when he returns to Uruk, by acknowledging the limits of a mortal being's life, he has nevertheless gained the maturity and wisdom to finally understand the great value of all he does possess.

SEEKING THAT WHICH HAS BEEN LOST

It is the terrible experience of loss—his loss of Enkidu and his fear of losing his own life—that impels Gilgamesh to embark upon his second quest, and thus this early Mesopotamian myth introduces a theme that is common to many tales wherein a quester searches for someone or something that is lost. In Egyptian tradition, for example, it is the loss of her beloved husband Osiris, murdered by his brother Set, that moves the goddess Isis to undertake two grueling journeys in search of his remains, and in the myths of ancient Greece, Orpheus sets forth on a perilous trip to the underworld to try to recover the wife that he has lost. Indeed, several tales from myth tradition describe characters' journeys to the dreaded land of the dead in search of family members who have perished. In a story told by North America's Iroquois people, the brave warrior Sayadio travels to the realm of the spirits to look for his younger sister, and in Indian tradition, the wise and generous Savitiri succeeds in persuading Yama, the lord of the dead, to release her husband from his underworld domain. Mythic characters also search for objects that are lost, and medieval tales from Europe recount the exploits of those many knights who embark upon sacred quests to find the Holy Grail. In Virgil's great Roman epic, it is the magnificent city of Troy that is lost, and Aeneas is the hero who undertakes his long and perilous journey so that he might found a new Trojan empire.

Like Gilgamesh, other questers who seek to recover that which is lost encounter obstacles that test their courage and determination. After Isis finally finds Osiris's corpse entombed in a massive tree within a distant land, Set once more steals the body, and, after chopping it into fourteen pieces, he scatters his brother's remains throughout the Egyptian kingdom. To restore her husband's body and resurrect him as the ruler of the dead, Isis must therefore summon her strength and will to begin her quest again. The journeys undertaken by Sayadio, Aeneas, and the knights who seek the Holy Grail are all ventures that extend over the course of many years and thus repeatedly test these questers' purpose and resolve. Indeed, to pursue his mission to its end, Aeneas must reluctantly forsake the woman that he loves, and when he does indeed leave Dido behind, she kills herself in her grief. Gilgamesh does not succeed in his efforts to restore Enkidu to life, and like the Mesopotamian hero, Orpheus too fails a test he must perform to free his wife from the underworld. When the loving husband proves himself unable to wait until Eurydice returns to earth before turning around to look at her, his moment of weakness costs him the goal of his quest. Savitiri, on the other hand, answers the questions that Yama poses to test her sincerity with such remarkable wisdom that the lord of the dead not only restores her husband to her, but also honors her virtues with his blessing.

IRISH AND GREEK ODYSSEYS

The Irish hero Mael Duin and the Greek warrior Odysseus are two other questers whose journeys take them months or years to complete and whose adventures in pursuit of their goals loom larger in the telling of their stories than do the outcomes of their quests. Indeed, when Mael Duin finally realizes the opportunity to achieve his objective, that of exacting revenge upon the warriors who have slain his father on the battlefield, he chooses to forgive them instead of taking their lives. As recounted in the *Odyssey* (eighth century B.C.E.), Homer's great epic, Odysseus's goal throughout the course of his adventures is simply to find his way from the ruins of Troy back to his kingdom in Ithaca, where his wife Penelope patiently awaits him. Accompanied by their crews, both of these adventurers make their journeys by sea, and as the winds and tides carry their ships to strange lands or magical isles, the seafaring heroes experience the many marvels of their voyages of discovery. Like those of other questers, these heroes' journeys are fraught with peril, and Mael Duin and Odysseus both encounter temptations that threaten to divert them from pursuing their goals. In the end, however, each completes his quest and returns home from his wandering with many tales to tell.

Voyage to the Otherworld

When Mael Duin sets forth to avenge his father's death, he heeds the words of a Druid who advises him to take with him a crew of no more than seventeen men. The quester's plans quickly go awry, however, when his three cousins swim out to sea and ask to join the expedition. Fearing that his cousins might drown, Mael Duin brings them on board and continues his journey to the nearby island where his father's enemies live. Just as he reaches its shores, however, a mighty storm sweeps the boat out to sea and carries Mael Duin and his crew into the uncharted waters of the Otherworld. A mysterious realm of exotic islands, the Otherworld is populated by giants, terrifying beasts, and many other kinds of magical beings, and it is here that the voyagers' great adventures begin. Although they dare not go ashore on some of the islands, Mael Duin and his crew visit thirty different places during the course of their travels and successfully elude dangerous predators that include gigantic ants, a monstrous horse with the legs of a dog, demons who race on horseback, flesh-eating blacksmiths, and ferocious, flaming pigs. The voyagers also observe many fabulous sights and visit gorgeous palaces that hold marvelous treasures. On one island they discover a beautiful crystal bridge, and on another, birds with human voices. On one island an immense eight-sided silver pillar rises from the sea to disappear into the heavens, and a waterspout full of salmon arches like a rainbow over another isle.

Temptations

Mael Duin's boat first goes off course when he adds his cousins to its crew, and on the tenth island that he visits, he loses one of his cousins. A sumptuous palace filled with treasures and inhabited by cats stands on this island, and Mael Duin's eldest cousin cannot resist his desire to steal a precious necklace. Although the cats do not harm the other voyagers, they swarm upon the thief and, glowing like hot coals, they reduce him to cinders. A second cousin leaves the crew when the voyagers stop on an island that is inhabited only by sorrowful people. Mael Duin attempts to rescue his relative from the crowd of weeping mourners all dressed in black, but he is unable to do so and must therefore leave him behind. It is Mael Duin himself who is reluctant to leave the island that is the home of many beautiful maidens who promise the voyagers eternal youth and freedom from all cares, for he becomes the lover of the maidens' queen. When his companions become homesick and beg to leave the island, Mael Duin finally agrees to go with them, but just as his boat is heading out to sea, the queen casts a magic ball of thread into the hand of her lover. Mael Duin is unable to let go of the ball, and the queen then draws the boat back to the shore. Finally, after nine months have passed and the voyagers have made numerous attempts to resume their journey, another member of the crew catches hold of the queen's ball. When the voyagers quickly cut off the hand that clutches the ball, Mael Duin and his companions take up their quest again and soon reach an island that is inhabited by crowds of joyful, laughing people. Mael Duin's third cousin goes ashore to explore this enticing place, and after he joins in the laughter and singing and then fails to return to his traveling companions, the men depart without him.

A Hero's Homecoming

After losing his three cousins, Mael Duin commands a crew of seventeen, the number originally stipulated by the Druid, and he is therefore able to chart his course once more and thus turn back toward Ireland. As the voyagers travel homeward, they pass the Blessed Isle, the land of the dead, but they do not go ashore there. They do pause, however, to speak with a hermit who sits alone on a rock in the sea, and this lonely figure promises them all safe passage if Mael Duin will relent and offer forgiveness to the men who killed his father many years before. Soon after they bid farewell to the hermit, one of Ireland's falcons appears in the sky, and by following its flight, the voyagers make their way to the island home of the very warriors that Mael Duin seeks. These men welcome the weary travelers as great heroes and beg Mael Duin to forgive the great injury they did him by killing his father. When he hears these words of regret, the avenger's anger indeed fades away, and after he makes peace with his old foes, they prepare a magnificent feast in honor of his heroism.

Another Violent Storm

Mael Duin comes close to realizing the goal of his quest just before the fierce storm drives his boat to the Otherworld, and Odysseus, too, comes within tantalizing sight of his goal just before tumultuous winds carry him off to distant lands. After leaving Troy, battling with the Ciconians, and escaping the lands of both the Lotus-Eaters and the Cyclopes, Odysseus leads his fleet to the realm of Aeolus, the guardian of the winds, and there he is given a bag of winds to use during his journey homeward. The breezes indeed carry the ships to the shores of Ithaca, where the smoke that rises from the chimneys of Odysseus's palace is visible to all, but while their leader is asleep, the curious sailors open Aeolus's bag and release all the winds at once. A violent tempest is produced by the furiously churning winds, and Odysseus's ships are blasted far out to sea once more. The voyagers encounter many great dangers as they continue on their journey, and, unlike Mael Duin, Odysseus loses his entire crew before he reaches Ithaca again, ten long years after he first sets sail from Troy.

Similar Temptations and Adventures

Interestingly, some of the adventures experienced by Odysseus and his men are similar to those of Mael Duin and his crew, both in the nature of the creatures they encounter and in the characteristics of the strange lands that they visit. Both groups of voyagers, for example, travel to places where the exotic fruits they consume produce intoxicating effects. When three of Odysseus's sailors eat the fruit that the Lotus-Eaters offer them, they lose all memory of their previous lives and homes and long only to remain in the company of their hosts and to eat of their fruit. Odysseus, who resists the temptation to taste the alluring fruit, rescues his companions before retreating in haste from the bewitching land of the Lotus-Eaters. The Irish voyagers also visit an island where the very aroma of its fruit causes a hypnotic drowsiness. Mael Duin eats the inviting berries and falls into a deep trance from which his men cannot awaken him, but, when he finally stirs, he is utterly refreshed. These voyagers soon discover that by mixing the fruit with large quantities of water, they can enjoy a delicious wine. Both groups of travelers also journey to lands inhabited by giants intent upon devouring them and must employ trickery to make an escape. After Odysseus blinds Polyphemus, the shepherd of the fearsome, one-eyed Cyclopes, he sneaks his men past the waiting monster by lashing them beneath the stomachs of the giant's sheep. Mael Duin also escapes hungry giants by means of deceit, for when he sees the monstrous blacksmiths waiting for his crew to land on their island, he quietly instructs his men to begin rowing backward while keeping the front of their boat pointed to the shore. The giant blacksmiths are indeed fooled by this ploy, and, like Polyphemus, they angrily hurl stones at the escaping voyagers.

Like Mael Duin, Odysseus is tempted to abandon his quest when he visits the kingdom of an enchanting woman and becomes her lover. Indeed, the Greek hero and his men remain in Aeaea at the palace of the sorceress Circe for an entire year before Odysseus, with Circe's assistance, at last resumes his journey. As it happens, Odysseus spends seven more years with another lover as well, for when his ship sinks and he is rescued from the sea by the nymph Calypso, she seduces him and then makes him her captive on the island of Ogygia. Finally, with the help of the goddess Athena, Odysseus is allowed to set sail once more, and after surviving yet another shipwreck, he makes his way home to Ithaca, where one last task awaits the mighty hero before he can realize his long journey's goal. To win back his beloved wife, Odysseus must pass the test that she devises, for after resisting for twenty years the entreaties of the many suitors who seek to replace her husband, Penelope finally agrees to marry the man who can string Odysseus's immense bow and shoot an arrow through the holes of twelve axes lined up in a row. Not one of the suitors can even bend his bow, but Odysseus, of course, performs this task with ease, dispatches all the troublesome suitors, and spends the rest of his long life at Penelope's side.

QUESTERS' GOALS

As accounts of the journeys undertaken by Gilgamesh, Isis, or Odysseus suggest, the heroes of myth embark upon their quests for many different reasons. For example, the great Greek hero Herakles travels throughout the world performing his labors because he is seeking personal redemption. By accepting tasks that serve the welfare of others, Herakles hopes to atone for having killed his own sons in a fit of madness. The Greek hero Jason travels to the distant kingdom of Colchis to secure the Golden Fleece in order to win back the throne stolen from his father and is successful in this quest because Medea helps him. Theseus, yet another Greek hero, journeys to Crete for the purpose of saving Athens' youth from the scourge of the Minotaur, and, with the help of Ariadne, he too achieves his goal. In Indian tradition, Siddhartha, the Buddha, undertakes a lifelong spiritual quest in which his goal is the enlightenment he finally achieves while sitting beneath the Bodhi Tree. While Gilgamesh does not set forth with the purpose of pursuing the youth-restoring plant that he finds and then loses, many other mythic questers search for a fountain of youth, and, indeed, one of Mael Duin's companions is fortunate enough to happen upon such a treasure during the voyagers' journey through the Otherworld: after bathing in a magical lake on one of the islands, Diurán, a member of the crew, remains young and strong for the rest of his long life.

Although Diurán preserves his youth by bathing in the refreshing waters of a lake, Celtic-Irish mythology also includes stories of questers' journeys to the Otherworld in search of a cauldron of rejuvenation that is sometimes called the Fountain of Health, and many scholars find a link between these ancients myths and the numerous accounts from the Middle Ages of the quest for the Holy Grail. Indeed, in the many versions of the Grail myth wherein the wounded Fisher King possesses the sacred vessel, its healing properties can restore the maimed ruler and his devastated kingdom. Represented in the tales popular throughout medieval Christian Europe as either the cup used by Jesus at the Last Supper or as the vessel used by Joseph of Arimathea to gather Jesus's blood, the Grail is the symbol of grace that is sought by knights determined to prove their worthiness and courage. Many tests await the knights who search for the Holy Grail, for the mysterious castle in which it is housed is difficult to find, and the journey they must undertake is a perilous one that takes them through many strange and distant lands.

THE QUEST FOR THE HOLY GRAIL

In most versions of the myth, a young, innocent knight happens suddenly upon the Grail Castle during the course of his long and perilous journey and gratefully accepts the hospitality that is offered him. The castle is the home of the Fisher King, ruler of the Waste Land, and the knight is quick to observe that his host is suffering from a painful wound and that his kingdom is in ruins. The young knight does not ask the Fisher King about the trouble that has come to him, nor does he realize that he is in the castle that houses the Grail until the sacred object is brought into his presence during a great feast. Because he is amazed by the spectacle that lies before him, or because he is too polite to question his host, or because he is too inexperienced to comprehend the significance of his circumstances, the young knight remains silent throughout the Procession of the Grail, and therefore when he awakes the next morning, it is to the discovery that the castle has vanished and the Grail is gone. In these stories, the knight who sees the Grail must demonstrate his worthiness by expressing his sympathy for the Fisher King and his awe of the sacred relic in the form of questions, for if he dares to speak, the king will be healed and his lands will be restored. To complete his quest, the knight who fails this test must gain wisdom from his experience and courageously journey forth once more in search of the Holy Grail.

See also Culture Heroes; The Underworld

THE RAINBOW

The manifestation of the rainbow, which is both a dramatic and an ephemeral event, figures in the myths of most cultural traditions, and several patterns emerge among ancient people's various interpretations of this natural phenomenon. The rainbow, perhaps because it appears suddenly and arches across the sky, is frequently associated with divinities and, as is the case in the story of Noah's flood, is sometimes regarded as the emblem of a divine covenant or sign. As a sign that appears in the heavens, the rainbow can be either propitious or sinister, for in some cultures it is linked to the underworld symbolism embodied in the figure of a creator serpent. Because the rainbow arches between the heavens and the earth, it is sometimes conceived as a bridge that, much like the World Tree, links these separate realms. In other myths the shape of the rainbow inspires its conception as an archer's bow or as a goddess's necklace strung with multicolored jewels.

EMBLEM OF THE GODS

In some traditions the rainbow is associated with particular deities or with divine animals. In Chinese culture, where the dragon is regarded as a water creature, the rainbow unites the heavens with the earth by serving as a symbol of the benevolent sky dragon that bestows the gift of rain. In Incan tradition the rainbow is associated with the sun god Inti, and in Greek myth the rainbow goddess is Iris, the divine messenger. Originally a weather deity, a goddess of the wind and rain, Iris is nonetheless best known as the celestial messenger who serves both Hera and Zeus. In light of her earlier incarnation as a weather god, it is especially fitting that Zeus sends Iris to summon Demeter when she, grieving over the disappearance of Persephone, causes the crops on the earth to wither and die. In some myths Iris is depicted as the personification of the rainbow itself, and in others the rainbow serves as the road she travels to deliver her messages. In either case the rainbow serves as an appropriate emblem for the messenger whose duties take her back and forth between the heavens and the earth. As messenger, the rainbow goddess is the harbinger of disaster as well as the instrument of good will. While Iris saves humankind from starvation by arranging the reconciliation of Demeter and Zeus, her presence, according to Ovid, also presages the mighty flood that only Deucalion and Pyrrha manage to survive.

The personification of a celestial deity in some cultures, the rainbow is sometimes said to be a member of a family of gods. Among Australia's Karnai people, for example, the rainbow is Binbeal, the son of Bunjil, the supreme deity and the creator of human beings. Australia's Kaitish people regard the rainbow as the son of the rain, and because the son attempts to prevent his father from falling to the earth, the people make ritualistic efforts to lure the rainbow from the sky when a rainfall is needed. In Andean tradition the rainbow is the husband of Mama Kilya, the goddess of the moon, and among the Finns and the Lapps, the rainbow is Rauni, a fertility goddess and the wife of Ukko, the mighty Thunder God. According to ancient Tibetan tradition, Shenrap, the founder of the Bon religion, first appears on the earth in the form of a rainbow.

THE RAINBOW SERPENT

In myths from Australia, Africa, India, Asia, Eastern Europe, and North and South America, the rainbow is associated with another animal, a great serpent symbolic of both water and the earth's fertility. Among Australia's indigenous peoples, the ancestral spirit of the rainbow serpent is linked to springs, waterholes, and winding streams and can be seen as the rainbow itself when the mighty snake arches upward to drink from the sky. The rainbow serpent, whose powers can be either benevolent or destructive, often plays a role in stories of the deluge or in tales of creation. In the tradition of the Djauan people, for example, the rainbow snake named Kurrichalpongo twists and turns to carve out the shape of the Wilton River and then floods the land to sweep away the rivals of the Djauan. In another tale the rainbow snake known as Ngalyod devours three birds that then peck a hole through its stomach to emerge as human beings. Yurlunggur, the rainbow serpent of the Yolngu people, is a creator deity who also forms features of the earth's landscape by carving out a vast river valley. The rainbow snake is known by many names within Australian tradition, and the tales of several peoples describe how this ancestral figure swallows the first people and then later spits them out to populate the world.

The figure of the serpent is also associated with the rainbow in parts of Africa, and some peoples, including the Zulu, recount stories in which the rainbow swallows cattle or devours human beings; among these peoples the rainbow signals danger, for it is thought that the giant serpent comes out to feed at the end of a storm. Among the Bantu-speaking peoples, however, the serpent is regarded as the beneficent bringer of rain, and in these traditions people of high social status often claim to be descendents of the rainbow. Although the rainbow serpent is sometimes revered as a culture hero or as a healer or is associated with creation, in the myths of the Luba people of central Africa, Nkongolo, the Rainbow King, is a cruel and merciless tyrant. The many stories of the Rainbow King recount his incestuous relationships with his twin sisters and his futile attempt to build a tower to heaven so that he might achieve immortality. Although many of his people are killed when the tower collapses, Nkongolo's own undoing comes about when he tries to murder a young man whose skill at running and dancing is greater than his own. The Rainbow King flees when the young hero, Kalala Ilunga, pursues him with an army, but his sisters reveal his hiding place and he is beheaded. According to the Luba, Nkongolo's spirit appears in the form of a monstrous serpent that can be seen as the rainbow in the sky.

While the association between the rainbow and the giant snake is in part evoked by the rainbow's shape, the fact that the serpent is commonly regarded as a water creature is also significant and provides an obvious link between the image in the sky and the source of the earth's life-sustaining rain. Indeed, in tales from Eastern Europe, the serpent as rainbow circulates earth's waters as it sucks up moisture from rivers, lakes, and seas and then spews it back upon the land as the falling rain. The Chinese dragon, a creature that is closely related to the serpent, also serves to link earth and heaven in this way. In Ecuador, the Canelos Quichua describe how the giant anaconda connects the earth's rivers with the sky when it assumes the form of the rainbow, and the figure of the serpent appears as well in myths from North American traditions. The Shoshone people, for example, regard the sky itself as an immense vault of ice, and whenever the great snake, which appears as the rainbow, rubs against the heaven, pieces of ice fall to the earth as the rain or snow.

SIGN FROM THE GODS

Celestial phenomena such as an eclipse or a bolt of lightning are sometimes interpreted as supernatural messages, and the rainbow, too, is regarded in some myths as a sign from the gods. When seen as a covenant, a heavenly message for those on the earth, the rainbow is a recurring feature in accounts of the flood. In the Hebrew story of the deluge, for example, the rainbow is symbolic of the promise to Noah and his descendents that never again will the world be completely inundated. In the Mesopotamian story of the flood recorded in *Gilgamesh* (ca. 2000 B.C.E.), the goddess Ishtar holds up her jeweled necklace after the waters have receded and promises that as long as she wears this gift from the sky god, she will never forget the time of the great flood. In the tale of the flood told by the people of North America's Yellowstone Valley, only those who are sheltered beneath the skin of a great white buffalo manage to survive. When the rains stop and the sun strikes the buffalo skin, it shrivels and shrinks until it becomes a rainbow arching across the sky. Formed from the sacred buffalo skin, the rainbow is a reminder of the Great Spirit's command that the people of the earth respect all the animals and live in harmony with them.

BRIDGES

In myths from several traditions, the rainbow is the bridge between the earth and the sky or between the world of human beings and the realm of the gods. Called

Bifrost in the Norse tradition, the rainbow bridge connects Asgard, the home of the gods, with Midgard, the land where people live. Heimdall, the sentinel of the gods, stands guard over Bifrost, the bridge that fallen warriors cross when they join the gods who gather in Valhalla. The rainbow serves a similar function in myths from Japan, where it is known as the Floating Bridge of Heaven. In this tradition the rainbow links the High Plain of Heaven, the home of the sky deities, with the Central Land of the Reed Plain, the world of the earth. As recounted in the *Kojiki* (A.D. 712) and elsewhere, Izanagi and Izanami—the first of the celestial divinities to dwell upon the earth—stand on the rainbow while they create a new home for themselves on the surface of the primordial ocean that lies beneath the bridge. Using the ornate spear that he has carried from the heavens, Izanagi stirs the primal waters. Then, when he raises the spear, the congealed drop that falls from its tip becomes the first of the islands that give form to the Central Reed Plain.

The rainbow also serves as a bridge in legends from Hawaii as well as in the myths of New Zealand's Maori people. According to these traditions, the souls of the dead pass over the rainbow bridge to enter paradise. In a story told by Africa's Dogon people, for whom the blacksmith is an especially important figure, the first smith carries his hammer and his anvil with him when he travels from the heaven to the earth on the rainbow bridge. The Navajo also recount tales of the rainbow bridge, and in one of them the twin sons of First Woman cross the Grand Canyon by using the bridge. In search of their fathers, the twins also journey to the end of the rainbow bridge to reach Sun-God's Turquoise House in the middle of the Great Water. The twins' use of the rainbow bridge to complete their heroic quest resembles the way the bridge is used in yet another cultural tradition. According to the Buryat people of Siberia, shamans seeking wisdom and the power to heal must travel the rainbow bridge to reach the spiritual realm.

ARCHER'S BOW OR SPARKLING JEWELS

While many people see a serpent in the shape of the rainbow, to others it resembles an archer's bow or a necklace made of jewels. In India the rainbow is the bow of Indra, the storm god, and among the Maori it is the weapon of Tu, the fierce god of war. On occasion the rainbow is described in Norse tradition as the bow of Thor—the fertility god who, like Indra, presides over thunder, lightning, and storms. Another weather deity, Ukko, the Finnish Thunder God, uses the rainbow to launch arrows that are bolts of lightning. In Hebrew tradition Yahweh is sometimes represented as carrying a bow, and the image of a rainbow hanging from the clouds is interpreted as a sign that Yahweh is not angry. Both the shape and the colors of the rainbow figure in its conception as a necklace strung with precious gems. Ishtar's necklace is the gift of her father Anu, the god of the sky, storms, and wind, and yet another daughter of the wind, the Norse goddess Freyja, also possesses a necklace that is sometimes said to be the rainbow in the sky. In Basque tradition, Mari, the fabulously bejeweled Queen of Heaven, appears as the rainbow.

COLORS

While several distinct patterns emerge within myth tradition's accounts of the rainbow, there are also idiosyncratic interpretations of its significance. For North

America's Mojave people, the colors of the rainbow represent a series of charms the creator deity must invoke before he can bring a rainstorm to its end. In Buddhist tradition the rainbow signifies the seven-colored ladder of the path to paradise, and in both Hindu and Buddhist Tantric traditions, it is in the light of the rainbow that earthly life is revealed to be an insubstantial illusion. In Christian tradition, the rainbow's colors are symbolic of the Holy Spirit's seven gifts to the church, the seven sacraments. Among the followers of Tibet's Bon religion, the *dmu*, the rainbow that intermittently appears and then vanishes, represents the fragile thread that links the heaven and the earth, and in Bon ceremonies the *dmu* is symbolically retied. The rainbow also plays a role in the tradition of alchemy, where it is said that the appearance of its colors signals the transformation of base metal into gold. According to a tale told by the Wik Kalkan people of Australia, red, the color thought to be the most vivid of the rainbow's hues, is added to heaven's arc to symbolize the menstrual blood that nurtures new life.

FORTUNE

The rainbow plays a role in folklore tradition as well as in the myths of many different cultures. Perhaps because of its association with the fertility of rainfall, the rainbow is often thought to be the source of a great treasure—throughout Europe, folk tradition holds that a pot of gold lies buried at the end of the rainbow. According to another European tradition, a person who walks under a rainbow or drinks water from a spring at its end will undergo a change of sex. In Africa, where the great serpent comes out to feed after a storm, it is thought to be dangerous to point a finger at the rainbow, and in Asia it is said that the person who steps on the end of the rainbow will be drawn up into the sky and then swept away. The rainbow can be a sign of either bad fortune or good luck, and in some folk traditions the bow that arches over water is seen as an ill omen, whereas the rainbow that touches upon the land is regarded as a favorable sign. By some accounts the presence of a double rainbow signals the arrival of sunny weather, but in China the more brilliant of the pair is said to be the male rainbow while the secondary arc represents the female; in Germany, the fainter rainbow in a pair is said to be the handiwork of the devil.

See also Deluge Motif; Messengers

SACRED MOUNTAINS

The mountain, one of the most dramatic features of the natural landscape, is revered in numerous cultural traditions. Reaching upward toward heaven, the mountain symbolizes spiritual ascent and is often regarded as the meeting place of the heavens and the earth. In the myths of certain cultures, the mountain is the *axis mundi*, the center of the world, and in other traditions sacred mountains are the pillars that hold the sky above the earth or support the world. Generally represented as holy places, the mountains of myths are frequently the homes of weather gods and other deities or the special places on earth where the gods make themselves manifest to mortal beings. Many stories tell of how people ascend sacred mountains to communicate with the gods or to receive revelations from them. In the tales of several traditions, ritual sacrifices are performed on the tops of mountains. In other narratives, people make pilgrimages to sacred mountains to seek spiritual enlightenment or to purify themselves. Mountains, furthermore, figure prominently in stories of the deluge, for those who find safety in an ark or a boat usually come ashore on a sacred peak.

While the mountains of a few myths are imaginary places, most accounts of sacred mountains refer to actual sites. The familiar image of a mountain veiled in heaven's clouds understandably inspires veneration within many traditions, but so too do such massive outcroppings of rock as Australia's Uluru (Ayer's Rock) or Wyoming's Devil's Tower among those peoples who live on the plains. Volcanic mountains, whose destructive power is often understood to express the displeasure of the gods, can inspire fear as well as veneration. For example, among the Aeta people of the Philippines, Mount Pinatubo is known as Apo Mamalyari (Father Creator). When the volcano erupted in 1991, the Aeta elders recognized that deforestation, geothermal drilling, and other acts of intrusion on their sacred mountain had angered the creator god. The Aeta therefore regard the eruption of the mountain as the means by which the gods punish those who desecrate the land.

In many cultures the sacred mountain performs a symbolic function strikingly similar to that of the World Tree, which characteristically links the earth with the sky or unites the three realms of heaven, earth, and underworld. In fact, the shape of the mountain, that of a pyramid, resembles the inverted cosmic tree described in Indian tradition. From a point high in the heavens, both the mountain and the inverted tree spread outward like the rays of the sun to embrace the earth. Both the sacred mountain and the cosmic tree are emblems of stability, and, like the top of the World Tree, the summit of the cosmic mountain is always said to be the highest place on earth. The eagle, king of the birds, often roosts at the crown of the universal tree or on *mons veneris*, the sacred mountain.

TEMPLES

In *The Myth of the Eternal Return* (1954), Mircea Eliade observes that the world's temples and holy towers are humanly constructed extensions of the concept of a sacred mountain. Like the mountain, these structures occupy a position central to their worlds and represent a place where earth and heaven meet. Indeed, ziggurats, cathedrals, pyramids, stupas, and pagodas are all mountain-shaped, and the traditional Japanese pagoda is built with seven stories that represent the seven stages of spiritual ascent. Egypt's pyramids, Mesoamerica's stepped pyramids, and Indonesia's Borobudur temple are among the many other examples of mountain-shaped structures that can be found around the globe. As Eliade further notes, the metaphoric relationship between the temple and the mountain can also be seen in the names of many temples, including the ancient Babylonian "House of the Mount of All Lands" or the contemporary mosque in Jerusalem known as the "Temple of the Mount." Not only do many temples carry a reference to a mountain in their names, but many are also built on the tops of natural or artificial hills.

PRIMAL MOUNDS

While the symbolic significance of the sacred mountain resembles that of the World Tree, the mountain can also be seen as an extension of the concept of the primal mound, the life-bearing earth that rises above the primordial waters in many creation myths. In Egyptian tradition, for example, the sun god Ra emerges from a golden egg that rests upon the primal mound, and scholars have therefore proposed that Egypt's mountainous pyramids represent the original primal mound. The mound, a mountain in miniature, is an elevation that signifies spiritual ascent not only in the form of Egypt's pyramids, but in other cultural artifacts as well. In addition to mountain-shaped temples or towers, ancient peoples also constructed monumental earthworks in the form of mounds. Indeed, England's Silbury Hill, the largest prehistoric mound in the British Isles, covers five acres and rises to an elevation of 130 feet. The artificial hills built by North America's mound-building cultures, the Adena, the Hopewell, and the Mississippians, apparently served as sacred places used for both worship and the burial of the dead.

HOME OF THE GODS

Sacred mountains are the dwelling places of the gods in a large number of cultural traditions. Mount Olympus, the highest peak in mainland Greece, is famous as the traditional home of the pantheon that bears its name (the Olympians), but other mountains are also significant in myths from Greece, a land of many mountains. For example, the Muses—the nine goddesses who inspire the work of artists, historians, and astronomers—are said to reside on either Mount Helicon or on Mount Parnassus. In Hindu tradition, Mount Kailash, a Himalayan peak, is the home of Shiva, who sits atop the mountain supporting the entire cosmos through the power of his will. Mount Alburz, described in ancient Persian myths as the first mountain to exist, is the home of Mithra, god of the sun. In Chinese tradition, Mount Kunlun, one of five sacred mountains and the source of the Yellow River, is revered as the dwelling place of the Lord of the Sky, the Lord of the Rain, and the Queen Mother of the West. Another sacred mountain, a volcano on the island of Bali, is said to have been created by the Hindu gods who moved there from Java when it turned to the Islam faith during the seventeenth century. Shrines dedicated to Gunung Agung, the "Great Mountain," can indeed be found in all Balinese temples.

The Mount Olympus that served ancient Greeks as a natural defense against invasions from the north becomes an imaginary place in the myths that describe it as the home of the gods. In these accounts, the Olympians live in brass houses made by Hephaistos and wear clothing woven by Athena and the Three Graces. They feast upon ambrosia and nectar at the golden tables in the palace of Zeus. Similarly, the Mount Kunlun of Chinese tradition is an imaginary place originally inspired by the Kunlun Range in western China. The mythical mountain where gods reside is described as towering nine levels high and containing doors in its side through which the winds blow. The Queen Mother's peach tree, the Tree of Immortality, grows in a garden on the mountain's slopes, and the red water that flows from Mount Kunlun bestows immortality upon those who drink it. Scholars have theorized that myths associated with Mount Kunlun and also with Mount Kailash in Tibet might well have been influenced by accounts of Mount Meru, the mythological sacred mountain of Indian tradition.

Perhaps the best known of the figurative sacred mountains, Mount Meru (or Sumeru) is important to followers of Hinduism, Buddhism, Jainism, and the Tibetan Bon religion. In all of these traditions, Meru is conceived as the center of the cosmos, with the layers of heaven rising above it and the layers of hell lying below it. Sometimes described as a golden mountain, Meru is said to be the paradise that is the home, in different accounts, of Vishnu, Indra, or Brahma. Mount Meru is always the world axis, and therefore the polestar shines directly above its peak. The mountain is sometimes described as rising from an immense plain and sometimes as emerging from an ocean of milk. In the accounts of the Shan people of Burma, Meru rests on the back of a gigantic fish. Qaf, the sacred mountain of Islamic tradition, offers another example of a conceptualized image of the mountain. Unlike Meru, which is the navel of the world, Qaf completely surrounds the earth, with Mecca at its navel.

REVELATIONS AND PILGRIMAGES

Not only the homes of deities, sacred mountains are also the sites of revelations and the objects of pilgrimages. In myth, the ascent of the holy mountain is a spiritual journey, promising purification, insight, wisdom, or knowledge of the sacred. Near the end of his earthly life, Gesar Khan, the divine warrior hero of the ancient Tibetan and Mongolian traditions, journeys to the sacred mountain. Sent into the world to combat the forces of evil, the battle-wearied god goes to Margye Pongri to meditate and seek purification before ascending into heaven. In Hebrew tradition, Moses climbs Mount Sinai to receive the divine revelations represented by the Ten Commandments, and, in the well-known Christian story, Jesus ascends the mountain to deliver the revelations offered in the "Sermon on the Mount." Like Gesar Khan, Jesus too ascends into heaven from a mountaintop: as recorded in the Acts of the Apostles, Jesus ascends from the Mount of Olives, near Old Jerusalem.

Pilgrimages to sacred mountains occur not only in myths, but also in the cultural practices of many peoples. In Tibet, both priests and lay pilgrims visit three holy mountains, Mount Kailash, Mount Labchi, and Mount Tsari, to seek spiritual enlightenment. Mount Fujiyama, a symbol of Shinto tradition in Japan, is also a site sacred to many pilgrims, as is the Hindu shrine on Mount Agung in Bali. Among the accounts found in myths, stories of the quest for the Holy Grail often feature a pilgrimage to a sacred mountain. In most narratives, the sacred relic is housed in the Grail Castle, which, like the temple, is an emblem of the sacred mountain. In some stories, however, the Grail Castle itself rests atop a sacred mountain known as Mont Sauvage, or Montsalvatch. While there are many theories about the location of the Grail's mountain, one suggests that it might be found in the Pyrenees, where there is a mountain called Monsalvat. In another interesting tale, one included in the Welsh narrative collection called the *Mabinogion* (1839), a strange pilgrimage is made to White Mount in London. In this story, followers of the Celtic hero Bran make their journey in order to bury their leader's severed head beneath the White Mount, a site thought to be the Tower of London, which is built of white stone.

INSTRUMENTS OF CREATION

Sacred mountains play unusual roles in tales from some traditions. In a myth from India, for example, a holy mountain is used to churn the Ocean of Milk. In the story, Vishnu appears on earth as the great tortoise Kurma and swims to the bottom of the milky sea. He then orders the gods to place Mount Mandara on his back and to use it as though it were a butter churn to stir up the milk. The process of churning with the sacred mountain produces many treasures: the moon, the tree of heaven, the white elephant Airavata, the goddess Lakshmi, and soma, the drink of the gods. In another account, that from the Dayak people of Borneo, the universe is created when two sacred mountains crash into one another. Gold Mountain, home of the lord of the lower realm, and Jewel Mountain, home of the lord of the upper realm, exist before creation begins. Each time the two mountains clash together, a portion of the cosmos comes into being. At the first meeting of the mountains, the clouds and skies are formed. When the mountains crash again, the features of the earth take shape, and then the sun, the moon, and certain animals are all created by the sacred mountains.

SACRED SITES

Myths about the sacred mountain are wonderfully various. For the ancient Egyptians, the mysterious Mountain of the Moon is the source of the precious Nile. In the Chinese and Mayan traditions, sacred mountains hold up the heavens. China's five sacred mountains are revered as embodiments of deities, and the Mayans' Pauahtun, god of the four directions, is represented as the mountains that support the sky. For both the Incas and the Aztecs, mountains are among the most sacred places in the world—and are the sites where they observe the rituals of human sacrifice. In Aztec tradition, Tlaloc, god of the rain, is personified in the sacred mountain that bears his name and honored in an annual festival that includes the sacrifice of children. Among the indigenous people of Australia, Uluru, the immense sandstone formation also known as Ayer's Rock, carries special significance. Shaped by a tremendous battle between the rock-python people and the carpet-snake people, Uluru is said to have been the last of the world's features to be created. In Australian tradition, all creation occurs during a period known as the Dreamtime, and, when the ferocious war between the snake peoples produces the sacred mountain, Dreamtime comes to an end.

FLOOD HEROES' SANCTUARY

In many traditions the mountain plays yet another significant role as the site where survivors of the deluge first return to land. While mountain peaks are obviously the first places to emerge when the floodwaters subside, there is nevertheless a special symbolism in the fact that, of all places on the earth, they reach closest to the heavens, the home of the gods. When the flood's survivors step back onto the earth and then build an altar to pay homage and give thanks, the mountain where they worship becomes a sacred place. In Judeo-Christian tradition Mount Ararat is the site of Noah's landing, and in the Greek tale of the flood, Deucalion and Pyrrha step ashore on the top of Mount Parnassus. Manu, the flood hero of myths from India, alights on a peak high in the Himalayas, and the slope he eventually climbs down becomes known as Manu's Descent. In other stories of the deluge, people are saved by the mountain itself, as it continues to rise high above the flood. In one such tale, that of the Araucanian people of Chile, the deluge occurs when two monstrous serpents test their powers in a contest: while one of the serpents causes the waters to rise, the other wins the contest by lifting up the mountain that offers refuge for the people. In a similar myth from Ecuador, Huacaynan Peak in the Andes is the sacred mountain that preserves the human race by magically growing ever higher as the floodwaters encroach.

LOST TOWERS

While the majestic image of a sacred mountain inspires awe in many cultural traditions, occasionally those narratives that describe the towering edifices built by human beings represent these artificial mountains as symbols of arrogance, folly, or dreams unfulfilled. In these tales, the act of constructing a tower that reaches to the heavens serves as a measure of humankind's aspirations, but when people's undertakings are perceived as overreaching, their ambitious enterprises are doomed to fail. Accounts of unsuccessful attempts to erect a towering ladder to the sky include the Hebrew people's story of the abandoned effort to construct the Tower of Babel and numerous tales of collapsed towers that come from various African traditions. Cautionary tales, these stories warn of the dangers of creating mountains that are then necessarily imbued with the symbolic significance of monumental places. Sadly, these early legends of lost towers strangely prefigure a more recent loss— that of the two towers lately destroyed in the city of New York. Indeed, particular features of the story the Hebrews record in Genesis are strikingly similar to cir-cumstances that surround the fall of the Twin Towers. In the ancient tale, the peo-ple who begin construction of their tower are united in their efforts and speak with one voice, but when they lose their common language and their common purpose, they also abandon their shared goal. Erected to represent the shared purposes of many peoples and named the World Trade Center to signify the unity of nations, the New York towers, like the Tower of Babel, have become emblems of a goal that is as yet unfulfilled.

See also Deluge Motif; The Quest; The World Tree

SEPARATION OF EARTH AND SKY

Stories of how and why the distant realms of earth and heaven come to be separated from one another arise in a surprising number of narratives from around the world. Many of the tales occur in the context of those creation myths wherein the earth and the sky are the primal parents who give birth to the universe or to the gods and the people who inhabit the cosmos. When earth and sky serve as the original parents, they must be separated to create a space where the world they engender can fully emerge. Sometimes earth and sky are separated before the birth of the world occurs, and sometimes the offspring of their union must separate the parents. In these tales, the separation of the earth and the heavens occurs as a stage in the process of creation. In other myths, however, the realms of earth and sky remain in close proximity to one another until the sky deity eventually withdraws from the earth or until the world's inhabitants devise a means to elevate the sky.

ORDER FROM CHAOS

In narratives from China and Egypt, the separation of earth and sky occurs early in the process of creation. According to one version of China's several creation myths, the universe begins to take shape when a cosmic egg breaks open and its white and its yolk start to separate. Yin, the white of the egg, rises to become the sky, and yang, the heavier yolk, sinks beneath to become the earth. To prevent yin and yang from merging once again into the formlessness of chaos, the primeval giant Pan Ku, who also emerges from the cosmic egg, spends eighteen thousand years hoisting the sky higher and higher up above the earth. Only when Pan Ku's task is completed and he has created sufficient space between the heavens and the earth for living beings to exist does the process of the world's creation continue. In the Egyptian account, where sky and earth are primal parents, there is no room for the sky goddess Nut to give birth until she is separated from the embrace of the earth god, Geb. Although in many other tales the children of the earth and sky separate their parents, in the Egyptian story it is the father of Nut and Geb who moves his children apart. When Shu, the god of the air, lifts Nut high above Geb, he not only makes it possible for her to deliver her children, but also for the process of creation to continue to unfold.

PRIMAL PARENTS

The Egyptian account of the separation of earth and sky is distinctive not only because the primal parents are separated by their father, but also because the earth in most myth traditions is conceived as mother and the sky as father. Among the many stories of the separation of earth mother and sky father by their children are examples from North America's Yuma people and New Zealand's Maori people. In the Yuma myth, sky father and earth mother are represented as husband and wife who produce twin sons. After their births, the twins' first task is to stand upon the body of their mother and lift up the sky. In completing the first of the tasks that lie before them, the twins successfully create the room they need to lead lives of their own. In the tale of the Maori, the task of separating the primal parents is exceptionally difficult, for the six sons of sky father Rangi and earth mother Papa lie smothered in their embrace: in the dark and moist space between their parents, the sons of Rangi and Papa have only room to crawl. When Papa raises her arm one day, and her sons catch a glimpse of the space beyond her, they decide that they must find a way to break free of their parents. Although the brothers consider killing father Rangi and mother Papa, Tane, the god of the forest, suggests that they be separated—and, after great effort, it is he who manages to pry his parents apart by standing on his head and pushing Rangi upward with his feet.

The task of separating sky from earth also falls to a son in a version of the ancient Greeks' creation myths, but in this case it is mother earth herself who contrives to be free of the sky's oppressive weight. According to this tale, the earth mother Gaea and the sky father Uranos are the primal parents who give birth to the three Hekatonchires, the three Cyclopes, and the twelve Titans, the first generation of the immortal gods. Gaea loves the children she has engendered, but her husband, who regards his offspring as a threat to his own power, buries them all deep within the earth where their mother cannot see them. Not only does Gaea sorely miss her children, she also suffers the great pain caused by carrying them within her own womb. When her sorrow and pain grow too great for her to bear, Gaea calls upon her offspring to overthrow their father and free themselves from their dark prison. Kronos, the youngest of the Titans, agrees to help his mother, and, using the sickle she has made for him, he castrates Uranos and thus separates the primal parents. The process of creation begins to unfold again after Uranos is deposed, for the Titans, freed from their mother's womb, give birth to a new generation of gods.

THE SKY'S RETREAT

When sky and earth are differentiated during the process of creation, cosmic order emerges from the formlessness of chaos. By separating yin from yang, Pan Ku creates space for the world to assume its shape, and by lifting Nut above Geb, Shu makes it possible for creation to unfold through the act of birth. By separating their parents, the children of sky and earth become participants in the process of creation; when they make room for the world to exist, they emerge from the undifferentiated unity of the void. In other myths, including a large collection of tales from western Africa, the people of the earth live just beneath the sky for some time after the process of creation has ended. In these stories, the sky deity eventually becomes annoyed with the behavior of human beings and retreats to a new home high up in the heavens. Unlike the creation myths that link the emergence of cosmic order to the differentiation of earth and sky, these tales explain how it occurs that the deities come to dwell at a great distance from the world they originally created. In other words, they account for people's recognition that their celestial gods have become remote from the mundane concerns of the world's inhabitants and therefore represent the differentiation of the sacred and the worldly domains.

In legends from throughout western Africa, the creator god first lives in a sky that arches just above the heads of the people on the earth. Because the sky is so readily available, the people begin to take advantage of it in various unseemly ways. In some accounts, women tear off a piece of the heaven to flavor their stews, and in others children wipe their dirty hands on the clouds in the sky, or hungry people rip off fragments of the clouds and eat them for food. In one story a woman tears a hole in the sky with her spoon, and in another a woman who is grinding meal inadvertently strikes the creator in the eye with the handle of her pestle. Needless to say, the sky deity eventually grows tired of these abuses, and, seizing the heavens, withdraws to a safe position high above the world. The retreat of the sky signals a separation between people and their deity, and, in the story of the woman and her pestle, the people try to build a tower that will once again bring them close to their god. The distance between the heaven and the earth is too great for them to span, however, and when the tower collapses, they fall back onto the earth, the place where they must live.

The withdrawal of the celestial deity, which marks an end to the time when the people's god lives among them, can be regarded as a variation of the recurring story of human beings' fall from grace. This theme is clearly represented in the image of the falling tower and can also be seen in a tale told by the Dinka people of the Sudan. In their myth, there is no want or hardship while the creator god resides just above his people's heads. The god provides the people's daily food and allows them to climb a rope that reaches down from his celestial realm. This golden age comes to an end, however, when a woman takes more grain than her fair share and grinds it with her pestle. When her pestle strikes blows against the sky, the god cuts the rope to heaven and moves high above the earth. After the departure of the creator god, disease, death, and hardship come into the world, and people must work hard to produce the food they need to live on the earth.

In the myth of western Africa's Fon people, it is the trickster Legba who causes the creator deity to withdraw from the earth. When the story begins, the creator goddess Mawu and her son Legba both live among the people of the earth. Legba,

169

who is his mother's servant and messenger, resents the fact that people thank Mawu when he performs a good deed on her behalf, but blame him when he carries out instructions not to their liking. The trickster therefore conceives a plan to humiliate his mother. Wearing Mawu's shoes, he steals yams from her garden and then informs her of the theft. Greatly angered, the goddess declares that the one whose footprints match those in the garden will be put to death. When it turns out that her own feet fit the print of the shoes, Mawu escapes the people's laughter by moving ten feet above the earth. This distance, however, is not great enough for Legba, who is still expected to perform as his mother's servant, and so he persuades an old woman of the village to dispose of each day's dirty dishwater by hurling it high into the air. Mawu, angered by this daily soaking, finally retreats to the celestial realm, and thus the trickster, by means of his cunning, effects the differentiation of the sacred and profane.

The creation myth of northeastern India's Minyong people describes both the separation of the earth and sky and the births of the sun and moon. According to this tale, the earth mother Sedi and the sky father Melo decide to marry at the beginning of the unfolding of creation. The couple's union, however, is not regarded as an occasion for celebration, for the beings who live between them grow fearful that they might be crushed when the primal parents join together to make love. These beings, including animals, and spirits known as the Wiyus, gather together to discuss their plight. Finally Sedi-Diyor, a great leader among the Wiyus, decides to drive the sky father far from the earth. Unlike those stories wherein the sky deity becomes increasingly annoyed or is tricked into departing, the Minyong account represents Melo's flight as an escape from peril. Indeed, Sedi-Diyor beats the sky father so severely that he is forced to seek safety high up in the heavens.

Two daughters are born to Sedi just as her husband disappears, but because the forlorn wife cannot bear to see her children, Sedi-Diyor provides a nurse to care for them. The infants thrive under the protection of their surrogate mother, and the faint light that emanates from them grows more radiant each day. Although Bomong and Bong, the daughters of earth and sky, eventually become the sun and the moon, the girls must grow to maturity before this occurs, and the interval that immediately follows Melo's separation from Sedi and the subsequent separation of the parents from their children is characterized by difficulties that test the wisdom of the Wiyus. Problems first arise when the young girls' nurse dies and they then die of grief. When this happens, the light the girls provide fades away with them and the world is left in darkness. In search of the lost light, the Wiyus, animals, and people dig up the nurse's corpse, and although most of her body has rotted, her two glowing eyes remain. Reflections of the dead children can be seen within the eyes, and so after carefully washing the orbs, the Wiyus summon a carpenter who can remove the images within them. Freed from their imprisonment, Bomong and Bong once again bring light into the world.

When Bomong becomes a woman and her full radiance shines forth, she sets out on a journey that takes her through the entire world. Daylight appears wherever she wanders, and the beings who live on the earth rejoice in her splendor. However, the Wiyus must confront yet another problem when Bong chooses to follow her sister's path and the world then becomes too hot and too bright. After the animals, people, and Wiyus meet and reluctantly agree that Bong must be killed, Frog performs the deed by slaying her with arrows. Unfortunately, Bong's death leads to further troubles, for when Bomong learns of it, she hides under a great rock and mourns for her sister. The world, of course, is darkened once again, and therefore Cock is dispatched to find the sun. Because Bomong agrees to leave her hiding place only when her sister is restored to life, the Wiyus once more call upon the carpenter to refashion Bong's body and recover some of its light. Bong becomes the moon when the carpenter completes his task, and as Bomong's light begins to shine again, Cock begins to crow.

HOISTING THE SKY

For North America's Snohomish people of the Pacific Northwest, the story of the separation of earth and sky serves to illustrate what is possible when the people work together. According to this myth, the creator originally makes many different groups of people and gives to each group a language of its own. Although the world's people cannot speak with one another, they all understand that their sky, which rests just above their heads, is too close to the earth. The leaders of the various tribes meet to try to solve the problem and agree that an effort to lift the sky will require that all the people, animals, and birds push in unison together. Because the tribes live far from one another and do not understand each other's tongues, the leaders must find a way to signal when it is time to hoist up the sky. After the tribes agree upon a plan, the people, using poles they have made from the tallest trees, all push together when they hear their elders cry out "Ya-hooooh!" Thus, working as one, the creatures of the earth succeed in raising the sky.

See also Creation Myths; Deluge Motif; Primal Parents

THEOMACHY

Theomachy, a word derived from Greek roots meaning *god* and *war*, is a specialized term used in myth study referring to accounts of great battles that are waged among deities and other primal beings. Although people are sometimes caught up in these cosmic struggles, the conflicts designated by this term characteristically originate with the gods. In some narratives, including those from the ancient Mesopotamian and Greek traditions, strife among the gods occurs during the process of creation and prior to the existence of human beings. In these myths, the usurpation of the original creators by a younger generation of deities is represented as necessary to the emergence of a cosmic order. Whereas wars lead to the beginnings of the world in the narratives from Mesopotamia and Greece, in other traditions, including those of the Norse, the Aztecs, and the Zoroastrians of ancient Persia, the great battles of the gods bring the world to its end. For both the Norse and the Aztecs, the death of the old order is followed by the birth of a new and different world, but in the apocalyptic vision of the Zoroastrians, the final battle between the lords of good and evil marks the end of time. In still other instances of theomachy in myth, the conflict between cosmic powers is represented as an unending struggle for mastery of the universe.

WARS AT THE BEGINNING OF CREATION

Babylonian Creation Myth

According to the *Enuma elish* (ca. 1100 B.C.E.), the ancient Babylonian epic, the battle for supremacy over all creation is waged between Marduk, the mighty god and hero, and one of his own ancestors, Tiamat, the primal mother. In the *Enuma elish* chaos first exists in the form of Tiamat, the personification of the salty waters of the primordial abyss, and her consort Apsu, who is the embodiment of the fresh waters. The mingling of the waters produces Anshar and Kishar, the parents of the gods, and from these beginnings the Babylonian pantheon arises. Trouble first occurs when Apsu, who is disturbed by the presence and the movements of the other gods, decides that he will kill them. Apsu's plans, however, are thwarted by his great grandson Ea, god of the earth, and after slaying the primal father, Ea takes possession of his crown. Creation continues to unfold as Ea and his wife Damkina produce their son Marduk and as Anu, god of the heavens, gives form to the mighty winds of the four directions. The winds, which toss and churn the primal waters, arouse the wrath of Tiamat, and she vows to avenge the death of her husband by destroying the unruly gods who are her descendents.

In the Babylonian creation myth, differentiation begins to take shape out of chaos when new life arises from the commingling of the primal waters. The process continues as the new deities make claim to their domains and Anu creates the four directions of the cosmos in the form of the four winds. The winds that play upon the water impose their own order on the great abyss, and Tiamat, the personification of formlessness, rises up to reassert the original state of chaos. The gods, threatened by the power of chaos to engulf them, call for a hero whose victory over Tiamat will mean that the process of creation can continue to unfold. When neither Ea nor Anu dares confront the primal mother and her minions, Marduk, the double god with four eyes and four ears, agrees to accept the challenge. In return for his heroism, Marduk demands kingship over the universe, the absolute authority to create order after chaos is subdued.

In preparation for the war, Tiamat creates an army of eleven venomous monsters that include demons, snakes, a mad dog, the scorpion-man, and the ferocious sphinx. Then, after making the god Kingu the leader of her monsters, she awaits the approach of her divine adversary. Marduk, determined to face Tiamat in single combat, arms himself with the four winds and with hurricanes and cyclones as well. He carries with him lightning and the flooding rainstorm and brings a net to ensnare the primal mother. Clothed in his shining armor and wearing his brilliant halos on his head, Marduk strikes terror in the heart of Kingu, who is unable to advance at the head of his forces. Left alone with Tiamat, the new king of the gods wraps her in his hurricane, and, when the gaping mouth of chaos opens to consume him, he unleashes all his winds into the abyss. Swollen by the winds and unable to close her mouth, Tiamat is helpless when Marduk draws his great bow and sends his swift arrow straight into her heart.

Marduk assumes the role of creator deity with Tiamat's defeat and fashions order out of chaos by using the two halves of her corpse to make the heavens and the earth. He forms mountains from the primal mother's skull and causes great rivers to spill forth from the empty sockets of her eyes. He then creates the sun and moon, sets the celestial bodies in motion, and divides time into days, months, and years. He transforms Tiamat's army of demons into statues of stone and uses Kingu's blood and bones to create a race of mortal beings made to serve the gods. By conquering Tiamat, whose victory over the gods would have resulted in the dissolution of the emerging world, Marduk, the king of the universe, earns the right to complete the process of creation. In the *Enuma elish*, whose great battle dramatizes the power struggle between the primal mother and the male god who ascends to kingship of the cosmos, a patriarchal order triumphs over the ancient vision of the mother goddess as the emblem of fertility. In representing Tiamat as the agent of disorder, the Babylonian epic portrays her as a monster that must be destroyed.

Greek Creation Myth

The Greek creation myth recounted in Hesiod's *Theogony* resembles the Babylonian account in its depiction of power struggles between the original creator deities and the succeeding generations of gods. In the Greek narrative, the great war among the gods occurs when Zeus, a member of the third generation of immortal beings, ascends to the kingship of the heavens by overthrowing his father Kronos and the other Titans. According to Hesiod, conflict first arises in the cosmos when Gaea the earth mother and Uranos the sky father give birth to their first children, the three Hekatonchires (Hundred-Handed Giants) and the three Cyclopes. Fearing the great strength and the talents of his offspring, Uranos binds them and confines them to Tartarus, the underworld that lies deep within the body of their mother earth. Gaea is angered by this treatment of her children, but she waits for her revenge until after the births of thirteen additional progeny, the immortal divinities known as the Titans. Then, after Kronos, the youngest of the Titans, agrees to free his brothers, Gaea gives him the sickle he uses to emasculate his father.

Kronos becomes god of the sky after usurping his father's authority, but he too is a tyrant who betrays his mother's trust when he fails to keep his promise to release his older brothers. Fearing that his father's fate could become his own, he swallows each of his own children just after they are born. Rhea, the sky god's grieving wife, finally turns to Gaea for help, and after her sixth child is born and carefully hidden away, she follows the earth mother's advice and tricks Kronos into swallowing a stone instead of their son, the infant Zeus. In the story told by Hesiod, the differentiation that occurs during the process of creation cannot be fully realized until there is sufficient distance between the heavens and the earth. As sky god, Uranos covers the earth and buries her first children in the darkness of her depths. When Gaea calls upon another child to create a space where creation can exist, Kronos the Titan also precludes the emergence of new life by swallowing his offspring. As in the *Enuma elish*, the primal earth mother is in conflict with the male god of the sky, but in the Greek narrative it is the sky deity rather than the fertility goddess who threatens to interrupt the unfolding of creation, and Gaea therefore looks to Zeus to overthrow the rule of Kronos and to free her children.

The war for the kingship of the heavens begins when Zeus gives Kronos a potion that causes him to regurgitate the gods that he has swallowed. Zeus's siblings side with him in the battle with the Titans—a war that is also known as the Titanomachy—and because the forces are well matched in both strength and cunning, neither can defeat the other during the first ten years of warfare. Gaea then turns the tide of the battle by telling Zeus about the immortal beings still imprisoned in Tartarus. When the Hundred-Handed Giants and the Cyclopes join the army of the gods, the Cyclopes bring with them gifts for their liberators: for Zeus there is the powerful thunderbolt, for Poseidon the three-pronged spear called the trident, and for Hades the magical helmet of invisibility. Armed with their new weapons and assisted by the giants, the Greek gods finally overwhelm the Titans with an onslaught that causes the earth itself to shake. When the Titans seek refuge in the depths of Tartarus, the Hundred-Handed Giants secure them in chains. In the world above, a new order is established when the kingdoms of the cosmos are divided among three of the immortal gods. Zeus, ruler of the sky, governs from high atop Mount Olympus, while Poseidon rules the realm of the seas, and Hades presides over the kingdom of the underworld.

DESTRUCTION OF THE WORLD

In myths from several cultures, enmities that exist from the time of creation ultimately erupt into tremendous battles that destroy the world. In Norse tradition, for example, the animosity between the gods and their enemies dates back to the creation of the cosmos, when Odin and his brothers slay the evil Frost Giant, Ymir, and use his dismembered corpse to shape the heavens and the earth. In the account of the Aztecs, whose creation myth describes the existence of four worlds prior to the emergence of the fifth and final one, the conflict between the two great creator gods, Tezcatlipoca and Quetzalcoatl, results in the creation and destruction of the first four of the five worlds. According to ancient Persian tradition, Ahura Mazda's perfect universe is flawed at the beginning of creation when Angra Mainyu, the Wise Lord's wicked double, appears in the world. Embodiments of the opposing forces of good and evil, Ahura Mazda and Angra Mainyu engage in a cosmic struggle that persists until the day of their final battle.

Ragnarok

Ragnarok, the last battle between the Norse gods and their many age-old foes, ends with the destruction of the world that Odin, Vili, and Ve originally created. When Heimdall the White God sounds his horn to signal the beginning of the fight, the gods and Valhalla's heroes converge on the Plain of Vigrid to confront the World Serpent, the Frost Giants, Fenrir the Wolf, Loki, and all their other fearsome enemies. Neither side prevails on the battlefield, where the heroes and the monsters all slay one another. Midgard, where human beings live, is demolished when the fire giant Surt sets the world ablaze, and only one man and one woman manage to survive the great conflagration. Although the world of the gods is gone forever by the end of the war, the new earth that in time arises from the sea provides a home for Ragnarok's two survivors, the primal parents of a new race of people.

Destruction of Four Worlds

Whereas great armies destroy the cosmos in the Norse myth, in the Aztec tale two powerful gods vie with one another for mastery over creation, and, in the course of their struggle, four different worlds are fashioned and destroyed. Black Tezcatlipoca, the second son of the primordial creators, rules over the First World, which is inhabited by a race of powerful giants. This world, however, is brought to its end when Quetzalcoatl, the creators' third son, strikes his brother and causes him to fall into the sea. When Tezcatlipoca emerges from the water, he does so in the form of the jaguar that devours all the giants and destroys the world. Quetzalcoatl is the ruler of the Second World, but when his brother kicks him and causes him to fall, a great wind arises and sweeps this world away. Although other gods preside over the third and fourth creations, the brothers persist in their battle, and Quetzalcoatl destroys the Third World in a rain of fire while Tezcatlipoca brings an end to the Fourth World by causing the two people who are the only survivors of its devastating flood to turn into dogs. Finally, having each destroyed two worlds in the course of the struggle, the brothers join with six other deities to re-create the cosmos in the form of the Fifth World.

Cosmic Struggle

In some myth traditions the history of the world unfolds within the context of a cosmic struggle. According to the ancient Persians, the conflict between Ahura Mazda, the Wise Lord, and his great enemy, the evil Angra Mainyu, lies at the heart of all existence. From the moment of creation, Angra Mainyu strives to destroy the cosmos and all that it contains as he seeks to overpower the god who is both his brother and his adversary. Ahura Mazda, who defends his creation through the course of his enemy's unrelenting assaults, must wait until Angra Mainyu is defeated before the universe can be restored to a state of perfection. The war between good and evil therefore continues as long as the world exists, for perfection is not possible within a universe that is flawed. Ahura Mazda and Angra Mainyu meet in their last great battle at the end of time, and on that Day of Judgment the world that contains the forces of death, disease, and darkness is at last destroyed. Cleansed of all its imperfections, Ahura Mazda's creation is a paradise within the timeless realm of eternity.

While the conflict between the Wise Lord and his evil twin ends in a final battle in the Zoroastrian worldview, in other cultural traditions the perpetual warring of cosmic forces is represented as a never-ending struggle. In one of the most common instances of this motif, sky deities in the form of powerful birds battle the gigantic serpents that rule the watery depths of the sea or the underworld. For example, the Kwakiutl people of North America's Pacific Coast recount stories of the war between the great Thunderbird and Sisiutl, the immense two-headed serpent that lives in the sea, and in similar myths from Africa, the mighty Lightning Bird battles the fearsome Rainbow Serpent in a contest for supremacy that neither creature wins. Unlike the cosmic struggle that shapes the course of human history in the Persian account, the conflicts between birds and serpents do not draw people into wars with one another. Rather, in observing the traditional enmity between these adversaries, human beings witness an elemental tension in the workings of the universe. Interestingly, the portrayal of enmity between serpents and birds that is a feature of many myth traditions is countered in the Aztecs' representation of Quetzalcoatl, the great creator god. Indeed, in Quetzalcoatl, whose name means "feathered serpent," the contrasting qualities of the bird and the snake are symbolically linked together.

THEOMACHY AND THE TROJAN WAR

Although the action in the *Iliad* (eighth century B.C.E.) focuses on a war between two heroic peoples, the Trojans and the Greeks, Homer's epic interestingly depicts the conjunction of this conflict and warring among the gods. In other words, while the struggle on earth unfolds throughout the epic's drama, another battle simultaneously rages in the celestial realm, where the deities are divided in their support of the mortals who fight below. While individual gods are often implicated in the affairs of the mortal warriors, as when Apollo instigates the dispute between Agamemnon and Achilles in the *Iliad*'s opening scene, it is in Book 20 that Homer fully portrays the extent of the deities' involvement in the Trojan War. Indeed, Zeus unleashes "the dogs of war" when he grants the gods permission to take sides in the conflict, and the theomachy that ensues pits the immortal defenders of the Trojans against those divinities that favor the Greeks.

See also The Apocalypse; Creation Myths; Separation of Earth and Sky

TRICKSTERS

Figures that scholars have characterized as examples of the trickster appear in the myths and folktales of cultural traditions throughout the world. Although the stories and legends that feature these characters do not necessarily identify them as instances of the trickster or even call them by that name, the term provides a useful means of classifying these recurring figures, and scholars have therefore defined several characteristics that they often share. For example, tricksters are typically sly and cunning characters who survive by their wits. While these figures customarily use trickery and deceit to advance their interests, they are not infrequently the victims of their own stratagems, and then they are shown to be ludicrously foolish: eager to take advantage of the gullibility of others, they often set themselves up to be dealt their comeuppance. These quick-witted characters, however, are wonderfully resilient by nature, and therefore they are usually able to overcome the problems they imprudently bring upon themselves. In other words, the trickster, who is both shrewd and silly, both the prankster and the laughingstock, is a consummately ambiguous character who embodies all manner of contradictions.

AMBIVALENT FIGURES

Indeed, the contradictions inherent in the figure of the trickster take many forms in myths and folktales. While tricksters are essentially loners, for example, they are also gregarious characters who use their remarkable sociability to charm those they hope to trick. Although they are greedy characters at heart, ones who characteristically watch for opportunities to promote themselves, tricksters are also capable of performing magnanimous acts of generosity and even self-sacrifice. Troublemakers who delight in the mischief they make and the confusion they introduce, tricksters are nonetheless often helpful characters, and in many myths they are indeed the culture heroes who provide humankind with the gift of fire. Their behavior, therefore, can be both destructive and productive, for while on one hand a figure like Coyote brings death into the world and unleashes a great flood, on the other hand he also helps to create the world and to protect it from monsters. Generally playful characters who relish chances to challenge rules or overturn conventions, tricksters can also act out of earnest purpose, as does the Norse trickster Loki when he maliciously sets in motion the events that inevitably end with the destruction of the world. Sometimes the instigators of beneficial change and sometimes the agents of misfortune or harm, tricksters are morally ambivalent figures whose contradictory impulses are expressed in both the good and the ill that they provoke.

TRANSGRESSORS

With no qualms whatsoever, opportunistic tricksters do not hesitate to cross the boundaries of propriety, decorum, or law, and thus they are outrageous figures who frequently play the part of outlaws by violating their society's conventions, mores, and taboos. Adventuresome characters who audaciously cross the borders of that which is familiar, tricksters impetuously venture into the realm of the unknown. As characters who can readily transcend all boundaries, tricksters often function as messengers, figures who travel between the realms of deities and mortals or between the worlds of the living and the dead. Many tricksters traverse another boundary as well, for they are frequently represented as shape-shifters who have the power to undergo metamorphosis, to cross from one material form to another. Indeed, these tricksters are able to appear in all manner of guises as they move among the shapes of animals, human beings, and objects or transform themselves from one sex to another. Inexhaustibly inventive, masters of the art of bricolage, tricksters not only transform their appearances to address their circumstances, but they also contrive—usually through lying, blustering, or brazenness—to change the conditions in which they find themselves. By using their wits to invert situations, tricksters are able to transform their surroundings, reducing order to chaos or creating harmony out of dissonance.

In stories from many cultures, the greedy nature of tricksters is depicted within the numerous bawdy accounts of their insatiable appetite for sex. Indeed, another significant characteristic of the trickster figure emerges in these myths, for most tricksters prove to be lusty and promiscuous characters that resourcefully draw upon their cunning and guile for the purpose of seduction. Often tricksters have families of their own, but they are nonetheless always watchful for the opportunity to satisfy their bodily urges, and they accordingly act without inhibition. References to various bodily functions are in fact commonplace in trickster tales, for in addition to the stories of tricksters' amorous encounters are those that detail their ribald behavior and their distinctly scatological propensities. Characters that show no reluctance to transgress a society's proprieties, tricksters are often depicted as outrageously lewd, irreverent, or blasphemous figures.

ROLES AND GUISES OF THE TRICKSTERS

The tricksters of myth appear as deities, human beings, or animals. Many of them are culture heroes as well as pranksters, and some of them are also creators or the helpers of creator deities. Although characters who share features of the trickster figure emerge in many cultural traditions, the cycles of trickster tales related by North American and African peoples provide especially rich accounts of this figure's antics and adventures. According to the traditions of several Native American and African societies, the trickster figure is an animal, often a seemingly unprepossessing creature such as the spider, hare, or weasel. While tricksters are generally represented as males, they sometimes possess androgynous attributes or readily assume the forms of females, and stories told by North America's Tewa and Hopi peoples feature two different coyote tricksters, Coyote Woman and Old Man Coyote. Another female character, Tsetse, the troublemaking goddess of lightning in tales from Africa's Bakuba and Boshongo peoples, also shares features of the trickster figure in her representation as an unpredictable and disruptive force.

NATIVE AMERICAN TRICKSTERS

Coyote

In Native American tradition, Coyote is the ubiquitous trickster who appears in tales recounted by many different peoples throughout the North American continent. Indeed, the numerous stories of Coyote's exploits and adventures greatly outnumber those told about any other tricksters. Almost all of the characteristics and roles of the trickster figure can be found in the plethora of myths that feature Coyote, for in one tale or another he is represented as creator, destroyer, culture hero, shape-shifter, prodigious lecher, prankster, or fool. According to the tradition of the Yokut people, Coyote and Eagle are the creators of both the earth and the first human beings. Surrounded by the primal waters at the beginning of time, the two creators send Turtle to the bottom of the sea to find the grain of sand they need to give shape to a new world. In this tale, Coyote also plays the role of messenger, for after he and Eagle have formed the first people and sent them forth to inhabit their creation, he travels among them to see how they are faring and must then carry back to Eagle the troubling news that in fact the human beings are eating up the earth. To save their creation, Coyote and Eagle dispatch Dove to search for a seed, and from this original kernel they produce all the crops that grow on the earth. In the Yokuts' origin myth, the creative tricksters Coyote and Eagle use the materials at hand—a single grain of sand and a single seed—to transform the world.

Coyote changes the world in destructive ways as well, and in the Navajo emergence myth it is he who causes Water Monster to flood the people's fertile underground home within the Fourth World. This is one of those occasions when the trickster's behavior leads to trouble for himself and others, for Water Monster angrily strikes back after Coyote first cheats him and then robs him. Moreover, in tales told by the Caddo and the Yakima peoples, it is Coyote who decides that all earthly life must end in death. While the trickster's actions in these stories undeniably bring the people much hardship and grief, what Coyote does is not without benefit as well, for in one myth the inundation of their home causes the people to ascend to the Fifth World, the immense, sun-filled land on the surface of the earth, and in the others it is in fact the presence of death that ensures that the living do not run out of space or food while dwelling on the earth. In keeping with the trickster's own ambiguous nature, the actions that Coyote takes in these tales assume a paradoxical significance insofar as their repercussions can indeed be regarded as blessings in disguise.

Although Coyote's thievery causes trouble in the Navajo account, in other tales the trickster's role as thief earns him renown as the celebrated culture hero who steals wonderful treasures that improve people's lives. According to the Klamath people, for example, the fire that Coyote steals from the monster Thunder provides warmth for human beings and makes it possible for them to cook foods that they had once eaten raw. In the tales of the Miwok, Coyote steals the sun and the moon, transforming the people's dark world into a place of light. Coyote steals summer in a story related by the Crow, and the warmth that comes with this precious gift causes the people's crops to blossom and then grow. In this myth, the former owners of summer threaten to wage war if the trickster refuses to return the great prize he has taken, and Coyote therefore suggests a compromise that is accepted when he agrees to give up summer for half of the year and to take possession of winter during that interval. In typical trickster fashion, Coyote of course seeks to realize as great an advantage as he can within his situation, and thus when he is confronted with the grim prospect of war, he shrewdly chooses to cut his losses. In a tale told by the White Mountain Apache, Coyote is not quite so cunning, for when he greedily hoards the tobacco that he steals, refusing to share it with the people, they outwit the trickster. Coyote is eventually enticed to exchange his tobacco for a young wife, but the people have the last laugh when the trickster discovers that the bride they have sent him is actually a boy dressed in women's clothing and that he has therefore traded his tobacco for nothing.

According to the traditions of the Sanpoil people, Coyote is the culture hero who provides them with their staple food by teaching them how to catch, cook, and preserve salmon, and in several tales he is portrayed as a great hero who slays fearsome monsters by relying on his cunning rather than on strength. For example, in a story related by the Nez Percé, Coyote kills seven flesh-eating giants at once by luring them into seven deep pits filled with molten metal, and after he has trapped them, the trickster changes the monstrous creatures into the peaks that are known as the Seven Devils Mountains. Able to change his own appearance when it suits his purposes, Coyote assumes the form of a tree in order to capture birds in a tale told by the Navajo, and in numerous accounts he uses this power while seeking to satisfy his unquenchable lust. In a tale told by the Shasta people, Coyote turns himself into a salmon to attract two unsuspecting girls who are walking beside a river, and in a story recounted by the Southern Ute, the devious trickster devises an elaborate ruse in which he changes his shape so that he can seduce his own two daughters. Although tales of the trickster often celebrate this figure's ability to subvert the authority of an established order, they can also reinforce a society's moral imperatives by representing the trickster as a negative example, and in this tale Coyote, who knows that he is flouting the incest taboo, is shown to pay for his terrible duplicity. Not only does the trickster incur the wrath of his wife, who wields a sharp knife as she furiously pursues him, but indeed he loses his two daughters, who out of their shame and sorrow ascend into the heavens to take the form of stars.

Other Animal Tricksters

Other tales from Native American traditions feature various trickster figures, among them such animal characters as Blue Jay, Crow, Fox, Mink, Rabbit Boy, and Tortoise. Iktomi the Spider, the trickster of the Sioux peoples, is known for first inventing language—and then using it to tell his lies. Yehl the Raven, the trickster among the peoples of the Pacific Northwest, is the inveterate thief who helps himself to the fish and clams of others, but who is also celebrated as the culture hero who helps humankind by stealing the sun, the moon, and fire and then sharing these precious treasures with all of the people. Lox, a sly troublemaker in the trickster tales of the Passamaquoddy people, is the thief and spoiler who can change himself from a wolverine into a badger or a beaver. Among the Algonquian peoples, the trickster Nanabozho, who is also known as the Great Hare, is both a mischief maker and a heroic monster slayer. A culture hero as well, the Great Hare is the teacher who instructs hunters in the skills they need to track and trap their prey. Indeed, Nanabozho is also the messenger who carries knowledge of the healing arts from the realm of the spirits to the people of the earth.

Shape-Shifters

While many Native American tricksters are characterized as animals, others are represented as human figures or as deities. Nanabozho, who can appear as a rabbit or other creatures, is often depicted as a giant in his human form, and Kwatyat, the trickster of the Nootka people, is a master of disguises who assumes a variety of shapes during the course of his adventures. Like other trickster figures, Veeho, Nixant, and Sitconski, tricksters in stories recounted by the Cheyenne, the Gros Ventre, and the Assiniboine peoples, are represented as lecherous characters, and many tales about them detail their sexual encounters. Old Man Napi, the foolish trickster of the Blackfoot people, is often tricked by those he attempts to deceive, and Wesakaychak, the trickster of the Cree, is an irrepressible braggart whose cockiness frequently lands him in trouble. Wakdjungkaga, the trickster of the Winnebago, is an inveterate wanderer who transforms the world through the mischief he makes as he roams the earth. Both Glooskap, the trickster of the Abenaki peoples, and Masaaw, a trickster figure among the Hopi, are deities who possess supernatural powers as well as the cunning that is characteristic of the trickster. Like Nanabozho, Glooskap is often depicted as a giant, and Masaaw, who is ruler of the underworld, appears as the frightening character who is known as the Skeleton Man on those occasions when he does not choose to change his shape.

AFRICAN TRICKSTERS

Animal Tricksters

As do the cycles of trickster tales told by North American peoples, those from African traditions describe how the trickster figure transforms the world through actions whose effects are sometimes helpful and sometimes deleterious. For example, according to one tale, the antics of Anansi, the trickster spider of the Ashanti people, unleash death upon the world, but in another story Anansi is the culture hero who persuades the creator deity to make a sun to warm the people and to then send the rains and winds to cool them whenever the sun becomes too hot. Anansi is also responsible for the creation of the moon, for when he asks the creator deity to provide time for the people to rest from their hard labor, the obliging god Nyame creates both the night and the moon. Africa's trickster tales are similar to those from North America in yet another respect, for the trickster figures of both traditions are often animals. Ture, the trickster of the Zande people, is also a spider, and Hlakanyana, the Zulus' clever trickster, resembles a weasel. The hare and the tortoise are trickster figures in the tales of the Bantu peoples, and Cagn, the praying mantis, is creator, trickster, and culture hero in the myths of the San, the people of the Kalahari Desert. One of those tricksters who possess shape-shifting powers, Cagn often assumes the forms of other animals. Yurugu the Jackal (the "Pale Fox"), the trickster of the Dogon people, is the troublemaker who brings disorder and unpredictability into the world after its creation.

Trickster Gods

In the traditions of West Africa's Fon and Yoruba peoples, the deities Legba and Eshu are the trickster figures who disrupt social order and violate taboos. Accounts of the antics of these divinities reveal that both are lecherous characters, and Legba in particular breaks sexual taboos by seducing his sister, his niece, and his mother-in-law. Both tricksters are messengers as well and travel between the realms of the heaven and the earth while serving as interpreters for the deities. Indeed, Legba and Eshu perform another office that is related to their roles as messengers, for both of these tricksters introduce the art of divination to the people of the earth and then act as mediators between human beings and the gods of fate. Figures who are also agents of change, Legba transforms the world by causing the sky deity to move to the heavens high above the earth, and Eshu overturns the world's original order by persuading the sun and the moon to reverse their positions. Although these trickster deities are often a source of trouble and confusion for humankind, they are nevertheless also credited with providing gifts greatly valued by the people. According to the Fon, Legba creates magical charms and teaches the people to make use of the powers of magic, and the Yoruba honor Eshu for giving them the sun as well as the sacred oracle of Ifa.

MONKEY TRICKSTERS

The monkeys Hanuman and Sun Wukung are trickster figures in myths from India and China. According to Indian tradition, the divine Hanuman is a clever shape-shifter who does not fully realize his own great powers until he is called upon to help Rama rescue his wife Sita from her vicious abductors, the demonic Rakshasas. One story about Hanuman's youthful years describes how he swallows the sun and then, in response to the pleading of the gods, opens his mouth to let it out again. In the *Ramayana* (ca. 300 B.C.E.), Hanuman is Rama's loyal messenger and the leader of the army of monkeys that finds Sita on the island of Lanka. When Hanuman is captured by the Rakshasas and they set his tail on fire, the trickster makes the best of his circumstances by using his flaming tail to burn down his enemies' city before making his escape. Whereas Hanuman, who fights along with

Rama to secure Sita's release, helps to restore order in the world, Sun Wukung, the monkey trickster of China, is a raucous and unruly character who brings disorder to the heavens, the earth, and the netherworld during the course of his outlandish adventures. The story of Sun Wukung's exploits, told in the sixteenth-century book, *The Journey to the West* (1592), shows the Monkey King to be a rascal and a thief as well as the resilient trickster figure who is able to outwit both the celestial gods and the lords of the netherworld before at last earning great honor through his service to them.

The remarkable adventures of Sun Wukung, the Monkey King, begin after he learns how to fly and how to change his shape into seventy-two different forms. After acquiring these powers, the Monkey King travels to the realm of the Dragon King in search of a mighty weapon, and through use of trickery he steals a wonderful magic wand. Transported to the netherworld as punishment for his deed, the indomitable Monkey King threatens to use his magic wand to wreak destruction upon the realm of the dead if he is not released, and when the rulers of hell are thus forced to set him free, he brazenly steals from them the ledger that lists the names of both the living and the dead. The Monkey King is summoned to the heavens after the Dragon King and the netherworld lords complain about the troubles he has caused them, and there he steals both the peaches of immortality and the potent elixir of life. With these heavenly treasures in his possession, the trickster is able to achieve immortality, and thus he survives when the gods chase him back to earth and attempt to execute him. Because the troublesome Monkey King cannot be put to death, he is imprisoned beneath a mountain for thousands of years and at last released when he agrees to accompany a devout Buddhist monk who plans to make a sacred pilgrimage to India. These odd traveling companions experience many harrowing adventures during the course of a journey that takes them fourteen years to complete, but when they finally return to China carrying the sacred Buddhist scriptures, the indefatigable trickster's reward is particularly gratifying, for the Monkey King is elevated to the status of a god.

TRICKSTER DEITIES

The trickster figure appears in the form of a god in myths from the Greek, Indian, and Japanese traditions. The Greek deity Hermes, messenger of the gods and traverser of boundaries, travels between the borders of the heavens and the earth and also crosses into the underworld as the psychopomp, the guide of the dead. The patron deity of thieves, Hermes is himself the thief who as a mere child steals cattle from the mighty god Apollo and then impishly absconds with Apollo's bow and quiver. According to Indian tradition, Krishna, the great hero who is born on the earth as the eighth incarnation of Vishnu, first earns his reputation as a prankster when he steals butter as a child. The "Butter Thief," as he is called, delights in playing tricks on his neighbors, and it is he, for example, who blithely steals the clothes of all the young women of his village while they are bathing in the river. A monster slayer who rids the world of various evil beings, Krishna kills both the bull-demon Arishta and the horse-demon Keshim during his earthly life. Susano, the storm god in the myths of Japan, is a notorious troublemaker who imperils all earthly life when he frightens his sister Amaterasu, the goddess of the sun, and she then withdraws into a heavenly cave and leaves the world in darkness.

Like other trickster figures, Susano, however, is more than a disruptive nuisance, for he is also both the monster slayer who tricks and kills a malicious, eight-headed serpent and the heroic figure that saves the world from a deadly plague.

Greek Tricksters

In myths from ancient Greece, characteristics of the trickster figure are apparent not only in the messenger god Hermes, but also in the Titan Prometheus, in the mighty hero Odysseus, and in the crafty Sisyphus, who is by some accounts the father of Odysseus. Prometheus, who helps Zeus overthrow Kronos and become the sky god, nevertheless defies his former ally when he chooses to serve as the protector and benefactor of humankind. When the deities and the first human beings meet to decide how they should share their food, Prometheus tricks Zeus into accepting animals' bones and entrails by covering them up with fat, and when Zeus takes this portion on behalf of the gods, the tasty meat is the portion left for the people. The angry sky god then withholds from human beings possession of the fire they need to cook their meat, but he is once again thwarted by the troublesome Prometheus, who steals fire from Hephaistos, presents it to the people, and teaches them how to use it for metalworking as well as for cooking. Odysseus, the warrior renowned for his cunning and guile, is the wily strategist who conceives the plan to trick the Trojans with the wooden horse, and thus it is he who finally brings an end to the siege of Troy. Before the war begins, however, Odysseus tries to avoid setting sail for Troy by feigning madness, and when his deception is revealed, he exacts his revenge by contriving to cause the death of the warrior who unmasks his scheme. According to some accounts, Odysseus inherits his sly nature from Sisyphus, the roguish trickster who extends the years of his life by tricking Thanatos, the god of death, and by outwitting Hades, the god who rules the underworld.

TRICKSTERS OF OCEANIA

The figure of the trickster also appears within the various myth traditions of Oceania. Maui and Olofat, the great tricksters in the myths of the Polynesian and the Micronesian peoples, are both fire bringers and accordingly culture heroes. Mischief makers as well, Maui transforms his brother-in-law into the first dog, and Olofat changes the shark into a menacing creature by giving it sharp teeth. Maui is also a lecherous figure who violates social taboos by committing incest, and Olofat is the troublemaker who instigates a fierce war among the deities when he visits his father, the god of the sky. Although these tricksters are often the agents of disorder within their communities, some of the changes they introduce are clearly beneficial. Maui, for example, increases the length of the day by slowing down the passage of the sun and provides new lands for people to inhabit by drawing up islands from the bottom of the sea. Olofat, who is the messenger of the sky god, serves human beings as their intermediary with the celestial deities. In myths from Australia, the figure of the trickster emerges in tales of capricious beings who work their mischief as they wander through the bush. The Ngandjala-Ngandjala, for example, take pleasure in ruining people's crops, and the Wurulu-Wurulu are the annoying thieves who often steal their honey. The Mimi, ancient trickster spirits who live within rocky cliffs, are credited with teaching the people's ancestors to hunt.

THE ENIGMATIC TRICKSTER FIGURE

The ambiguous nature of the trickster figure is represented in especially dramatic fashion in the Norse tradition, where the inveterate troublemaker, Loki, is both friend and enemy of the gods, both creator and destroyer. Companion to Odin and Thor, Loki shares many of their adventures, and after he persuades the dwarves to fashion marvelous treasures, he bestows great gifts upon these gods: he gives Odin the invincible spear, Gungnir, and the golden ring called Draupnir, and he gives Thor the finest gift of all, the mighty hammer Mjollnir. Loki is, however, as unpredictable as the fire for which he is named, and thus he also proves to be the adversary of these gods and, ultimately, the agent of their doom. Loki first endangers the gods when he helps a giant abduct Idunn and steal her apples of eternal youth, for without the precious apples, the gods begin to age. It is the trickster himself, however, who saves the gods from growing old and dying when he reverses his actions and snatches the goddess from the giants, returning her and her apples to the home of the gods. The changeable trickster thus works his mischief both on the gods and on their eternal enemies, the giants. A lecher and a shape-shifter, Loki seduces goddesses, giantesses, human beings, and even plants and animals, and changes his shape into many different forms. Indeed, this trickster possesses the power to transform his sexual nature, for while he is the father of numerous offspring, he is also the mother who gives birth to Sleipnir, Odin's magnificent, eight-legged horse. Liar, thief, and prankster as well as helper of both the giants and the gods, Loki is finally the instrument of change, for when he brings about the death of the old world, a new one is born in its place.

See also Animals in Myth; The Apocalypse; Creation Myths; Culture Heroes; Gods; Messengers

TWINS, PAIRS, AND DOUBLES

Symbols of duality, the twins that appear in tales from many cultures serve several different functions within myth tradition. In some narratives twins embody the opposing powers of good and evil, and in others they represent the harmonious conjunction of complementary powers. In either case the presence of twins signifies differentiation through their manifestation as two distinct characters rather than one. The twins whose relationship is defined by opposition characteristically engage in a struggle for supremacy, while those who act in concert are usually depicted as remarkably resourceful heroes whose combined skills and ingenuity prove too great for the adversaries they encounter. Interestingly, in several tales where twins appear as beneficent culture heroes, they eventually assume the form of the sun and moon or a pair of stars. In other narratives a subtle twinning is implied when contrasting figures are clearly paired or when a character obviously serves as the double, or alter ego, of another being. In a few myths the differentiated selfhood of twins is embodied in a single figure, usually a creator god.

GOOD AND EVIL TWINS

Good and evil twins compete to shape the features of the world in a motif that recurs within certain Native American creation myths. In similar versions of a story told by the Iroquois, Mohawk, and Huron peoples, for example, wickedness and hardship are introduced into the world by Evil Twin's acts of creation. According to the Iroquois origin myth, after Atahensic, the Sky Woman, falls from the heavens and eventually comes to rest on the back of Great Turtle, the earth-diver Muskrat carries from the bottom of the primal sea the grains of earth from which the world then grows. In time Sky Woman gives birth to a daughter, Earth Woman, and when she is made pregnant by the West Wind, her children are the twins who complete the creation of the world. Evil Twin, determined to thwart his brother and to be the firstborn son, bursts from Earth Woman's side while she is giving birth to Good Twin, and thus their mother dies during her delivery of the boys.

In a variation of the Ymir motif, Good Twin shapes the sun from Earth Woman's face and uses the back of his mother's head to make the moon and the stars. When the sun begins to shine, squash, beans, and corn sprout from the portions of the corpse that lie buried in the earth, and Good Twin beseeches Thunder to provide life-sustaining rain to nurture these plants. The twins are the creators who must prepare the earth for the people who will live there, and thus each contributes according to his nature. In his land to the west, Evil Twin shapes treacherous mountains and creates huge, predatory creatures that include bears, wolves, mosquitoes, and snakes. In the east, Good Twin makes meadows and lakes and populates his land with fat deer, buffalo, rabbits, and birds. Although neither twin can destroy what the other has made, each has the power to make subtle changes, and thus Good Twin reduces the size of his brother's monstrous beasts, and Evil Twin causes Good Twin's plump animals to become thinner. When Evil Twin's favorite creation, the thirsty toad, swallows all the water in the land, Good Twin creates rivers by piercing the creature's bloated body, and, to assist the people who will soon travel those streams, he gives them each two currents that flow in opposite directions. Evil Twin, however, does not wish to make life easy for the people, and so he removes one of the currents from each of the rivers and adds waterfalls and rapids to create extra dangers.

Displeased with what his brother has made and angered by the ways Good Twin has changed his own creations, Evil Twin eventually proposes that the two fight to the death for supremacy over the world they have shaped. When Good Twin, who has been warned in a dream of his brother's treachery, suggests that their contest be a race rather than a battle, Evil Twin agrees—upon the condition that the loser will be killed. It takes the brothers two days to complete their grueling race, and when Good Twin is the first to cross the finish line, he knows that Evil Twin will surely kill him if his life is spared, and therefore he slays his lifelong opponent. Upon his death the malicious creator becomes the Evil Spirit in the Land of the Dead, and Good Twin, the benevolent creator, shapes the first man and woman from the soil of the earth. These primal parents, the original Iroquois people, give birth to the six pairs of children who in time found the great nations of the Mohawk, Oneida, Onondaga, Cayuga, Seneca, and Tuscarora peoples, all the members of the Confederacy of the Six Iroquois Nations.

According to the Yuma people of North America's Southwest, good and evil creator twins emerge from the depths of the primal waters. Kokomaht, the good twin, is the first to stand upon the surface of the primordial ocean, and because he already knows that his brother is vicious, he instructs him to open his eyes as he swims up through the salty sea. Thus, when the evil twin finally reaches the water's surface, his capacity to produce mischief is greatly reduced by the fact that he is blind. Bakotahl, the "Blind One," is nevertheless able to introduce evil into the world that Kokomaht creates, and it is he who is responsible for unleashing the whirlwind that carries all disease. Kokomaht stirs the primal waters to create the earth, and from its mud he then gives form to the first human beings. Bakotahl also attempts to shape people from the mud, but his imperfect creations, which have no hands or feet, must dwell in the water as fish and other creatures. Kokomaht, who knows that the earth will become too crowded if people do not die, wisely teaches them how to die through the example of his own death. The evil Bakotahl, who cares nothing for the people's welfare, withdraws to the depths of the earth, and there he continues to make trouble with his earthquakes and volcanoes.

Several tales from Melanesian peoples offer accounts of the rivalry between a clever creator and his foolish twin. Although the incompetent brother does not intend to introduce evil through his creations, the mistakes that he makes as he competes with his twin are nonetheless the source of much trouble in the world and serve to explain certain flaws in creation. In one of these accounts, for example, the wise twin To Kabinana produces beneficial gifts while To Karvuvu, the maladroit twin who attempts to emulate his brother's acts, unfailingly wreaks havoc with his creations. When To Kabinana uses coconuts to make the world's women, To Karvuvu quickly follows his example; because he unwittingly turns his coconuts upside down, however, the noses of the race of women that To Karvuvu produces are all monstrously malformed. To Kabinana carves a wooden fish that leads other fish to the shore where people can easily harvest them, but the wooden fish that To Karvuvu then carves becomes the deadly shark that devours the people's fish and often threatens their lives too. Like the creator brothers of the Native American traditions, the twins of Melanesian myths act at odds with one another, and thus the world that they shape contains both good and bad features.

CREATORS VERSUS DESTROYERS

In the ancient traditions of both Egypt and Persia, the world is conceived as the site of a never-ending struggle between the powers of creation and those of destruction, and in these cultures' myths, pairs of opposing figures embody this essential conflict. For the Egyptians, Osiris, fertility god and emblem of ordered creation, is opposed by his brother Set, god of the barren desert and the disorder it represents. Disorder threatens to prevail when Set murders Osiris, the ruler of the earth, and then attempts to seize control of his brother's kingdom. However, a balance between the forces of creation and destruction is restored when Osiris is resurrected as the ruler of the afterlife and his son Horus assumes his father's earthly throne. In Persian tradition the opposing figures of Spenta Mainyu, the creator of life, and Angra Mainyu, the demon of death, embody the culture's vision of a cosmic struggle between good and evil. Spenta Mainyu, known to the Zoroastrians as Ahura Mazda, battles his wicked adversary until the end of time and finally destroys him on the Day of Judgment. According to one version of the tale, Ohrmazd (Ahura Mazda) and Ahriman (Angra Mainyu) are the twin sons of the primordial being known as Zurvan-i Akanarak, or "Infinite Time."

Interestingly, in several of the myths where twins represent opposing powers, the brother who is the embodiment of disorder and destruction begins his struggle for supremacy by determining the time of his own birth. Like Evil Twin in the Iroquois tale, the Persian figure of Ahriman seeks to be the firstborn son, for he knows that Zurvan has promised to give this twin the power to rule the earth. Ahriman therefore forces his way out of Zurvan's body and makes his claim to power by representing himself as his brother Ohrmazd. Zurvan, however, is not tricked by the wicked twin's duplicity and, although he must honor his pledge and grant Ahriman supremacy during the first nine thousand years of the world's existence, at the end of that epoch Ohrmazd at last overthrows his evil brother. According to Egyptian tradition, Set chooses to be born on the third day of the five during which his mother Nut delivers her offspring, and he too leaves his mother's body by violent means: like Ahriman and Evil Twin, Set cuts a hole in his mother's side rather than waiting to emerge as his siblings do through a natural birth.

LIGHT VERSUS DARKNESS

The dualistic vision of the cosmos that is expressed in the Persian and Egyptian myths of opposing pairs is also evident in tales from the Baltic Slavs, where Byelobog, the white god, personifies all goodness and Chernobog, the black god, represents the presence of evil within the world. According to this tradition, Byelobog, who is the deity of light and day, appears only during the daylight hours and can be recognized by his flowing white beard and dazzling white clothes. The beneficent white god helps travelers find their way through the dark woods, assists with the harvest, and bestows the gifts of fertility and wealth, while the black god of night spreads misfortune and hardship throughout the land. In this contrasting pair of gods, the dualistic nature of earthly existence is thus symbolized.

The eternal conflict between good and evil that is represented in the opposing figures of the white and black gods also appears in Slavic creation myths that describe a similar struggle between the forces of light and darkness. In one Russian tale, for example, the bright lord of light originally rules over heaven, and the wicked Tsar Santanail governs the dark realm of the earth. Tsar Santanail fashions the first people from clay but cannot breathe life into them, and when the bright lord brings the people to life, he takes them with him to his celestial kingdom. After Tsar Santanail is successful in tempting the people to return to the earth, the armies of the forces of light and darkness engage in a mighty battle that lasts for seventy-seven days before the bright lord of heaven defeats the dark demons of the earth. In triumph, the victor hangs his brilliant sword high up in the sky, and there it shines brightly in the form of the sun. Tsar Santanail and his demons must hide whenever the sun lights up the world, but when the darkness falls, the minions of evil emerge and roam throughout the earth.

In Aztec tradition the relationship between another contrasting pair of creator deities, Quetzalcoatl and Black Tezcatlipoca, is more complex than that portrayed in the myths where opposing figures wholly embody the powers of creation and destruction. Generally represented as a great culture hero and an emblem of life and fertility, Quetzalcoatl nevertheless performs acts of destruction, and Tezcatlipoca, who is associated with darkness, conflict, change, and death, is nonetheless also a revered protector deity as well as a creator god. While these figures are often foes, sometimes they act in concert as a pair of heroes. As adversaries, each god destroys the world created by his brother, but, as allies, the two work together to create the fifth and last world of the Aztecs. In one version of this creation myth, Quetzalcoatl and Tezcatlipoca slay and dismember the flesh-eating monster Tlaltecuhtli to shape the heavens and the earth and, in another account, they take the form of gigantic trees that hold the sky above the earth. As a reward for their joint efforts to create the Fifth World, their father Ometeotl makes Quetzalcoatl and

Tezcatlipoca the rulers of the heaven's stars and provides the Milky Way that serves as their path through the sky.

HERO TWINS

While Quetzalcoatl and Tezcatlipoca are often depicted in Aztec myths as a pair of either opposing or complementary figures, according to tradition it is Xolotl, the dog-headed deity whose feet are turned backward, who is Quetzalcoatl's unlikely twin brother. Xolotl, whose name means "Twin," is the god of both twins and deformities and characteristically serves as the psychopomp, the guide who leads the dead on their journey to Mictlan, the Aztec underworld. As the god of fertility and life, Quetzalcoatl possesses attributes that are very different from those of his twin, and therefore the two are generally represented as an opposing pair. However, after the creation of the Fifth World, these twins are the heroes who travel together to the underworld to recover the bones needed for the creation of a new race of human beings. To gather the bones of the people who were destroyed at the end of the Fourth World, the twins must outwit Mictlantecuhtli, the treacherous ruler of the underworld who is loathe to let them leave his realm. Quetzalcoatl evades the traps laid by the skeleton god, however, and when the twins successfully complete their dangerous task, they mix the pulverized bones with the blood of the gods to create the Aztec people.

The Aztec twins' exploits in the land of the dead resemble those of Hunahpu and Xbalanque, the Mayan Hero Twins who also outwit the rulers of the underworld, the terrible Lords of Xibalba. Unlike the twins of myth who represent opposing forces, the culture heroes whose adventures are detailed in the *Popol Vuh* (ca. 1558) share a common goal, the task of preparing the world for the creation of human beings. To fulfill their mission, the twins must rid the world of monsters and avenge the deaths of their father and his twin by defeating the fearsome death gods who rule in Xibalba. Before making their descent to the underworld, the Hero Twins destroy Vucub Caquix (Seven Macaw) and his two destructive sons, all pernicious monsters who proclaim themselves the rulers of the earth. While the twins, who are both skillful hunters, make use of their blowguns to wound Seven Macaw, they must rely upon their cunning to finally overcome their adversary and his malicious sons.

The guile practiced by the Hero Twins during their earthly conquests also stands them in good stead when they reach the underworld, where the death lords try to destroy them by means of the trickery they earlier employed to kill their father and their uncle, another pair of twins. Hunahpu and Xbalanque, however, cleverly escape the perils of the Hot Seat, the House of Gloom, the House of Knives, and the other obstacles they confront in Xibalba, and then, posing as dancers and magicians, they use trickery of their own to slay Hun Came (One Death) and Vucub Came (Seven Death), the greatest of the underworld's gods. When the remaining inhabitants of Xibalba plead for mercy, the heroes spare their lives after first receiving their promise that they will not demand the blood sacrifice of human beings. Then, carrying with them the remains of their uncle and their father the maize god, the twins return to the earth that at last lies ready for the creation of the Maya, the people made from corn. To light the world they have prepared for the first human beings, the Hero Twins ascend to the heavens and there they assume the forms of the sun and the moon.

CELESTIAL BODIES

The Mayan culture heroes are by no means the only set of twins associated with celestial bodies in myth tradition. According to the ancient Greeks, Apollo and Artemis, the twin offspring of Zeus and the Titan Leto, are the gods of the sun and moon. As sun god, Apollo carries the epithet Phoebus, or "shining one," and his twin Artemis is Phosphoros, or "bearer of light." Known for their skill as archers, Artemis is also the goddess of the hunt and her twin is the hero who slays the monstrous dragon Python with his silver arrows. In some versions of another Greek myth, Zeus is also the father of the heroic twins who eventually become the constellation known as Gemini. Called the Dioscuri, or the "striplings of the god," Castor and Pollux (Kastor and Polydeukes) travel with the Argonauts, join in the hunt for the Calydonian Boar, and rescue their kidnapped sister Helen before becoming twin stars in the sky. In Australian tradition, twins known as the Wati-kutjara ("two men") become the constellation Gemini after they also perform heroic acts on earth. Iguana-men, Kurukadi and Mumba are the ancestral spirits who save a group of women from being ravaged by the moon man, Kulu. In this myth, not only do the twins ascend into the heavens, but the women also leave the earth to become the stars known as the Pleiades.

The Aztec deities Quetzalcoatl and Black Tezcatlipoca are also associated with both the stars and the sun, and some myths recount how Quetzalcoatl assumes the form of the morning star. The lord of the evening star is Quetzalcoatl's twin, the dog-headed Xolotl, and he is said to oversee the daily passage of the sun through the underworld. In Indian tradition the morning and the evening stars are another pair of twins, the horsemen of the sun known as the Asvins. According to tradition, each night the Asvins ride through the sky to prepare the way for the coming of Aruna, the god of the dawn. Twin goddesses personify the morning and evening stars in tales of the Slavic peoples: Zvezda Dennitsa ushers in the sun each day, and her sister Zvezda Vechernyaya signals the rising of the moon. The Hero Twins of Hopi myths perform yet another important task, for they are called upon to place the stars in the heavens during the process of creation. The Hero Twins carefully arrange patterns in the sky and thereby create the Milky Way and the great constellations. Before they can finish their work, however, Coyote the trickster loses patience with their artful planning, and, seizing all the remaining stars, he scatters them helter-skelter all about the heavens.

DIFFERENT FATHERS

In several myth traditions twins are depicted as the offspring of different fathers. The great Greek hero Herakles, for example, is the son of Zeus, while his twin brother Iphikles is the son of the mortal hero Amphitryon. Likewise, by some accounts Pollux is the son of Zeus, while his twin brother Castor is the son of the mortal king of Sparta. Although Iphikles accompanies his twin during several of Herakles' heroic adventures, it is the other pair of heroes, Castor and Pollux, who prove to be inseparable in Greek and Roman myths. Indeed, when the mortal Castor is killed during the twins' final battle, Pollux asks that he be permitted to share his own immortality with his beloved brother. Zeus grants his son's request, and thus the warrior twins are always seen together within the constellation known as Gemini ("The Twins").

Other pairs of twins who are engendered by different fathers also join together in pursuit of adventure, and in some accounts these brothers embark upon a quest to seek the recognition of their fathers. In one such tale told by the Tupinamba people of Brazil, Ariconte and Tamendonare do not know which twin is the son of the divine Maira Ata, and they therefore set forth together to search for the god. When they find the deity, Maira Ata requires that the twins prove themselves before he will acknowledge them, and thus the two help each other to survive a series of ordeals. When one brother is crushed by a rock, the other restores him, and when one is torn into pieces, his twin reassembles the body parts. By working together the twins complete their appointed tasks, and, because each of them proves to be worthy, Maira Ata finally accepts them both as his sons. In a Native American myth with a similar motif, the Navajo twins Monster-Slayer and Born for Water undergo an arduous journey in search of their fathers, Sun-God and Water-God. With the help of Spider Woman, the Navajo twins safely pass through canyons whose walls threaten to crush them and through beds of reeds whose leaves are as sharp as knives, and, finally, they cross the Rainbow Bridge that leads them to the Turquoise House of the fathers who rejoice to welcome them.

DESTINIES OF TWINS AS RULERS

Although similar myths from the Greek and Roman traditions recount stories of twins who are destined to be rulers, the tales from these two cultures have very different endings. The Greek myth of Amphion and Zetheus resembles the Roman story of Romulus and Remus in that both sets of twins are taken from their mothers and left to die in the wild when they are infants. Rescued by a shepherd, Amphion and Zetheus grow up to become the heroes who save their mother from slavery and then reign jointly as the kings of Thebes. At first rescued and nurtured by a wolf, Romulus and Remus are then also raised by a shepherd, and they too grow up to become mighty warriors and the leaders of the people. In time the people call upon the twins to found a new city, but the brothers quarrel before they can build it, and Romulus kills his lifelong companion. Thus, authority in Rome, the city that is named for its founder and first ruler, is represented as a power that cannot be shared. Whereas Romulus and Remus use their doubled power to defeat their enemies and unify their people, the ending of their story suggests that within Roman culture the authority vested in the king is not to be divided.

PAIRED COMPANIONS

As in the example offered by *Gilgamesh* (ca. 2000 B.C.E.), the ancient Mesopotamian epic, certain of myth's paired characters are linked neither by their parentage nor by their opposition to one another. Because Gilgamesh, who is young, arrogant, and impetuous when he first ascends his throne, interferes too much in the lives of his subjects, the gods decide to enlarge his experience by creating for him a companion who is his equal in both strength and courage. Thus Enkidu, the man formed from clay, becomes the youthful king's double and the heroic warrior who helps him slay the ferocious giant Humbaba as well as the mighty Bull of Heaven. The king's ally, however, is more than a heroic companion, for Enkidu also serves as Gilgamesh's alter ego, the voice that at first questions the wisdom of the quest to seek adventure by confronting the dangerous Humbaba. Later, when the heroes have insulted the gods by destroying the sacred Bull of Heaven, Enkidu performs yet another service, for it is he who pays for the pair's deed with the price of his life. Bereft over the loss of his other self, the figure that shared all the heroic adventures of his youth, Gilgamesh sets forth alone on the journey that will lead to his acceptance of his own mortality, and, when he returns from his travels, he at last possesses the wisdom, experience, and maturity of a great and much-beloved king.

GENDER DUALITY

In many myth traditions the duality of the sexes is represented in the form of male and female twins. The Greek deities Apollo and Artemis are an example of such a pair, as are the Norse twins Freyr and Freyja, god and goddess of fertility. Not surprisingly, male and female twins also frequently appear in creation myths. According to ancient Egyptian cosmology, creation originates with the four pairs of primal twins known as the Ogdoad. Deities that personify the chaos from which the cosmos emerges, the Ogdoad includes Nun and Naunet, god and goddess of the primal waters, Kek and Kauket, twin deities of darkness, Amon and Amaunet, who symbolize invisible powers, and Heh and Hauhet, god and goddess of infinity. Male and female twins indeed play a prominent role in Egyptian accounts of creation, for after the sun god emerges from the primal waters, he gives birth to another pair, Shu and Tefnut, the god of air and the goddess of mist. These deities then become the parents of the twins Geb and Nut, the earth god and sky goddess who give birth to Osiris and Isis, the first great rulers of Egypt. In a similar account, the Dogon people of Mali trace their origins to the Nummo, the two pairs of male and female twins who are the offspring of the earth and Amma, the creator deity.

Occasionally principles of duality are expressed in a single mythic figure. The creator deity of Africa's Fon people, for example, is the twin-faced Mawu-Lisa, an androgynous god whose female essence, Mawu, is linked to the moon, and whose male identity, Lisa, is associated with the sun. According to tradition, Mawu-Lisa gives birth to all the gods in the Fon pantheon, and male and female twin deities are the first of these offspring. Another double figure comes from India, where the divinities Vishnu and Shiva are sometimes embodied as one in the form of Harihara. The wheel that the twin god carries in his left hand symbolizes Vishnu (Hari), and the trident that he bears in his right hand is an emblem of Shiva (Hara.) Ardhanarisvara, another Indian deity, is an androgynous being in whom Shiva is embodied as half male and half female—and thus possesses the creative powers of both god and goddess. In Roman tradition, the two-faced Janus, guardian god of doorways, gazes into the past with one pair of eyes and looks to the future with his other pair. In all of these deities, differentiated qualities are twinned within a single incarnation.

See also The Apocalypse; Creation Myths; Culture Heroes; Ymir Motif

THE UNDERWORLD

The myth traditions of most cultures not only explain the origins of life in their accounts of creation, but they also address, in tales that describe a world of the dead, the question of mortal beings' destiny once their earthly lives have ended. That an underworld is commonly envisioned as the realm of the dead is not surprising, for inherent in such a conception of it is an acknowledgment of the world's natural cycle of life and death that eventually culminates in the earth's absorption of all creatures and crops. In other words, the ground that receives the bodies of the dead is frequently conceived as the place where their spirits continue to exist. According to the accounts of some cultural traditions, the sun passes into the underworld at the end of each day, and thus the land of the dead lies to the west, where the sun makes its descent into the netherworld. Although the underworld is sometimes depicted as a site of torment, it is not always represented as the place where the dead are punished and can indeed be regarded as the realm where souls are rewarded or simply as the land that the dead inhabit. In some myths the underworld is seen as the permanent home of the dead, and in others it is the temporary residence of spirits that await reincarnation and a return to life or resurrection at the end of time. According to the accounts offered by several cultural traditions, the dead are judged in the underworld, and thus it is there that the ultimate fate of a soul is determined.

JOURNEY TO THE UNDERWORLD

While admission to the underworld is characteristically forbidden to mortals, tales from many traditions describe the perilous journeys that people or deities make to the realm of the dead. Known as the harrowing of hell or the descent motif, the journey to the underworld requires great courage and resolve, for the heroes who undertake it do not know if they can ever find their way back to the world of the living. Heroes who make a descent sometimes do so to rescue someone from the land of the dead or to seek the counsel or wisdom of an ancestor who dwells there. Some heroes travel to the underworld to capture, fight, or slay a fearsome monster, and others seek the precious objects or magical powers that can often be obtained by journeying to the netherworld. The journey itself is an arduous one, for most of the underworlds of myth tradition are separated from the world of the living by great mountain barriers and bodies of water. Boats are often necessary to cross rivers, lakes, or seas, and in many cultural traditions a ferryman of the underworld carries the souls of the dead to their destination. Bridges or gates present additional obstacles, and these entryways are usually guarded by terrifying sentinels. According to the myths of several traditions, those mortals or gods who do make their way to the underworld must refuse all food and drink there, for after consuming the food of the dead, it is no longer possible to return to the earth.

JOURNEY OF THE DEAD

If the journey undertaken by heroes who visit the underworld is an arduous one, so too is the trip made by the dead, as it is described in the accounts of many myth traditions. Indeed, quite often the dead are assisted in their journey by a guide known as the psychopomp, the "bearer of souls." While the psychopomp is usually a god, in some tales animals accompany the dead or serve as messengers that travel between the earth and the netherworld, and in stories from Africa, for instance, the hen is often the guide of the dead or their messenger. In many cultures the living also assist the dead by providing them with sturdy shoes or supplying them with the clothing, food, weapons, or other provisions that they need to travel in comfort. For example, in ancient Greek tradition the dead are customarily provided with a coin that can be used to pay Charon, the underworld boatman, for passage across the rivers that border the kingdom known as Hades. And in the ancient Egyptian culture, where the underworld is envisioned as a place where crops are grown, the dead who carry with them a *shabti* (a small figurine) are thereby provided with a servant who can labor in the fields that nourish the dead.

REGIONS OF THE UNDERWORLD

Frequently a deity presides over the underworld as lord of the dead, and some myths offer vivid portraits of the landscapes of these chthonic (underground) kingdoms. Sometimes the netherworld's terrain is divided into various separate regions, and in several instances the underworld consists of multiple layers. These geographical divisions within underground kingdoms can signify hierarchies among the populations of the dead, and in both Greek and Norse traditions, for example, the spirits of dead warriors enjoy a special status: according to the Greek myths, the shades of the great heroes dwell in Elysium, the realm of the blessed, and in the tales of the Norse, the brave warriors killed in battle all gather in Valhalla, the mead hall of the slain. The Greek and Norse underworlds both feature layers as well, and in the Greek tradition, the lowest region of Hades, Tartarus, is the abyss where the wicked and the enemies of the gods are eternally punished for their heinous crimes. Although Niflheim, located at the bottom of the Norse underworld, is not a place of punishment, it is the forbidding land of ice and fog that is the home of Nidhogg, the monstrous serpent that devours corpses and viciously gnaws at the roots of Yggdrasil, the great Tree of Life. The Christian vision of Hell that is offered in Dante's *Inferno* (1472) does represent the underworld as a place of torment, and in the hierarchical organization of this realm's terrain, sinners are assigned to one of Hell's nine levels as punishment for their earthly deeds. Thus the uppermost layers of Hell are inhabited by the lustful and the gluttonous, while the lower levels are reserved for those evildoers whose crimes are more onerous.

THE GREAT BELOW

The earliest descriptions of a chthonic realm inhabited by the dead appear in ancient Mesopotamian myths. According to these tales, the goddess Ereshkigal, sister of the sky goddess Inanna, becomes ruler of the underworld when she is abducted and carried there after the separation of the earth and sky. Ereshkigal's kingdom, the Great Below, is conceived as an egalitarian place where all the dead, both gods and human beings, suffer the same grim lot, for the denizens of this land all wander naked through the dark, eating of the dust that affords them nourishment. Although some myths make reference to the seven judges of the underworld, the Great Below is not a place where the dead are judged and punished, and the judges that preside there serve to prevent those who enter their kingdom from ever leaving it. The first accounts of a descent to the underworld also appear in the Mesopotamian myths, and the story of Inanna's journey to the netherworld includes passages that detail many of the features of her sister's chthonic realm. According to various versions of the accounts that tell of her descent, Inanna, like all others who travel to the Great Below, dies upon reaching her destination. However, the great goddess who oversees the earth's fertility is indeed restored to life and rescued from the underworld, and her lover then takes her place in the land of the dead.

The Great Below, as it is described in the tales of Inanna's descent, can be reached by traveling the Road of No Return. Seven locked gates are positioned at intervals along this passageway, and at each of the gates Inanna must remove articles of clothing and jewelry so that, by the time she passes through the last of the gates and enters the underworld, she is completely naked and thus divested of all the accouterments of her life as goddess of the sky. Inanna is guided in her passage through the seven gates by Namtar, the messenger of the underworld whose duty it is to lead living beings to the place of death. In the dark underworld, Ereshkigal sits upon her throne with her seven judges in attendance, and, in some versions of the myth, it is when the judges gaze upon Inanna that she becomes a corpse. In these accounts of the tale, the judges play another role as well, for after the goddess is restored to life, they insist that she be accompanied by the demon guardians of the underworld when she returns to the Great Above. Because the ferocious demons travel with her, Inanna cannot evade the judges' demand that she name a substitute to take her place in the netherworld, and thus she chooses Dumuzi, the lover who shows no sign that he has mourned her death.

THE DUAT

Descriptions of the ancient Egyptians' conception of the underworld can be found in numerous funerary texts that contain instructions for the journey to the netherworld and provide the spells and incantations that all travelers need to escape the dangers they must confront. According to Egyptian tradition, the sun god enters the underworld in the west each night, and the twelve hours it takes him to complete his journey correspond to the twelve regions within the chthonic realm. The underworld, known as the Duat, resembles the world on the surface of the earth, and indeed a mighty river that is an extension of the Nile flows through this domain. Judgment is passed on the souls of the dead within the underworld, and to reach the place of judgment at the throne of Osiris, the god who rules the Duat, the dead must travel on the sun god's barque to Sekhet Hetepet, the sixth region within the netherworld. The barque that ferries the dead is guided by the boatmen Aken and Mahaf, whose head faces backwards, and underworld guardians stand sentry at the seven gates through which the dead must pass after they leave the boat. According to tradition, the dead must speak the names of those who guard the Duat's portals before they can enter Osiris's Hall of Justice and learn the destiny of their souls.

The jackal-headed god Anubis is the psychopomp who leads the souls of the dead to the Scales of Justice where their hearts are weighed, and Thoth, the ibis-headed god of wisdom, records the judgments that are made in the Hall of Justice. Osiris, with his sisters Isis and Nephthys at his side, watches from his throne while Anubis places an ostrich feather from the headdress of Maat, the goddess of truth and justice, on one side of the scale. Anubis then places the heart that is being judged on the scale's other side, and if it is heavy with the weight of its owner's misdeeds, it is consumed by Ammit, the monster whose epithet is "devourer of the dead." One of the demons of the underworld, Ammit is a female with a crocodile's head, a lion's torso, and the hindquarters of a hippopotamus. If the weight of a heart does not tip the scale, its owner's body is resurrected and sent to the Field of Rushes, a fertile land where crops are grown. Although there are dangers in this realm—demons, burning lakes, giant beetles, and crocodiles—those who live there can protect themselves by reciting spells. Because crops are planted and harvested in the Field of Rushes, there is much work to be done, but those who bring *shabtis* with them to the underworld can use them as their servants.

THE BRIDGE OF CHINVAT

While the underworld envisioned by ancient Persia's Zoroastrians is a place of both judgment and punishment, it is not the permanent home of the dead, for, according to tradition, all souls are finally redeemed at the end of time. Before the apocalyptic destruction of the earth, however, the dead travel to the Bridge of Chinvat in the underworld, and there Rashnu, the guardian of the bridge, Sraosha, the god of obedience, and Mithra, the god of light, add up all the good and evil deeds performed by the dead during their earthly lives. After the reckoning is made, the souls approach the bridge, and those who led good lives on earth perceive it as a broad expanse that is easy to traverse. Escorted by the goddess Daena and her two guardian dogs, these souls pass into a paradise known as the House of Song. When the deeds of the dead are equally balanced between good and evil, the bridge these souls perceive is a narrower one, and it leads them to a gloomy limbo known as Hammistagan, the "Place of the Mixed Ones." To the souls whose evil deeds outnumber the good, the bridge appears as a narrow ledge, too treacherous to cross, and indeed these souls all fall from the Bridge of Chinvat into a place of suffering deep in the underworld. In Zoroastrian tradition, the punishment endured by the wicked cleanses them of evil, and therefore they are resurrected and the underworld is utterly destroyed on the final Day of Judgment at the end of earthly time.

HEL

In some cultural traditions the underworld assumes the name of the ruler of the dead, as it does in the myths of the Norse, where Hel, the daughter of the trickster Loki, is queen of the netherworld. Hel, who is described as half living and half rotted in putrid decay, holds dominion over all of the dead except those who fall on the battlefield and are led by the Valkyries to Odin's great hall of dead heroes. According to Norse tradition, even slain deities who do not die in battle must make the trip to Hel, and thus that is where Balder goes after he is murdered. Although the Norse underworld is not a place of punishment, Hel is a gloomy and forbidding realm that is encircled by high walls. Garm, the snarling, slavering hound of Hel, guards Valgrind, the underworld's gate, and when Valgrind is occasionally left open, the dead swarm out and hasten back toward Midgard, the land of the living. Balder makes his voyage to the underworld when the ship that is his funeral pyre sinks down to Hel, but Hermod, who is sent by the gods to plead for Balder's release, makes his descent on horseback, and the account of his journey provides a vivid description of the underworld.

To reach Hel, Hermod must cross its many barriers, and thus he travels for nine days over the high mountains, deep chasms, and icy rivers to the north. When he finally reaches the great river Gjall on the border of the underworld, its bridge, the Gjallarbru, is guarded by the fearsome hag Modgud, who is a skeleton. Modgud usually demands blood as the toll for passage across her bridge, but when she learns of Hermod's mission, she allows him to proceed. After passing this obstacle, Hermod makes his way through the Iron Wood, a forest of blackened, dead trees with knife-like metal leaves. Rather than stopping at the gate that is guarded by Garm, Hermod spurs his horse, Sleipnir, to leap over Hel's high walls, and there he finds Eljundnir, the underworld's ghastly hall of death. The scene there is a grim one, for Hermod is surrounded by the rotting corpses that feed at Hunger, the great table in dark Eljundnir, and he must wait for the queen to rise from Disease, the bed in which she rests. In time Hel does grant the gods' messenger an audience, however, and she even agrees to release Balder if all the world will weep for him. In respect to the goal of his quest, Hermod's journey to the underworld is therefore successful, and in the end it will be the trouble-making Loki who sees to it that Hel will never have to honor her promise to the gods.

HADES

Hades, another underworld kingdom that bears the name of its ruler, is the realm of the dead in Greek tradition. According to the accounts of the ancient Greeks, the dead begin their journey to Hades when they are buried, for those who are not buried remain on the earth as wandering ghosts. After burial, the souls of the dead are led by the god Hermes, the psychopomp, to the great river that marks the border of Erebus, the upper region of Hades. To cross the river, sometimes represented as the Acheron and sometimes as the Styx, the shades must pay a fee to Charon, the ferryman of the dead, for those souls that do not possess a coin are left milling in the crowds that gather on the river's banks. After crossing the river, the dead travel on to the netherworld's place of judgment at the intersection of three roads, and there Rhadamanthys, Minos, and Aeacus, three sons of Zeus, decide which path each shade must take to complete the journey. One road leads to Elysium, the realm of the blessed, and another to a limbo that is called the Fields of Asphodel. The third path descends to Tartarus, the region at the lowest level of the kingdom, and it is there that evildoers are punished for their deeds.

Tartarus is enclosed by an immense bronze wall, and perpetual night cloaks this realm in darkness. The palace of Hades and Persephone, king and queen of the underworld, lies within the wall, and Cerberus, the fierce, three-headed hound, is the guardian of their domicile. The great abyss, a pit so deep that it is said to be bottomless, is also located within the bounds of Tartarus, and it is into this abyss that Zeus casts the Titans when he defeats them in his battle for supremacy. The punishment inflicted in Tartarus is everlasting, and thus Ixion turns forever on his wheel of fire there, and Tantalus perpetually reaches for the food and drink that he can never grasp. The hideous Erinyes (the Furies), the avengers of the dead, stand beside the throne of Hades, and when they are summoned by the gods, they rise up from the underworld to pursue and punish those among the living who commit heinous crimes. Winged goddesses in black, blood-soaked robes, the fearsome Erinyes particularly seek out those who slay members of their own families, and thus it is they who torment Orestes for the sin of killing his mother Clytemnestra.

REINCARNATION OF THE DEAD

The realm of the dead is conceived as an underworld in many other cultural traditions, including that of ancient China. According to the oldest of the accounts from China, the underworld lies beneath Taishan, the great northeastern mountain. As it is described in later myths, the land of the dead, with its principal city of Feng-Tu, is ruled by the ten Yama kings, the Lords of Death. At the entrance to the netherworld, three bridges separate the world of the living from that of the dead. Gods cross to the kingdom of the Yama Lords on a golden bridge, and the souls of the just pass over on a silver one. The third bridge, made of wood, is too flimsy to support the souls of the wicked, and these therefore plunge into the foul river that lies far below. Although the souls that reach the kingdom of the dead are all eventually reincarnated, those that fall from the wooden bridge are consumed by the vicious brass snakes and the fierce iron dogs that lurk in the nasty river. The Yama kings preside over ten courts, and all who reach their domain stop first in the Court of Judgment to account for the deeds of their earthly lives. Those souls that are immediately ready to return to the world of the living are then sent to the tenth court, where the Wheel of Transmigration releases them back to the earth. The other eight courts are places of punishment, and the dead who suffer in them are cleansed of all their sins before they too are sent to the Wheel of Transmigration.

Before leaving the land of the dead, all souls drink the Brew of Oblivion, and thus they return to the earth with no memories of a former life.

In the myths of Japan, the goddess Izanami reigns as queen of Yomi, the realm of the dead, and in Indian tradition, Yama is the ruler of the underworld. Like the Chinese kingdom of the dead, the Japanese underworld is a place where souls are cleansed of their wickedness, and thus the dead suffer in the hellish regions of Jigoku before they are reborn to earthly life. According to Hindu tradition, the souls of the dead must cross over the river Vaitarani to reach Yama's kingdom. Two ferocious, four-eyed dogs stand guard at the entrance to the ruler's palace, and the dead must get past these beasts to move on to the room where they are judged. Chitragupta, the scribe of the underworld, reads aloud a list of the deeds committed by the dead, and Yama then determines the fate of their souls. Some souls are sent to dwell in the heavens, others are reborn to a new life on the earth, and the souls of the wicked are condemned to punishment in one of the twenty-one hells of the underworld. A fearsome deity who sometimes visits the earth accompanied by his dogs, Yama carries a noose that he uses to wrench souls from the bodies of those who are dying.

UNDERWORLD COMMUNITIES

Although some African peoples envision the realm of the dead as a heavenly kingdom, others describe it as an underworld domain, and often it is conceived as the temporary dwelling place of those who are eventually reborn to earthly life. In a tale told by southern Africa's Wacago people, for example, a young girl who enters the underworld when she drowns in a pond resides there happily for some time until she expresses her desire to return to the earth. A kindly old woman then guides the young girl to the pool where she drowned, and from there she is able to find her way back to the world of the living. The netherworld, as it is represented in myths from Africa, closely resembles the world of the living, and this is also the case in the accounts of those North American peoples who conceive of the land of the dead as an underworld. According to the traditions of the Zuni, the Hopi, and the Tewa peoples, the dead return to the underworld from which their ancestors once emerged, and there they dwell in a community of spirits. To reach the village in the underworld, the dead must travel to the *sipapu*, the hole through which their ancestors climbed when they originally ascended to the surface of the earth. According to Hopi tradition, the *sipapu* can be found on the floor of the Grand Canyon.

MICTLAN

Whereas the netherworlds of African and North American myths are generally not represented as terrifying places, the underworlds of Mesoamerica's Aztec and Mayan traditions are both portrayed as forbiddingly sinister realms. According to the accounts of the Aztecs, it takes four years to make the journey to Mictlan, the land of the dead, for many obstacles await those who travel there. To reach their destination, the dead must first cross a raging river that churns through a precipitous chasm, and to accomplish this task, they need the assistance of a yellow dog. They must then cross wide deserts and great mountains and pass through thundering cliffs that grind together with crushing force. In a terrifying region of freezing cold, the dead must dodge the obsidian knives that are carried by the icy winds, and throughout their long journey they are constantly threatened by monstrous dragons and other fearsome creatures. To help them confront these numerous ordeals, the dead travel with a "soul companion," a dog that is placed in their graves when they begin their journey. Mictlan itself is a cold, dark, and dreary boneyard that is ruled by Mictlantecuhtli and his queen, Mictlancihuatl. Both dreadful figures, the lord of the underworld is a gory skeleton, and his cadaverous wife wears a skirt that is made of writhing snakes. According to tradition, poisonous serpents are the only food that is available in the kingdom of the dead.

XIBALBA

Like Mictlan, the underworld of the ancient Maya is a loathsome realm, and the journey that the dead must make to reach it is long and perilous. As it is described in the Mayan epic, the *Popol Vuh* (ca. 1558), the land of the dead, Xibalba, is ruled by the Lords of Death and their demonic minions. The *Popol Vuh* presents an account of the journey to the underworld that is undertaken by the Hero Twins, and the story of their descent details the many obstacles that they must overcome before they can return to the world above. Like the path to Mictlan, the road to Xibalba passes through deep chasms and over raging rapids. The twins must also cross rivers of blood and streams of oozing pus. They must pass through a region of spiked thorns and do battle with armies of fierce scorpions. Finally, when they enter the kingdom of the Lords of Death, they must draw upon their cunning to survive the many trials with which they are tested. During their visit to Xibalba, the clever Hero Twins indeed escape death in the House of Gloom, the House of Knives, the House of Cold, the House of Jaguars, the House of Fire, and the House of Bats, all places of torture within the underworld. When the Hero Twins at last kill One Death and Seven Death, the leaders of the Lords of Xibalba, the power of the other demons is greatly diminished, and thus, although the underworld continues to exist, those who live in the world above are released from paying tribute, in the form of human sacrifice, to the Lords of Death.

See also The Afterlife; The Apocalypse; Culture Heroes; Descent Motif; Emergence Motif; Fertility Myths; Gods; Goddesses; The Quest; Twins, Pairs, and Doubles

THE WORLD TREE

Images of the tree, a natural symbol of growth and resilience, recur throughout myth and folklore tradition. In its deciduous form, the tree commonly represents the earthly life cycle of birth, death, and regeneration and can therefore be seen as a symbol of these natural processes in fertility myths associated with the earth mother or in the rituals by which she is honored. Fruit-bearing trees, in particular, often serve to represent the earth's fecundity. For example, the apple, commonly associated with love and regeneration, is the fruit of rejuvenation in myths from the Nordic, Greek, and Celtic traditions. In its evergreen form, the tree is an emblem of longevity or immortality. Rising high into the sky (another symbol of immortality), the tree invites metaphoric connections to both the heavens and the earth. Indeed, because the tree is deeply rooted in the earth and yet reaches toward the sky, numerous myth traditions have conceived the existence of a cosmic tree, a World Tree that links the heavens with the earth.

THE AXLE TREE

Also called the axis, the axle tree, or the Tree of Life, the World Tree serves as the central pillar of the cosmos, the *axis mundi* that unites the realms of the natural and the supernatural, the temporal and the eternal. Characteristically, the World Tree is rooted in the underworld, the place of the dead; from there it passes through the earth, the home of the living, and then it climbs into the sky, the realm of the immortal beings. It is in the World Tree, in other words, where all planes of existence can be seen to intersect. It can therefore be regarded as a metaphor for the whole of creation or, as it were, as a microcosm of the entire universe. Many depictions of the tree thus represent it as containing objects that symbolize the multiplicity of the cosmos. In some myths the World Tree serves as a bridge that provides travelers passage from one realm to another.

The World Tree sometimes grows in paradise and sometimes on a sacred mountain, both sites where the earth and sky are often said to meet. In almost all traditions that describe a cosmic tree, it rests at the center of creation—thus serving as the very axis of the world. In some accounts a sacred spring bubbles up from beneath the tree, and in some instances a snake lies coiled at its base. In many cases birds perch in the branches of the tree, and often a particular bird associated with the Tree of Life is symbolically significant. Indeed, within the ornate iconography of the World Tree, birds can also represent heavenly messengers or even the incarnations of souls. Occasionally other animals reside in or near the tree; in the Norse tradition, for example, a squirrel scampers up and down the trunk of Yggdrasil. In several traditions a particular kind of tree, one that is especially significant to a people's way of life, is specified as the cosmic tree. Yggdrasil is an ash tree, for example, the same tree as the one used to create Ask, the first man in Norse myths, and in Egypt the Tree of Life is the fig, an important source of food and a symbol of fecundity. While the World Tree might bear fruit, olives, almonds, or other foods, sometimes the stars, moon, and planets hang from its branches.

YGGDRASIL, THE WORLD ASH TREE

The best known among mythological cosmic trees is perhaps Yggdrasil, the World Ash Tree of the Norse tradition. The center of Norse cosmology and both the Tree of Wisdom and the Tree of Life, Yggdrasil also plays a role in the plots of several tales from Norse tradition. The tree's name, for example, means "Horse of Ygg" and refers to the occasion when Odin ("Ygg" is another name for Odin) is hanged from the tree so that after nine days of suffering he might gain knowledge of the sacred runes used for writing and divination. The tree is also featured in the story of Ragnarok, the great battle that signifies the twilight of the gods, for in many versions of the myth, Yggdrasil still stands at the end of the battle, after the giants and the gods have destroyed one another. Hiding in its branches are Lif (life) and Lifthrasir (desiring life), the man and the woman who become the primal parents of the generations that will live in the new world.

A world in itself, Yggdrasil is composed of a landscape that is described by Snorri Sturluson and others in extraordinary detail. The earth, called Midgard in Norse cosmology, is a circle of land surrounded by the boundless water that is the home of the World Serpent. In the very center of the land stands Yggdrasil, supported by three roots that are all nourished by sacred springs. One root reaches to Asgard, the home of the gods, and is fed by the sacred spring of Urd, also called the Well of Fate. The Norns, or Fate Maidens, live beside this spring, and it is there as well that all the gods meet in their daily council. A second root extends into Jotunheim, the realm of the Frost Giants, and this root is nourished by the sacred spring of Mimir. Whereas the Well of Fate supplies knowledge of the past, present, and future, Mimir's spring is known as the source of all wisdom. (Odin, in fact, once desires to drink wisdom from this well, and, in another act of self-sacrifice, gives up one of his eyes in order to do so.) The third root is nourished by the spring of Hvergelmir, the source of all the great rivers in the world. This root reaches to

Niflheim, or Hel, the region of the dead and is constantly threatened by the serpent Nidhogg, who tries to destroy Yggdrasil by gnawing on its root. Although the serpent beneath the cosmic tree is sometimes a symbol of fertility, Nidhogg, who is the gods' enemy, represents the forces of disorder and destruction.

If the serpent that lives at the base of Yggdrasil is a common feature in accounts of the World Tree, so too is the bird that dwells high up in its branches. Fittingly, it is the eagle, king of all the birds and traditional enemy of the snake, which perches near the top of the Tree of Life. Because the eagle and Nidhogg are deadly foes, the two take delight in tormenting one another. The messenger that scurries up and down the tree ceaselessly delivering the insults exchanged by the serpent and the eagle is, appropriately enough, the incessantly chattering figure of Ratatosk the squirrel. A mighty stag feeds on the branches of Yggdrasil, and the goat that grazes nearby produces the mead that Odin serves to his warriors. It is said that Yggdrasil produces honey that falls to the earth and that it is the source of the dew that covers the ground. When Lif and Lifthrasir seek refuge in the Tree of Life, they find that they can survive there by eating and drinking the dew of Yggdrasil.

All of the animals associated with the Norse cosmic tree are symbolically meaningful. The sharp-sighted, high-flying eagle is a traditional symbol of the sky and thus is the embodiment of spiritual aspiration. Air is the eagle's element, just as earth is that of the serpent, a creature that sometimes represents the earth's fecundity, but that can also embody, as in the instance of Nidhogg, the will to destroy. Although the squirrel is regarded as a fertility symbol in Japan, in European myths the squirrel is associated with the rodent family and therefore represents that which is vicious and malicious. In the role of messenger, Ratatosk is the busybody that seeks to stir up trouble between the realms of sky and earth. The mighty stag (in some depictions of Yggdrasil, four harts stand among the branches) serves as another benevolent symbol and is emblematic of nobility and purity. Aptly, the stag's branching antlers represent in miniature the branching spread of the Tree of Life itself. The female goat is a symbol of nurture and nourishment—and, as the source of Odin's mead, provides nectar for the gods. Mead, of course, is made of honey, the honey that drops from Yggdrasil, and the tree's life-sustaining dew signifies the promise of renewal.

BIRDS AND SERPENTS

While other accounts of World Trees are not always as richly detailed as the Norse depictions of Yggdrasil, many do share certain of its features. The cosmic tree of the Ngaju Dayak people of Borneo, for example, repeats the pattern of the serpent and the bird. In this case it is a hornbill that nests at the top of the tree and a water snake that lies coiled at its base. The tree has golden leaves and fruit of ivory, and, like the Norse Tree of Life, unites the heavens and the earth. In the folk art of the Slavic people of the Volga region, the immense bird that crowns the Tree of Life is an emblem of the mother goddess. The Mongolian World Tree is supported by a dragon, a close relative of the snake. In fact, it is said that ancient Mongols refused to kill a snake for fear of offending the World Tree's dragon, the master of all snakes. Unlike Nidhogg, who represents disorder, the dragon beneath the tree is a benevolent symbol of both strength and power. The Persian cosmic tree is the Saena, or the Tree of Many Seeds, and, like Yggdrasil, is threatened at its roots; in the myths of the Zoroastrians, a frog is seen as the emblem of evil as it gnaws at the roots of the source of all abundance.

TREES OF LIFE

In China, images of the Tree of Life arise from several different traditions. In one of its versions, the cosmic tree is a peach, bearing the fruit that symbolizes immortality within the Chinese culture. Xi Wang Mu, the Queen Mother of the West, tends the Tree of Immortality in her gardens on the sacred mountain Kunlun, which is itself the site of paradise. Each of the peaches produced by this tree requires six thousand years to grow and then ripen to maturity. In another account, the Tree of Sweet Dew grows at the center of the world. Like the dew of Yggdrasil, the pure nectar of the tree symbolizes rejuvenation and renewal. Yet another tree, the Tree of Jianmu, is associated with myths about Fu Xi, one of China's culture heroes. The Tree of Jianmu grows in the center of the plain of Duguang, an earthly paradise at the center of the world. The trunk rises miles high into the sky before it branches into a canopy in the realm of heaven. Fu Xi, the only one who can climb the Tree of Jianmu, is the traveler between the heaven and the earth, and the cosmic tree thus serves him as a bridge. When Fu Xi returns from his celestial journeys, he often brings with him valuable gifts for his people.

TREE OF KNOWLEDGE

Among other narratives in which the Tree of Life is said to grow in paradise is the Hebrew story recorded in chapters 2 and 3 of Genesis. There, the fruit of the Tree of Life also affords immortality. When Adam and Eve eat of the fruit of another tree, the Tree of the Knowledge of Good and Evil, they are expelled from the Garden of Eden so that they cannot partake of the fruit produced by the Tree of Life. In this story the two trees of Eden represent dualism in Near Eastern thought, for corresponding to the Tree of Life is a tree of death, the tree whose forbidden fruit makes those who eat it mortal. In the account in Genesis, the pair of trees stands side by side in the center of paradise. A serpent is also present, and when it entwines itself around the tree that is the antithesis of life, it reveals itself to be an embodiment of anarchy and death. In Islamic tradition, yet another tree of immortality, the sidrah tree, occupies the noblest site in paradise.

EARTH AND SKY

While many cultural conceptions of the World Tree share common features, there are as well some interesting variations among accounts of the tree's significance. For example, in the myths of the Mixtec of Mesoamerica, the pygmies of Africa, and the Micronesian people of the Gilbert Islands, human beings are born from the Tree of Life. The account of the Gilbert Islanders is particularly interesting because it also incorporates both the Ymir motif and the theme of the separation of earth and sky. In this story Nareau the Younger summons all beings into existence, but creation cannot proceed because the great weight of the heavens rests upon the earth. To separate the earth and sky, Nareau the Younger kills his father and uses his spine to support the heavens, and it is the spine of the corpse that becomes the World Tree from which human beings are subsequently born. The tree, in this tale, separates as well as joins the realms of earth and sky, and the cosmic tree also serves this function for the Warao, the Shipibo, and other peoples of South America. According to another account from South America, however, the World Tree holds the heavens close to the earth until it is cut down. In the myth of the Chamacoco, fathers climb the great tree to gather honey for their children. Angry because no one offers honey to her fatherless children, a widow transforms herself into an insect and gnaws through the tree. The heaven flies high above the earth when the tree that holds it close crashes to the ground, and the fathers who are carried upward by the sky become the sun and moon and stars.

SOURCE OF THE DELUGE

The source of human life in some cultural traditions, the World Tree is also, in a few instances, the source of the great deluge. The African pygmies, for example, tell of the time when there is no water in the world. While it is resting beneath the cosmic tree, a chameleon grows curious about a murmuring sound that comes from inside the trunk. When the creature chops open the Tree of Life, the water that pours forth inundates the earth. Born of the tree, the first man and the first woman are carried out into the world by the mighty flood, and, when the waters soon subside, they become the parents of the pygmy people. Although the deluge typically cleanses the world by completely destroying it, in this myth, as in that of the Ackawoi people of South America, the flood transforms the world without causing its annihilation. Appropriately, the Tree of Life in this narrative both gives birth to humanity and also produces the water that is indeed a necessity of life.

In the tale of the Ackawoi, another myth in which the cosmic tree is linked to the deluge, Makonaima creates animals and birds and then places in their midst a wonderful tree that bears all the edible fruits of the earth. He then sends his son Sigu to rule over his creation. Sigu decides to cut down the Tree of Life so that its many fruits can be spread all around the world. When he does this, however, water begins to pour forth from the stump. Sigu quickly seals up the trunk, but a monkey removes the covering and the flood cannot be stopped. Sigu protects all the birds and animals throughout the terrifying night while the waters surge, but when the morning comes and the flood is gone, it becomes obvious that the world has been transformed. Changed by the ordeal they have suffered, the birds and animals are all different in either their appearance or their behavior. The monkey, for example, prefers to remain in the trees after the night of the flood. And because the floodwaters disperse the seeds of the World Tree to the far corners of the earth, the once simple task of gathering food becomes a difficult one for all the animals and birds.

COSMIC TREES

Like the tree of the Ackawoi, the World Tree of ancient Persia produces much more than a single fruit. Called the Saena Tree, or the Tree of Many Seeds, this tree bears the seeds of all the plants of the world. The tree rises from the primal waters of Vourukasha, the cosmic sea that lies above the earth, and, when the mighty Saena Bird that nests within its branches flaps its gigantic wings, seeds tumble to the earth below and take root in its fertile soil. Whereas the seeds in the Ackawoi myth are dispersed by the water, those in the Persian account are carried by the air. To protect the tree's aquatic roots from the frog that tries to gnaw them, ten fish called the kar keep a constant vigil. Ready to do battle should the frog appear, the kar serve the same function as that of the Norns, the Fate Maidens who restore the roots of Yggdrasil whenever Nidhogg attempts to destroy them. Positioned high above the earth that receives the bounty of its spreading boughs, the Saena Tree is the cosmic tree that nurtures all life within the world.

In very ancient cultural traditions, such as those of China or India, conceptions of the World Tree change over time. For India's Buddhists, the Bodhi Tree (or Bo Tree) is the sacred fig under which Gautama Buddha receives enlightenment. The Upanishads, however, describe a much earlier version of the cosmic tree. A symbolic representation of the entire universe, this tree is inverted so that its roots reach deep into the sky and its branches spread down across the earth. Rooted in the timeless heavens and branching downward toward the temporal world, the cosmic tree suggests that eternity is the true origin of all mortal life. While most World Trees symbolically link or separate the realms of earth and sky, India's ancient version of the tree serves as the manifestation of the Brahman, infusing all creation with that which is eternal. Like the rays of heaven's sun, the branches of its tree reach down to touch the earth.

RITUALS AND TRADITIONS

Images of a World Tree occur in cultures from around the world, and the symbolic significance of the concept of the cosmic tree is frequently expressed in rituals and traditions. In European cultures, for example, the springtime celebration of fertility traditionally includes an emblem of the axle tree in the form of the maypole. The maypole, like the World Tree, represents the center of the cosmos, and the dancers who unwind streamers as they circle it symbolically enact the unfolding of creation. Similarly, the Arandan people of northern Australia use a decorated pole, the *tnatantja* pole, to symbolize the cosmic tree in their religious ceremonies. The Mandan people of North America also use a symbol of the World Tree in their rituals, and, in the ancient traditions of the Mongols, a symbol of the cosmic tree plays a role in the initiation rites of the tribal shaman. The shaman, it is said, is able to ascend the World Tree in the form of an eagle. Therefore, when a new shaman is initiated, he dons the eagle's feathers and climbs up the pole at the center of his tent. When he emerges from the smoke hole, which represents the crown of the cosmic tree, he asks the gods to help him to protect all living beings.

Echoes of the World Tree also appear in myth's references to sacred trees or to trees associated with the central figures in fertility myths. Among the sacred trees that belong to the gods, for example, are those that produce the golden apples of immortality. In Greek tradition the sacred apple tree belongs to Hera, a wedding gift from the earth mother, Gaea. Hera plants her tree in a secret place, far to the west in the Garden of the Hesperides, and it is there that Herakles must travel when he searches for the apples. The goddess Idunn tends the sacred tree in Norse tradition, and the golden apples she offers to the gods keep them from aging. In the myths of the Irish, the sacred apple tree can be found in the Otherworld, the invisible realm that becomes the home of the Tuatha De Danann after they are defeated by the Milesians. As an emblem of renewal, the sacred tree also plays a role in many fertility myths, especially those that feature the dying god of vegetation. In Egyptian tradition, for example, Isis first finds Osiris's body embedded within the sacred tamarisk tree, and, in some versions of the myth, she is able to revive him when she frees him from the tree. Attis, the Phrygian vegetation god, is hanged from the sacred pine, a symbol of agricultural fertility, and Aeneas, the great Roman hero, carries with him into the underworld the sacred golden bough that is also a symbol of the earth's fertility.

See also Deluge Motif; Fertility Myths; Sacred Mountains

YMIR MOTIF

A myth motif that features the dismemberment of a primordial being, usually a god, the Ymir motif is named after the Frost Giant Ymir, the first living creature in Snorri Sturluson's thirteenth-century account of the Norse creation myth. Although the dismemberment theme derives its name from the Norse tradition, instances of the use of the body parts of a corpse to create the world or to produce a source of food occur in tales from many different cultures. Creation myths, which depict the emergence of existence from a primordial void, usually represent creation as a process, a series of evolving stages wherein out of nothingness the recognizable world gradually assumes its shape. In a surprising number of creation stories, one stage of the process involves the formation of that which is new from the dead remains of an older form of existence. In stipulating the use of a corpse to engender something new, the Ymir motif introduces the cycle of birth, death, and regeneration that is central to earthly life. It also serves the etiological function that lies at the heart of all myth in that it sets out to explain how the world comes to assume the form that it takes.

NORSE TRADITION

According to Norse tradition the primal void that exists before creation begins is called Ginnungagap (yawning abyss—or, in some translations, deceiving gap). In the first stage of creation, Muspelheim (destroyers' home) and Niflheim (fog home) emerge from the void. Characteristics of Iceland's landscape are reflected in these images of the world, for Muspelheim is a fiery, volcanic region, and Niflheim is a place of ice and venomous frost. Ymir, the first Frost Giant, comes into being where the two worlds meet and the flames of Muspelheim thaw the venomous frost that covers Niflheim's ice. Another creature, Audhumla the cow, also appears from the thawing ice, and her four streams of milk provide nourishment for Ymir. A vicious being born of Niflheim's foul mists, Ymir becomes the father of all the evil Frost Giants when another generation of monsters is formed from his sweat.

Buri, the grandfather of the gods, emerges in a later stage of the creation myth. Because Audhumla hungers for the salt embedded in Niflheim's frost, she licks at a block of ice until Buri is fully exposed. Buri gives birth to Bor, and Bor marries Bestla, a daughter of the Frost Giants. Bor and Bestla then become the parents of the first generation of Norse gods, for their children are Odin, Vili, and Ve, the three brothers who slay and dismember Ymir. After they kill the father of the Frost Giants, the gods carry the corpse to the middle of Ginnungagap and then make use of it to fashion the world. They shape the earth from Ymir's flesh, and they use his bones to make the mountains. Ymir's teeth become stones, his hair is made into the trees of the forest, and his blood is used to form the rivers and the oceans. The gods use Ymir's skull to create the vault of the sky, and they place his brains there, to become the clouds. The maggots from Ymir's flesh are made into a race of dwarfs, and his eyebrows are used to create the barrier between Jotunheim, the land of the Frost Giants, and Midgard, the rest of the earth.

While the Norse tale of the death, dismemberment, and reshaping of a primordial monster provides the exemplary instance of the recurring theme known as the Ymir motif, this creation myth also offers an interesting variation on the deluge motif. Stories of a flood not infrequently accompany accounts of creation, and indeed the Norse myth presents an unusual version of the flood. When Odin, Vili, and Ve kill their enemy, the blood that surges from the giant swells into a mighty river. All but two of the Frost Giants are drowned in the deluge, and the two that survive, Bergelmir and his wife, are only spared because they are able to make their escape in a boat. Like Noah and his wife, or Deucalion and Pyrrha, or any of the other pairs who are the sole survivors of the flood, Bergelmir and his wife in time become the parents of the new generation of their race, and the Frost Giants who are their offspring are the ones who do battle with the gods. The Norse myth is not only distinctive in its version of the flood, but also in its account of creation by dismemberment, for the corpse of an evil creature is rarely used to shape the world.

CHINESE TRADITION

Although Chinese tradition includes several versions of creation myths, one of the best known uses the Ymir motif to explain how the world acquires its features. The story of Pan Ku (or Pan Gu) begins, characteristically, with the existence of chaos. Chaos is contained within a cosmic egg, but when the process of differentiation begins, when yang begins to move apart from yin, Pan Ku, the creator being, breaks open the shell and emerges from the cosmic egg. Pan Ku is a giant, but there is no room for him to stand upon the earth, for the sky weighs heavily upon it. Recognizing that creation cannot proceed until the earth (yin) is completely separated from the sky (yang), Pan Ku, who grows ten feet taller every day, pushes the sky and earth apart for eighteen thousand years. Using a hammer and a chisel, he also carves hills and valleys and riverbeds on the surface of the world.

After eighteen thousand years have passed, Pan Ku finally tires of his labors and lies down to sleep. The giant dies in his sleep, but his service as creator does not end with his death, for the features of the world take their shape from his corpse. Pan Ku's breath becomes the wind and clouds, and his eyes the sun and moon. His voice turns into lightning and thunder, and his sweat becomes the rain and dew. Earth's soil is formed from his flesh, its stones are made of his teeth and small bones, and plants and trees are created from the hair of his body. The hair of his head is turned into the planets and stars, and the blood from his veins becomes rivers and oceans. The five sacred mountains that hold up the sky take their shape from Pan Ku's arms and legs and torso, and the vault of the heavens is made from his skull. The giant's bone marrow is turned into pearls and other precious gems, and the mites from his body are formed into people.

BABYLONIAN TRADITION

The story of Pan Ku features two significant myth motifs, the recurring theme of the separation of earth and sky and that of creation from the body of the corpse. In the Assyro-Babylonian account of creation that is recorded in the *Enuma elish* (ca. 1100 B.C.E.), the Ymir motif occurs in conjunction with another common theme, that of the theomachy, or the war among the gods. In the Babylonian myth, life is born of the mingling of the primal waters. Father Apsu, as fresh water, and mother Tiamat, as salt water, together produce Mummu, the mist that lies above them, and then Anshar and Kishar, who become the parents of the god of the sky. The son of the sky god becomes god of the earth, and, when he too has sons of his own, a family of gods occupies the cosmos. In time, conflicts arise between the younger gods, who are unruly and disruptive, and their primeval parents. When Ea, the earth god, kills Tiamat's consort, Apsu, the mighty salt-water mother seeks revenge on the gods.

To do battle with the gods, Tiamat creates an army of dragons, storm demons, venomous serpents, and other monstrous creatures. Both the god of the earth and the god of the sky attempt to defeat Tiamat and her rebellious hordes, but neither can succeed. Finally, on the condition that he be named the ruler of all the gods, Marduk, the son of the earth god, confronts Tiamat in single combat. With the help of the winds and his own magic powers, Marduk overcomes the primeval mother who represents the forces of anarchy, and, in so doing, establishes order in the cosmos. Like Odin and his brothers, Marduk dismembers his slain enemy and uses parts of her corpse to configure the world. The king of the gods slices the primeval mother in half and uses one part of her body to create the sky and the other part to form the earth. He makes the sky's clouds from Tiamat's saliva, and he uses her head to create earth's mountains. Finally he fashions Mesopotamia itself, by causing the two rivers, the Tigris and Euphrates, to flow from her eyes.

AZTEC TRADITION

The Ymir motif also appears in a version of the Aztec creation myth. According to this tale, the creator deities Quetzalcoatl and Tezcatlipoca assume the form of gigantic serpents to overcome Tlaltecuhtli, the primordial monster whose rapacious appetite for flesh threatens the creation. Tlaltecuhtli, an androgynous creature possessed of multiple gaping maws, is generally described as a female monster. Sometimes represented as a razor-toothed caiman of immense proportions, this insatiable figure uses her many fearsome mouths—including those positioned at her elbows, knees, and other joints—to gnash her prey to pieces. Determined to rid the world of a deadly scourge, Quetzalcoatl and Tezcatlipoca seize Tlaltecuhtli, tear her body apart, and then create the heavens when they hurl half of the monster's corpse high into the sky. From the top half of the body, other gods—those dismayed by Tlaltecuhtli's dismemberment—carefully fashion the earth and its features. Trees, large flowers, and herbs grow from the monster's hair, and small flowers and grasses come forth from her skin. Mountain ranges arise from the spines of her caiman's back, and her eyes produce earth's wells and its bubbling springs. Great rivers flow from Tlaltecuhtli's mouth, and from her nose the gods shape all the hills and valleys. When they use Tlaltecuhtli's body to fashion the life-sustaining earth, the gods reawaken her monstrous appetite for flesh—and thus blood sacrifices are necessary to satisfy her hunger.

SACRIFICE

The theme of creation by sacrifice is frequently associated with the Ymir motif. In fact, the death of Pan Ku, which leads to the formation of the world, might be regarded as a form of self-sacrifice. The idea of sacrifice is particularly important in the Indian tradition, and several of the hymns in the *Rig Veda* (ca. 1000 B.C.E.) touch upon this theme. In the account of Purusha, for example, a primordial being is ritually sacrificed and dismembered to create the world. A being that possesses one thousand heads, one thousand eyes, and one thousand feet, Purusha brings into existence the very gods and priests who perform their rituals over his gigantic body before they offer him in sacrifice. Indeed, Purusha is the universe itself, and three-quarters of his being exists in eternity. When the gods sacrifice and dismember Purusha, it is one-quarter of his being, his mortal manifestation, which is used to create the world and to establish its order.

The gods and the sages slice Purusha's body into many pieces, and these are all used to produce both the features of the cosmos and the beings that inhabit it. The world begins to take its shape when the sky comes from the primordial giant's head, the air from his navel, and the earth from his feet. Purusha's eyes become the sun and his mind becomes the moon. Indra, king of the gods, comes forth from his mouth, and he is followed by Agni, god of sacrificial fire, and then all the members of the priesthood. The breath of the giant being takes the form of Vayu, god of the wind, and those who are warriors come from his arms. Traders and farmers are formed from Purusha's thighs, and the servants of the world come from his feet.

ORIGINS OF FOOD

Myth's recurring themes of sacrifice and dismemberment are also frequently linked together in fertility tales or in traditional accounts of the origins of food. In a story told by the Marind-Anim people of New Guinea, for example, the killing of a young maiden produces a rich array of staple foods. According to this myth, the maiden Hainuwele is one of the earth's primordial beings. Born of a coconut palm, she possesses the power to produce from her body wonderful gifts of dishes, bells, and coral. Perhaps because they envy Hainuwele's talent, the men gather together and slay her after she bestows her gifts at the community's great festival. The maiden's corpse is cut into pieces that are buried, and in time many varieties of tubers and other edible foods grow from her body parts. Hainuwele's arms, however, are used to make a door through which the people must pass when the time comes for them to make their way to the realm of the dead.

In similar tales from the Japanese, Mayan, and Peruvian traditions, new foods are also produced from the body parts of sacrificial victims. The Japanese story of Ogetsuno can be characterized as a fertility myth, for this figure is indeed the goddess of food. Like Hainuwele, Ogetsuno produces gifts of food from her body before she is killed. Her suitor, however, is disgusted by this practice and thus slays her with his sword. From Ogetsuno's forehead comes a field of millet, and from her stomach rice. Wheat and beans grow from her loins, and a horse and ox, the animals needed to plough the earth, arise from her head. Also a fertility tale, one version of the Mayan myth of the Hero Twins represents their father, One Hunahpu, as the deity of maize and thus a fertility god. According to this variant of the tale, One Hunahpu's severed head becomes an ear of corn, and when his sons travel to the underworld in search of his remains, they are then engaged in a quest to find their people's staple food. In the myth from Peru, food for human beings also comes from a victim of sacrifice, in this tale a newborn baby. Although the creator god Pachacamac makes the first man and woman to live on the earth, he does not immediately provide them with food. When the first man dies of starvation, Pachacamac impregnates the woman and then kills and plants their child. The baby's teeth sprout as maize, its bones grow into manioc, and its flesh produces both beans and gourds.

Myths from some cultures feature other variations in their accounts of dismemberments. For example, the coconut, an important food for the people of the South Pacific's Mangaia Island, is said to come from an animal—a decapitated eel. In this story a young woman falls in love with the Father of Eels and enjoys his company for a long time before he informs her that he must die. When that time comes, the young woman fulfills her lover's desire that she cut off his head and plant it in the ground. From the two halves of the severed head grow two coconut palms laden with fine fruit, and, as in the other tales, a death therefore leads to regeneration. In yet another variation, one that comes from the Inuit peoples, a victim of dismemberment is transformed into a spirit when she is pushed from a boat and sinks into the sea. Several versions of the story of the young woman whose fingers are chopped off when she attempts to climb back into the boat are told by different groups of Inuit peoples. Among the Oqomiut, for example, the woman is called Sedna, and it is her father who disfigures her, and the Netsilik Inuit know the young woman as Nuliajuk, an orphan girl whose fingers are chopped off by her playmates. In all the stories, however, the girl's severed fingers turn into seals, whales, and walruses—the sea mammals hunted by the people—and the girl becomes the spirit of the sea and the ruler of the underworld.

See also Creation Myths; Fertility Myths

GLOSSARY

Allegory   Allegorical narratives, stories that possess two levels of meaning, are commonplace in myth tradition. In these tales, an understanding that is of moral, philosophical, or cosmological significance is expressed in the unfolding of the stories' plots.

Animal Master   A recurring figure in myth tradition, the animal master—usually a deity or spirit and sometimes the god of the hunt—oversees and protects the animal kingdom. In tales from several of the world's cultures, this tutelary figure also performs the duty of punishing human beings who wantonly kill animals or who otherwise fail to show respect for their fellow creatures.

Animism   A term derived from the Latin word for "spirit" or "soul," animism is the belief that spiritual powers inhabit all of creation. According to an animistic conception of the universe, natural phenomena and objects are, like living beings, possessed of a soul.

Anthropogony   A type of creation myth, the anthropogony recounts the story of the origin of human beings.

Apocalypse   Myths of the apocalypse envision a catastrophe that destroys the world. According to most apocalyptic visions, a new world or a changed order of existence emerges after the old cosmos is destroyed. For this reason, the apocalypse is usually conceived as an event that, like the deluge, cleanses the world of imperfection or corruption.

Archetype   Myth's archetypes include the recurring figures, motifs, or themes that appear within the world's diverse cultural traditions. Carl Jung, whose theories have interested many myth scholars, proposes that mythic archetypes arise from the "collective unconscious," a repository of human beings' shared psychological experiences.

Assimilation   Myth assimilation occurs when a cultural tradition adopts beliefs, deities, or tales that have arisen in another tradition. Cultural material that is appropriated in this way is then frequently altered to serve the purposes of the society that assimilates it.

Astromorphosis   Astromorphosis is the transformation of a being into a star, a planet, or a constellation. Myths from around the world describe the metamorphosis of deities, human beings, or animals into celestial objects.

Axis Mundi   The *axis mundi*, an object or location that is perceived as the center of the world, commonly takes the form of a sacred mountain or a World Tree within myth traditions. In some cultures, the *axis mundi* is the site upon which a temple is erected.

Bestiary   The bestiary, a catalogue or treatise containing illustrations and descriptions of both real and imaginary animals, was popular in Europe during the Middle Ages.

Chaos   The state of nothingness that exists before the creation of the cosmos, chaos is typically conceived as a primal void. Creation myths describe the emergence of the world's order from a state of chaos, and myths of the apocalypse envision a return to chaos when that order is destroyed.

Chimera   The mythical beast known as the Chimera, said to have been slain by the Greek hero Bellerophon, has lent its name to the fantastic creatures of myth whose bodies are composed of parts from different animals. While the Chimera itself is described as being part lion, part goat, and part serpent, the chimeras of myth tradition include instances of many other kinds of hybrid creatures. In European tradition, chimeras are commonly described in the bestiaries and depicted in the gargoyles that date from the Middle Ages.

Chthonic World   Located beneath the surface of the earth, the chthonic realm, or underworld, is recognized in many myth traditions as the land of the dead, and thus myth's chthonic deities are those who rule the underworld. Although the chthonic world is generally regarded as the site of death's dark, infernal powers, it is often seen as the source of life as well, for it is within the chthonic regions that the earth's crops are annually reborn.

Cosmic Egg   The primal void is conceived as an egg, an emblem of fertility and birth, in some creation myths. In these tales the universe emerges from the cosmic egg.

Cosmogony   A type of creation myth, the cosmogony recounts the story of the original emergence of the universe.

Cosmology   A people's understanding of the nature of the universe is expressed in its cosmology, its conception of the order of the whole of creation. Whereas the universe is commonly perceived as consisting of three separate worlds, a heavenly, an earthly, and a celestial realm, some peoples describe a cosmic order that contains a greater number of worlds or levels of existence.

Creation *Ex Nihilo*   Creation *ex nihilo*, the fashioning of the universe from a state of nothingness, most commonly occurs when the creator deity either speaks or thinks the cosmos into being.

Culture Hero   Stories of culture heroes, the divine, human, or animal figures whose remarkable deeds serve to promote or to safeguard a society's welfare, occur in myth traditions from around the world. The fire bringer, the flood hero, the founder of a dynasty, or the teacher who provides instruction in the arts of hunting, fishing, or agriculture, the culture hero can also be the courageous monster slayer who saves a society when it is endangered.

Deluge Motif   A universal myth, the story of a great flood that inundates the earth can be found in the myth traditions of numerous different cultures. According to many of these tales, the flood cleanses the world of imperfection or corruption, and earthly life begins anew after the waters have receded and the survivors of the deluge, the "flood heroes," repopulate the world.

Descent Motif   Stories of a living being's descent to the underworld, the land of the dead, appear within the myth traditions of many different cultures. This journey, also referred to as the "harrowing of hell," is typically undertaken by a hero who is engaged upon a quest.

Diffusion   Theories of myth diffusion, which account for certain similarities among tales recounted by different peoples, trace the ways in which myths are carried to new populations. Myths are often spread, for example, when discrete societies engage in trade with one another or when one people conquers another.

Earth-Diver   In creation myths that feature the earth-diver, an animal or deity swims to the bottom of the primal waters to gather the particles of dirt or sand that are then used to form the earth.

Emergence Motif   According to some creation myths, earthly existence begins when human beings or animals journey from subterranean worlds to emerge upon the surface of the earth.

Epic   Long, narrative poems that ceremoniously recount the deeds or the adventures of the outstanding heroes of particular societies, epics characteristically affirm the essential values and express the worldviews of the cultures that produce them.

Epithet   An epithet is a descriptive word or phrase that expresses an attribute or quality that is characteristic of a person or an object. In epics or other forms of storytelling, the epithet can either stand alone or accompany the name of the person or object to which it refers.

Eschatological Myth   Narratives that envision the end of the world, eschatological myths are concerned with last things or final events and often describe the coming of the apocalypse and the destruction of the earth.

Etiology in Myth   As narratives that offer explanations of origins and causes or afford reasons for the occurrence of events, myths are characteristically etiological in nature. Additionally, a common category of tales, including "just so" stories and similar explanatory accounts, particularly addresses questions of how animals have acquired their peculiar traits or how features of the landscape have assumed their shapes.

Euhemerism   An explanation of the origin of myths, euhemerism posits that traditional narratives are exaggerated or symbolic accounts of events that took place in the distant past or mythologized accounts of real persons who have been deified or represented as great heroes through the act of storytelling. Euhemerists, for example, trace the origins of narratives featuring King Arthur's heroic exploits back to the history of a real person.

Fable   The fable, a short narrative that often features animals as characters, typically serves as a cautionary tale or one that focuses attention on a moral value. Part of many societies' folktale traditions, fables characteristically offer wisdom or advice in storytelling form.

Fairy Tale   The fairy tale, a fantastic story that is usually recounted to children, is part of the folktale traditions of numerous cultures.

Fetish   Because a fetish is an object that is believed to be inhabited by spirits, it is considered to be imbued with magical powers. A fetish is most commonly a small object that can afford protection or otherwise serve its owner as a charm.

Flood Hero   Flood heroes are the survivors of the devastating deluge that is described in myths from around the world, and, after the flood, these survivors are the heroes who repopulate the earth.

Folklore   A people's folklore tradition, which can include customs, folktales (or märchen), traditional dress, sayings, dances, or other art forms, is generally distinguished from its traditions of ritual and myth. Although such a distinction is often somewhat arbitrary, scholars use it to discriminate between a society's secular practices and the forms through which it expresses beliefs that are sacred.

Funerary Texts   Funerary texts, such as the Egyptian *Book of the Dead* (ca. 1550 B.C.E.), contain information about the land of the dead and the afterlife. Because they are intended to serve as guides for souls undertaking perilous journeys to the netherworld, funerary texts are commonly interred with the dead.

Giantomachy Like theomachy, a war among the gods, giantomachy, the battling of giants or titans, occurs when supernatural beings fight one another.

Harrowing of Hell Stories of the harrowing of hell appear in numerous myth traditions. In these tales, a living being journeys to the land of the dead, braving the dangers of the netherworld to fulfill a quest.

Legend While myths recount events that are believed to have unfolded in the remote past or in another time, legends are stories of more recent occurrences. Typically, tales of memorable persons and events are embellished and exaggerated as legends grow and spread through the act of storytelling.

Märchen Märchen, the folktales of a people, are part of a society's folklore tradition.

Metamorphosis Metamorphosis is the transformation of the form of a living being or an object by magical power or by supernatural means.

Monogenesis Certain myths, according to the theory of monogenesis, originally arise in one culture and are then spread to others through the various processes of myth diffusion.

Monotheism Judaism, Christianity, and Islam are all examples of religious traditions founded on monotheism, belief in a single, supreme deity.

Myth Narratives that account for a people's beliefs, ritual practices, and values or provide explanations of natural or supernatural phenomena, myths express a society's conception of the nature of the world. As stories that embody the systems of belief that shape the practice of religions, myths are commonly regarded as sacred narratives.

Myth Motif Comparative studies of traditional narratives have identified a number of myth motifs, recurring images or thematic elements that are components of myths from around the world. Also called "detail motifs," these images, archetypal figures, or repeated themes appear in a variety of contexts within stories told by many different peoples.

Pantheon All the gods of a particular people are collectively regarded as a pantheon, and thus the term is used only in reference to the deities of polytheistic traditions.

Polygenesis Comparative studies of myths have revealed that the presence of recurring themes within the narratives of different peoples can be understood either as instances of polygenesis, the independent emergence of tales that contain similar motifs, or as instances of the diffusion of thematic elements that originate in a single tradition and are eventually assimilated by other peoples.

Polytheism In polytheistic traditions, those characterized by a people's belief in more than one god, divine responsibilities are commonly divided among deities. Within these traditions, for example, one god or goddess might rule the heavens while another presides in the underworld. When a people's belief system includes multiple divinities, the pantheon often consists of a number of lesser deities in addition to the major goddesses and gods.

Primal Parents According to some creation myths, primal parents give birth to the world or to the first deities or race of human beings. In the creation myths of several cultural traditions, the primal parents are represented as father sky and mother earth. Primal parents also appear in many stories of the deluge, for when the flood heroes who survive the destruction of the earth are a man and woman, these figures typically become the parents of a new race of human beings.

Psychopomp The conductor of souls to the land of the dead, the psychopomp is a recurring figure in myth tradition. Usually a deity, the psychopomp guides the dead on their journey to a place of judgment or to their new home in the afterlife.

Ritual Significant features of a culture's myth tradition are often expressed in its rituals, the ceremonial acts that, when repeatedly observed, serve a symbolic purpose. A people's deities, for example, are commonly honored or appeased in rites of sacrifice, and the observation of fertility rites is a customary practice in many agricultural societies.

Shabti The *shabti* of ancient Egyptian tradition is a figurine that was customarily buried with the dead. As servants in the afterlife, *shabtis* performed manual labor in the land of the dead.

Shaman A community's shaman typically serves as an intermediary between the material world and the invisible, spiritual realm. According to the traditions of various shamanistic societies, this intermediary is able to draw upon supernatural powers to perform magic, to effect healing, to control phenomena, or to foretell events.

Shape-Shifter Shape-shifters possess the ability to change their appearance, to transform themselves into other living beings, or to take the form of objects. Many of myth's deities possess shape-shifting powers, and the recurring figure of the trickster is almost always described as a shape-shifter. In addition to deities and tricksters, demons or other malevolent spirits are commonly represented as shape-shifters.

Sipapu According to the traditions of North America's Pueblo peoples, the *sipapu* is the hole through which human beings originally emerged when they traveled from the underworld to establish a new home on the surface of the earth. Because the land of the dead lies in the underworld, spirits must pass through the *sipapu* on their journey to the afterlife.

Theogony A type of creation myth, the theogony offers an account of the origins of a people's primordial deities.

Theomachy Accounts of theomachy, war among the gods, occur in a number of the world's myth traditions. Although human beings characteristically play no part in these battles, conflicts among the deities are nonetheless represented in some tales as having repercussions for mortal beings.

Theriomorphosis Theriomorphosis occurs when a deity or a person is transformed into an animal.

Totem An animal, plant, or object that serves as an emblem of a family or a clan, a totem symbolically expresses a social group's kinship with an entity in the natural world. According to some cultural traditions, members of a clan are the descendants of the totem.

Transmigration of Souls In cultural traditions whose conceptions of the afterlife envision the reincarnation of the dead to another earthly existence, the transmigration of the soul, or metempsychosis, occurs when a soul passes from one body to another. Transmigrated souls can be reembodied as human beings, animals, plants, or even inanimate objects.

Tutelary God Myth's tutelary gods are guardian deities that watch over and protect people, animals, places, or objects. In many cultural traditions the tutelary gods include domestic deities that oversee the welfare of the hearth and home.

Universal Myth Certain categories of narratives are widespread throughout the world's myth traditions, and those recurring accounts that independently arise in numerous disparate cultures are regarded as universal myths.

Ymir Motif The Frost Giant Ymir, a primordial being from the Norse tradition, has lent his name to a motif found in myths from around the world. In tales that include this motif, the dismembered corpse of a deity or of another supernatural being is used to fashion features of the world.

ADDITIONAL READINGS

ANNOTATED BIBLIOGRAPHY

Helbig, Alethea K., and Agnes Regan Perkins, comp. *Myths and Hero Tales: A Cross-Cultural Guide to Literature for Children and Young Adults*. Westport, Conn.: Greenwood Press, 1997.

CROSS-CULTURAL ANTHOLOGIES AND COLLECTIONS

Bierlein, J. F., ed. *Parallel Myths*. New York: Ballantine Books, 1994.

Elder, John, and Hertha D. Wong, eds. *Family of Earth and Sky: Indigenous Tales of Nature from around the World*. Boston: Beacon Press, 1994.

Eliot, Alexander. *The Global Myths: Exploring Primitive, Pagan, Sacred, and Scientific Mythologies*. New York: Continuum, 1993.

———. *The Timeless Myths: How Ancient Legends Influence the World around Us*. New York: Continuum, 1996.

———. *The Universal Myths: Heroes, Gods, Tricksters and Others*. New York: Meridian, 1990.

Leeming, David Adams, ed. *The World of Myth*. New York: Oxford University Press, 1990.

Robinson, Herbert Spencer, and Knox Wilson. *Myths and Legends of All Nations*. Savage, Md.: Littlefield Adams Quality Paperbacks, 1990.

Rosenberg, Donna, ed. *World Mythology: An Anthology of the Great Myths and Epics*, 3rd ed. Lincolnwood, Ill.: NTC Publishing Group, 1999.

SINGLE-TRADITION ANTHOLOGIES AND COLLECTIONS

Abrahams, Roger D., ed. *Afro-American Folktales: Stories from Black Traditions in the New World*. New York: Random House, 1985.

Bierhorst, John. *The Mythology of North America: With a New Afterword*. New York: Oxford University Press, 2002.

Curtis, Vesta Sarkhosh. *Persian Myths.* Austin: University of Texas Press, 1993.

D'Aulaire, Ingri, and Edgar Parin D'Aulaire. *D'Aulaires' Book of Greek Myths.* New York: Doubleday Books for Young Readers, 1992.

———. *D'Aulaires' Norse Gods and Giants.* New York: Doubleday, 1967.

Edmonds, Margot, and Ella E. Clark, eds. *Voices of the Winds: Native American Legends.* New York: Facts on File, 1989.

Erdoes, Richard, and Alfonso Ortiz, eds. *American Indian Myths and Legends.* New York: Pantheon Books, 1984.

Frobenius, Leo, and Douglas C. Fox. *Folk Tales and Myths of Africa.* New York: Dover Publications, 1999.

Hamilton, Edith. *Mythology.* Boston: Little, Brown, 1942.

Leeming, David, and Jake Page. *Myths, Legends, and Folktales of America: An Anthology.* New York: Oxford University Press, 1999.

Morford, Mark P. O., and Robert J. Lenardon. *Classical Mythology,* 7th ed. New York: Oxford University Press, 2003.

Spence, Lewis. *The Myths of Mexico and Peru.* New York: Dover Publications, 1994.

Squire, Charles. *Celtic Myths and Legends.* New York: Gramercy Books, 1994.

Taube, Karl. *Aztec and Maya Myths.* Austin: University of Texas Press, 1993.

DICTIONARIES AND ENCYCLOPEDIAS

Baumgartner, Anne S. *A Comprehensive Dictionary of the Gods: From Abaasy to Zvoruna.* Avenel, N.J.: Wings Books, 1995.

Bently, Peter, ed. *The Dictionary of World Myth.* New York: Facts on File, 1995.

Carlyon, Richard. *A Guide to the Gods.* New York: William Morrow, 1981.

Cotterell, Arthur. *A Dictionary of World Mythology.* New York: Oxford University Press, 1990.

———. *The Macmillan Illustrated Encyclopedia of Myth and Legends.* New York: Macmillan, 1995.

Evans, Bergen. *Dictionary of Mythology: Mainly Classical.* New York: Dell, 1970.

Gill, Sam D., and Irene F. Sullivan. *Dictionary of Native American Mythology.* Santa Barbara, Calif.: ABC-CLIO, 1992.

Hirschfelder, Arlene, and Paulette Molin. *Encyclopedia of Native American Religions.* New York: Checkmark Books, 2000.

Jones, Alison. *Larousse Dictionary of World Folklore.* New York: Larousse, 1996.

Leeming, David Adams, with Margaret Adams Leeming. *A Dictionary of Creation Myths.* New York: Oxford University Press, 1994.

Lurker, Manfred. *Dictionary of Gods and Goddesses, Devils and Demons.* Translated by G. L. Campbell. New York: Routledge, 1996.

Mack, Carol K., and Dinah Mack. *A Field Guide to Demons, Fairies, Fallen Angels, and Other Subversive Spirits.* New York: Henry Holt, 1998.

Wilkinson, Philip. *DK Illustrated Dictionary of Mythology: Heroes, Heroines, Gods, and Goddesses from around the World.* New York: DK Publishing, 1998.

Willis, Roy, ed. *World Mythology.* New York: Henry Holt, 1993.

SPECIALIZED STUDIES AND COLLECTIONS

Baring, Anne, and Jules Cashford. *The Myth of the Goddess: Evolution of an Image.* New York: Penguin Books, 1993.

Caldecott, Moyra. *Myths of the Sacred Tree.* Rochester, Vt.: Destiny Books, 1993.

Cowan, Tom. *Fire in the Head: Shamanism and the Celtic Spirit.* New York: HarperCollins Publishers, 1993.

Dundes, Alan, ed. *Sacred Narrative: Readings in the Theory of Myth.* Berkeley: University of California Press, 1984.

Edwards, Carolyn McVickar. *The Storyteller's Goddess: Tales of the Goddess and Her Wisdom from around the World.* New York: HarperCollins Publishers, 1991.

Eliade, Mircea. *The Myth of the Eternal Return or, Cosmos and History.* Translated by Willard R. Trask. Princeton, N.J.: Princeton University Press, 1991.

Erdoes, Richard, and Alfonso Ortiz, eds. *American Indian Trickster Tales.* New York: Penguin Books, 1998.

Gimbutas, Marija. *The Language of the Goddess.* San Francisco: Harper & Row, 1989.

Greene, Liz, and Juliet Sharman-Burke. *The Mythic Journey: The Meaning of Myth as a Guide for Life.* New York: Simon & Schuster, 2000.

Greer, John Michael. *Monsters: An Investigator's Guide to Magical Beings.* St. Paul, Minn.: Llewellyn Publications, 2001.

Hyde, Lewis. *Trickster Makes This World: Mischief, Myth, and Art.* New York: Farrar, Straus and Giroux, 1998.

Hynes, William J., and William G. Doty, eds. *Mythical Trickster Figures: Contours, Contexts, and Criticisms.* Tuscaloosa: University of Alabama Press, 1993.

Jung, Emma, and Marie-Louise von Franz. *The Grail Legend.* Princeton, N.J.: Princeton University Press, 1998.

Knapp, Bettina L. *Women in Myth.* Albany: State University of New York Press, 1997.

Larrington, Carolyne, ed. *The Feminist Companion to Mythology.* London: Pandora Press, 1992.

Leeming, David, and Jake Page. *God: Myths of the Male Divine.* New York: Oxford University Press, 1996.

———. *Goddess: Myths of the Female Divine.* New York: Oxford University Press, 1994.

Linderman, Frank B. *Indian Why Stories.* New York: Dover Publications, 1995.

Mascetti, Manuela Dunn. *The Song of Eve: An Illustrated Journey into the Myths, Symbols, and Rituals of the Goddess.* New York: Simon & Schuster, 1990.

Mercatante, Anthony S. *Zoo of the Gods: Animals in Myth, Legend and Fable.* New York: Harper & Row, 1974.

Patton, Laurie L., and Wendy Doniger, eds. *Myth and Method.* Charlottesville: University Press of Virginia, 1996.

Puhvel, Jaan. *Comparative Mythology.* Baltimore, Md.: Johns Hopkins University Press, 1987.

Rockwell, David. *Giving Voice to Bear: North American Indian Myths, Rituals, and Images of the Bear.* Niwot, Colo.: Roberts Rinehart Publishers, 1991.

Sproul, Barbara C. *Primal Myths: Creation Myths around the World.* New York: HarperCollins Publishers, 1991.

Turner, Alice K. *The History of Hell.* New York: Harcourt Brace, 1993.

SPECIALIZED SERIES

Myth and Mankind. Amsterdam: Time-Life Books BV, 2000.

INDEX

About the Author

LORENA STOOKEY is Assistant Professor in the English Department at the University of Nevada, Reno, where she teaches courses in mythology, poetry, and literature. She is the author of *Louise Erdrich: A Critical Companion* (Greenwood 1999).